MW00995844

Eastside Kid

To Hugh.

I hope you enjoy my memories of the Eastside. I am very fond of Dawn and Greg.

Kind Regards

David Bowen

3-16-15

St. Florian Church and surrounding houses, Hamtramck, Michigan

Eastside Kid

A Memoir of My Youth from Detroit to Congress

David E. Bonior

PROSPECTA PRESS

Prospecta Press
P.O. Box 3131
Westport, CT 06880
www.prospectapress.com

Book and cover design by Barbara Aronica-Buck.

Cover (and page ii) photo by Balthazar Korab, courtesy of The Library
   of Congress.
Andy and Vance Bonior, page 71, courtesy of Luis Vera.
St. Veronica, page 80, courtesy of Caitlin Conner.
Sacred Heart Seminary, page 112, courtesy of Caitlin Conner.
John Lewis and David Bonior, page 157, courtesy of Marty LaVor

Hardcover ISBN: 978-1-63226-011-6
Ebook ISBN: 978-1-63226-012-3

For my sister, Nancy Anne Bonior,
and my brother, Jeffrey John Bonior.

Be kind, for everyone you meet is fighting a hard battle.
– Ian Maclaren

Contents

The Strength of Roots

by Kathy Gille and Ed Bruley

T his is a book of very personal memories from a man who became a very public leader. It is more than a coming-of-age story of a boy growing to become an adult; it is the story of a time and place. *Eastside Kid* is a portrait set in an America undergoing a transition from working class to middle class.

It is the story of family, told in the voice a father might use in reminiscing with his children about what he has seen and done in his life. But underneath, there is another narrative about American democracy and the grounding—in culture and community—of a local, grassroots approach to politics that would have a decisive impact on the national stage.

We worked with David Bonior from his first congressional campaign to his last days as the Democratic whip, a powerful position— the second-highest-ranking leader of his party in the United States House of Representatives.

In his years in Congress, David was known as a tough, principled champion of progressive causes—so much so that many people in Washington assumed he came from a solidly Democratic, even liberal, district.

When they found out that his home base was a conservative-leaning swing district (one that had voted overwhelmingly for George Wallace in 1972 and that eventually gave the nation a new political term— Reagan Democrat), they would puzzle over how David could win thirteen straight elections to Congress.

They did not know what it meant to be an Eastside Kid.

Growing up on Detroit's East Side and its suburbs, David came to know in his bones what it means to be the underdog. It was natural that he would identify with other underdogs and give voice to their causes throughout his career. And it was a given that he would be ready to take on tough political challenges.

From David we learned to practice a politics that was focused more on community than on ideology. We watched as the star athlete turned his disciplined, competitive skills to the task of building and quarterbacking a political team. We loved being part of that team.

This is a book about roots, a theme we always came back to in the more than two decades we worked for David. Know where you come from. Make connections door-to-door, in schools, churches, union halls, at backyard barbecues. Get the kids and the whole family involved. Trust that people will respect you if you listen to them and speak their language. And, something that is sorely neglected in today's politics, help people get organized.

In David's first campaign and every year for more than twenty-five years, we had a symbol that represented this approach to politics. We would hand out small pine seedlings. Each little seedling came with a tangled trail of roots, usually far more extensive than the little branch of green needles that would grow to become a pine tree. We would carefully wind the strands around the taproot, pack them in dirt, and squirt them with water. In the strength of the roots, we knew, lay the future of the tree.

Over the years, hundreds of volunteers walked door-to-door with these little trees and their well-tended roots. "Yes, it's real. It's ready to plant. It's for you from your congressman, David Bonior." And we would, of course, add a political pitch: "It symbolizes our connection to community. Our hope for the future." In the process, we built a political organization based on kinship, commitment, and community.

We will let David tell you more about how these pine seedlings grew and what he achieved in politics when he writes his next volume on his congressional career. In this first volume, he has dug deep into his memories of family, and the people and places that shaped him. He has told us a rich, tender, at times humorous and at times painful but always heartfelt story of the roots that grounded the man whose passion for the underdog would make a difference in so many lives across the nation and around the world.

CHAPTER 1

Memory Repressed

My Mother, Her Surgery, and This Book

Recently my sister, Nancy, and I were discussing my mother's death in 1960 at the age of thirty-seven. In the two years before this conversation, as I composed the chapters that follow, I had spent many hours immersed in a systematic review of my early life. During that process, I recalled and recorded much about my mother's passing: I remembered the day she died; I remembered the heart attack she had suffered less than three years earlier. But between those two major events, another had taken place: Mother's open-heart surgery, performed several months after the attack. When Nancy described the circumstances surrounding the surgery, I realized that, for over half a century, I had repressed nearly all memory of them.

As I listened to Nancy, elements began to seep back into my consciousness. But there were still blank spots. Supplementing what I recovered with details recalled only by Nancy, I was able to reconstruct the story of the surgery.

Mother's weak heart had begun to sap her stamina prior to the heart attack, but afterward she became fatigued even more easily. Simple, everyday activities were beyond her capacity. She was unable to climb the steps at St. Veronica to attend Mass. She was unable to perform basic chores on behalf of her family—her husband, her three children, and her father, who lived with us.

Her health was slipping away, and we were all worried. Her doctors decided to operate.

As the date approached, the surgery became the number-one topic in our family, but in the years following her death, I somehow blocked from my memory not only the surgery but also our concern in the weeks before it. Nancy explained to me that the operation took eight hours. I don't know exactly what was done, but I do know that in the 1950s, open-heart surgery was new. It had not been practiced and repeated and refined to the point where, today, it's a serious and complicated but nonetheless routine procedure.

Following the surgery, Mother remained in the hospital for quite a while—weeks, probably—to begin her recuperation. Nancy, eleven at the time, recalls both of us visiting Mother there; I, then thirteen, don't. Nancy further reminded me that after Mother came home, she spent

Mother, in her late twenties

much of each day resting in bed, and that our father and grandfather instructed us to be quiet in the house. "Do not disturb Mother," they would say. Nancy told me that this state of affairs went on for months, changing dramatically the rhythms of our daily lives.

How could I not remember? Why had I buried these memories?

In the process of writing this manuscript, I had recalled the long scar running down the middle of Mother's chest; I'd seen it while she'd sunbathed in the backyard. The connection of the scar to the surgery may seem obvious, but until my conversation with Nancy, that visual memory had brought forth little recollection of the operation that had caused the scar—the scar marking where a medical team had opened up my mother's chest, then sewn it back together again after some eight hours of maneuvering inside. I'd buried in my memory vault all the images and conversations I'd been too scared to confront. When Mother suffered her heart attack, I was afraid she would die and we would lose her forever. Two short years after the surgery, we did lose her forever. It seems that locking these occurrences away was a means of shielding myself from the anguish of the loss.

The fragility of my mother's health was one of the central themes of my upbringing. Another was the paucity of verbal communication in our household, especially on the part of my father and grandfather. Each man's demeanor was serious, his sense of discipline strict. Only our mother and our baby brother softened the sober atmosphere of our home.

Mary McGrory, the longtime political columnist for the *Washington Post*, once described me in print as "funereal." The description didn't please me, but I knew it to be true. That was my look, all right. When I gazed in the mirror, I saw the stern faces of my father and grandfather staring back. My early childhood had been happy; I'd found joy in my narrow world filled with family, sports, and the Roman Catholic Church. But adolescence, and my mother's illness, changed my visage. I'd learned my father's and grandfather's lessons well.

The tragedy of my mother's early death notwithstanding, I was able to scale, sometimes just barely, the heights necessary to advance in life and end up with a long career in government service. I reached the highest levels of leadership in our federal government. I sat and spoke with presidents of the United States, heads of state and government from around the world, fellow congressional leaders, and thousands of my Michigan constituents. We discussed the most significant issues facing our communities, our nations, our world. Through it all I pushed myself to never forget that I was an Eastside kid, a son of Detroit's working class who grew up loving underdogs. If I tried to do anything during my years in government, it was to fight for those underdogs.

What I accomplished in Congress was and is important; recalling my achievements there is important, too, and will fill a second volume. But understanding and remembering what came before—the people, places, and events that shaped me; the maze I had to navigate to get to Washington—is no less significant. I've reached a point in life—I am sixty-nine years old at this writing—at which I've decided to take stock. In reviewing my history, some memories have come easily, some through the aid of friends and family members interviewed for this project, and some barely at all. Unearthing the happy memories, as well as the painful ones, has helped me to better understand my failures as well as my successes. Going back through my early life, trying my best to figure out what I was thinking at a given time and why—"elbowing my way into memory," in the words of the Israeli writer Fania Oz-Salzberger[1]—has presented its own rewards, although not without discomfort. Fortunately, the satisfaction has far outweighed the discomfort.

Here is the story of my youth. It starts with my grandparents and my parents, with large and small towns in Ukraine and Poland, and with an American town where I took my first step, said my first word, and learned the fundamental life lessons that made me the legislator I was and the person I will always be.

---

1 Fania Oz-Salzberger and Amos Oz, "A Compelling, Chutzpadik History Of 'Jews And Words.'" Interview on National Public Radio, December 1, 2012.

CHAPTER 2

Immigrants from Europe, Citizens of Hamtramck

My Grandparents, My Parents, and Their American Hometown

BLUE FENCES: LOOKING FOR ROOTS

Christmas came five days early to John Gavreluk in 1926. On December 20, in the Circuit Court of Wayne County, Michigan, my maternal grandfather held up his right hand and was sworn in as a citizen of the United States of America. His certificate of naturalization describes him as "32 years old, white with ruddy complexion, and five feet nine inches tall."

For previous citizenship, the certificate names two countries: Austria and Poland. The listing is correct even though he was, in fact, Ukrainian. He was born in 1894 in the rural village of Stetseva, near the foothills of the Carpathian Mountains, close to the Romanian border. Stetseva was located in the province of Sniatyn, which was part of Galicia, an area ruled before World War I by Franz Joseph I, emperor of the Austro-Hungarian Empire.

I had long wanted to see and experience for myself my family's roots in Eastern Europe, so during the summer of 2011 my wife, Judy, and I—together with Nancy, her daughter, Eva, and Eva's husband, Hooman—took what turned out to be an emotional and eye-opening trip to Ukraine, home to my ancestors on my mother's side, and Poland, where my father's family originated.

Judy and I flew to Newark airport, where we joined Nancy, who lives in Staten Island, New York, for our overnight flight to Munich. In Munich we were to connect with a flight to Lviv, Ukraine; there we would meet Eva and Hooman, who had traveled there earlier. Our plane was several hours late in departure, making us anxious about making our connection. We were right to be worried. As soon as we got off the plane in Munich, we raced through the airport toward the gate for the plane to Lviv. We arrived just in time to see the gate agent lock the door to the jetway. Out of breath, we searched for the rebooking agent, who told us that although there were no more flights that day to Lviv, she could get us on a flight to Timisoara, Romania, and on a flight from there to our destination. As bummed as we were about missing our flight, we decided to look upon the detour as an opportunity to experience a brief taste of Romania.

When we landed in Timisoara, the tiny waiting room in the tiny terminal was filled with people mostly on their way to other locations in Eastern Europe. The babushkas around us, with their peasant dresses and kerchiefs around their heads, formed a stark contrast to the stylishly clothed passengers we had seen in Munich. After a wait of two hours, we flew to Lviv. I occupied a window seat for the hourlong flight, and as we departed I gazed out, looking for signs of Falticeni, Romania, where Judy's father was born and raised. As we crossed into Ukraine, I repeated the exercise, looking for the foothills of the Carpathian Mountains, for I knew that my grandfather's village was down there somewhere. From twenty thousand feet it was easy to let my imagination run wild and conjure up visions of Judy's father, who was Jewish, as he rescued his mother and his two sisters from the Nazi-trained Romanian Iron Guard. Or to see my grandfather behind a horsedrawn plow, cutting furrows into the rich soil during the hot and muggy Ukrainian summer.

None of us slept much during the journey, so we arrived in Lviv exhausted. But we had tickets to see Verdi's *La Traviata* at the palatial Lviv Opera House. Our guide, Olga, met us at the airport and whisked us over to the theater, where we caught the last two acts and were united with Eva and Hooman. It was an impressive and dramatic way to begin our visit to Lviv.

After the show we checked into an elegant boutique hotel, the Leopolis. The rooms, service, and food were outstanding, making the accommodations the best in all my stays over the years in Eastern Europe. But as tired as we were, we could not wait until the next day to experience this captivating Ukrainian city.

The next two days were devoted to tours. There was much to see in Lviv, the City of Lions. Lviv is one of those jewels that travel guides rave about. It is a city of over eight hundred thousand that traces its glorious history back seven hundred and fifty years. During that time it served as the capital of the region of Galicia. *Lviv* is the Ukrainian name for the city; it was known as *Lvov* when dominated by the Poles and *Lemberg* when the Germans exercised control. It is a stunning city that managed to make it through World War II without much destruction. Krakow, its neighbor just one hundred and eighty miles away, had similar good luck.

Our two days were spent at the Rynok (Market) Square, at an assortment of churches, including the old Armenian Cathedral, the structurally magnificent Boim Chapel, the picturesque St. Michael's Cathedral and grounds, and the Dominican Church. On Sunday we went to Mass near our hotel, at the Church of Transfiguration, a tall, copper-domed edifice from the early eighteenth century. Lviv has over a hundred churches, many of them striking in both their architecture and the artwork inside. Beautiful museums and universities add to Lviv's reputation as an architectural and cultural gem.

Wandering through High Castle Park, up in the hills overlooking the city proper, and along Svobody Avenue, we saw wonderful green spaces, as well as monuments celebrating the heroes of the nation's history, such as the bard of Ukraine, Taras Shevchenko. In our short stay we took a fascinating tour of the Lychakiv Cemetery, famous for the beauty of many of its tombstones amidst a bucolic, hilly setting. The cemetery is also home to moving sites such as the memorial to the liberation movement of the Ukrainian people.

On our third day in Lviv, our party—minus Hooman, who left us for work, but including Olga and our driver, Roman—set off by car for Stetseva. The ride took three and a half hours, much longer than I had imagined.

As we approached the simple village, the first thing that stood out for me was the honolulu blue color of the poles and fences of the farms we passed. This same color was painted on the fence bordering the cemetery where the generations of the Gavreluk family rested. At first, the color created a jarring juxtaposition with the pastoral setting. Then it hit me: this blue was half of the national color scheme, blue and yellow. With that realization, the color began to grow on me—it was as though the broad, blue Ukrainian sky had been casting its heavenly hues on my forebears and the land they had inhabited. It also happens to connect with the land of my birth, for it's the blue seen in the uniforms of the Detroit Lions.

Cemetery in Stetseva

With a population today of some three thousand, Stetseva is set at an elevation of about eight hundred feet, on terrain that rolls gently to the Carpathians. The economy is little changed from what it was a century ago, when my grandfather left: primarily agriculture, including the cultivation of basic vegetables and grain and the raising of some livestock and, in small ponds, fish. The farms I saw were small, probably providing not much more than subsistence.

Before leaving home, I'd asked the travel agent to make contact for us with a family in Stetseva. The first house we visited was the home of a village elder, Sinovia, whom I took to be about eighty years old. With a broad, welcoming smile she took a liking to me right away, saying I reminded her of her late husband. She and her daughter-in-law couldn't have been more generous with their hospitality. We sat down to a table full of dishes like dumplings (*pirogi*) and stuffed cabbage (*holubsti*); fish, tongue, and hard-boiled eggs; beets, radishes, and other homegrown vegetables. We also had ample opportunity to sample Ukrainian vodka. The house was decorated with beautiful Ukrainian linens, hand-embroidered by our hosts. We purchased several, which now grace our own homes.

After about an hour of this amazing feast, one Steve Gavreluk, found for us by Sinovia, arrived. We went with him to pick up his sister, and then we visited the cemetery, situated at the edge of the village. Not only the fence surrounding the grounds was painted blue; so were the large main gate and numerous smaller fences that enclosed family plots of graves. The cemetery was larger than I'd expected—about the size of a football field. Although the grass was about a foot high, it didn't seem overgrown—swaying in the gentle Ukrainian breezes, it created, with the wheat fields beyond, an image I couldn't help thinking of as amber waves of grain. The cemetery was memorable, saying much about Stetseva's history. Set into many of the gravestones and markers, under glass, were photographs of the deceased, or poems or letters. I was moved being there with the remains of so many people I did not know but felt somehow linked to—even if, sadly, we came up empty in our search for information about our grandfather.

From the cemetery we went to the Gavreluks' home. The three residents of the household—Steve, his wife, and his sister—spoke as much English as we spoke Ukrainian, i.e., none. But through Olga and many shots of vodka, we communicated well enough. An injured leg from a road accident had recently caused Steve to retire after a career of driving large trucks throughout Russia and Eastern Europe. His wife, a pretty woman, had also just retired—she'd been involved in the artificial insemination of cattle on a large industrial farm. His sister worked in farming, too. The collapse of the Soviet Union and the Soviet economy had hit the Gavreluks hard. They supplemented meager pensions with the output of their farm—consuming most of it, but also selling some eggs and vegetables.

Steve was built like my grandfather and me, with the same body, skull, and large forehead—or perhaps I made these crude observations because I was straining to make a connection to this place and these people. Given that my grandfather had left a century earlier, I held little hope that we'd find someone in the village who remembered him, but I did think we'd find someone who had heard of him. We didn't. The Gavreluks we visited had never heard his name mentioned, nor had anyone else to whom we spoke during our visit to Stetseva.

I tried to picture him in the heat of a summer's day, working the long, fertile furrow of rich Ukrainian soil just beyond the cemetery gates. Or in the frigid cold of a long winter's night, with his arms wrapped tight around his torso. And then I thought how anxious he must have been, how scared, as he prepared to leave for North America, knowing he might never return to this village, the only home he'd ever known.

Before my grandfather died in 1979, he left me some old letters. Over the years, he'd been in touch with his family in Ukraine. We never shared a conversation about these relatives other than the countless times I heard him describe them as "peasants." I was excited to have the letters—surely they would yield some clues to my grandfather's family. Without making copies, I sent the letters off for translation to the Harvard Ukrainian Research Institute, in Cambridge, Massachusetts.

After six months I inquired about them, only to be told that they'd been lost and could not be found. I should have taken them to my friends at the Ukrainian Cultural Center in Warren, Michigan.

I still kick myself.

COLD BONES: GRANDPA

Before emigrating in 1912, my grandfather, who had only a third-grade education, spent most of his time laboring in the fields that ringed Stetseva. The work was hard, the winters frigid, the summers scorching. Most likely he never ventured outside of Galicia, but he must have longed to escape his dreary, arduous life. The political dynamics of the Austro-Hungarian Empire were volatile—a situation apparent to villagers in Stetseva, even if they could not see that a world war was in the offing. John and millions like him from central, eastern, and southern Europe wisely saw a better future waiting for them. Their task was to muster the courage and resources to make the long journey west, across Europe and across an ocean, to a new life in the New World.

"Every act of immigration is also an act of betrayal," wrote the journalist Ron Charles.[1] Nevertheless, Ukrainian immigrants in the early twentieth century, like those of so many other countries, tried to keep faith with the land of their birth, establishing ethnic enclaves in Canada and the United States. His route of travel once he arrived in New York suggests that my grandfather knew of these communities in Canada before leaving Ukraine. Perhaps the knowledge that he would not be alone when he arrived on the other side of the world eased the pain of separation.

Grandpa was eighteen when he left Stetseva. In the ship's manifest for his journey, I found in the list of the vessel's 2,012 passengers not

[1] Ron Charles, "Andre Aciman's 'Harvard Square,' reviewed by Ron Charles," *The Washington Post*, April 9, 2013.

only his name but also the names of two other eighteen-year-olds from Stetseva. It's reasonable to surmise that John Gavreluk, Mikolaj Ajawink, and Stanislaw Swierkosi left their village together, heading for the other side of the Atlantic. They might have begun the journey by traveling to Lviv, the Galician capital, where they could have boarded a train west. More likely, however, they traveled first to a much closer city, Ivano-Frankivska. Named after the great Ukrainian writer and poet Ivan Franko, the city today is the gateway for tourists visiting the Carpathians. It's probably where my grandfather began his railroad journey: eight hundred and fifty miles, to Antwerp, Belgium.

Antwerp was a primary embarkation port for emigrants bound for North America. I recall my grandfather saying that he sailed in steerage, or perhaps he used the phrase "third class." The cost of a steerage ticket to New York was somewhere between forty and fifty US dollars, which today would amount to around a thousand. And that didn't include rail fare to Antwerp. Clearly, he'd had to work long and hard to save enough money for his passage.

John Gavreluk sailed on the SS *Lapland*, a busy liner that carried more than two thousand passengers each time it crossed the Atlantic. Records indicate that large numbers of Poles and Ukrainians sailed under her flag to New York Harbor. The *Lapland* arrived on March 12, 1912, a month before the sinking of the *Titanic*. After the survivors of that disaster reached New York, the *Lapland* was commissioned to bring the crew members back to England. In 1917, with Europe at war, the ship hit a mine but made port in England. After repairs, the vessel was put to use transporting Allied troops. It was refurbished after the war and resumed ferrying civilian passengers across the Atlantic. Douglas Fairbanks and Mary Pickford, the foremost motion-picture stars of their era, began their honeymoon on board in 1920.

I don't think I'm going out on a limb when I say that the two screen idols enjoyed a more comfortable voyage in their luxury stateroom than my grandfather did in steerage. I remember his bemoaning the heavy seas—the ride must have been sickening for him, stuck belowdecks in a steerage compartment crowded with men, women, and children. My guess is that this was the first and only time he traveled by boat.

It must have been frightening and disorienting, on the ship and after he arrived, to be without family and without facility for the English language. He would never become comfortable expressing himself in English, and his inability to communicate his thoughts would haunt him for the rest of his life. But it wasn't the language barrier alone that kept him from expressing himself. My father spoke Polish, which is similar enough to Ukrainian that Grandpa could have spoken with him in depth about what he was thinking. Yet to my knowledge he never did. For one thing, I'm not sure the two men liked each other very much. Whatever the cause of Grandpa's difficulty in communicating, I always had the impression that he had something important to say but could not find the words. His feelings and ideas were like prisoners locked inside him; none of us knew how to unlock the heavy prison door. By day we could see the frustration well up in him. By night we could hear his emotions explode—his nightmares were audible throughout the house.

> Well, I came to America because I heard the streets were paved with gold. When I got here, I found out three things: first, the streets weren't paved with gold; second, they weren't paved at all; and third, I was expected to pave them.
> – "Old Italian story" now posted at Ellis Island Museum

On March 18, six days after he'd landed at New York Harbor, immigration officials at Ellis Island approved John Gavreluk for entry into the United States of America. He didn't stay long in the USA, however. Instead, he immediately set out for Canada—by train, probably, from New York City to the Canadian border, and then on to Montreal. The large cities of eastern Canada—Montreal and Toronto, Hamilton and Windsor—contained growing communities of Ukrainian immigrants. Organizations like the Ukrainian Self-Reliance League and the

Ukrainian Catholic Brotherhood helped new arrivals find homes and jobs—my grandfather found work in the nickel mines in Sudbury, Ontario. Word of these communities must have been what led him to Canada.

Somewhere along the way, John Gavreluk met Effie Malanech; they were married on November 24, 1918, in Sault Ste. Marie, Ontario, a city on the St. Marys River just across from Michigan. Witness to the handsome couple's wedding were Mike Leczuk, who would be a lifelong friend, and Annie Lennox (not the singer). Soon their first child, my aunt Nellie, was born—in a setting that was, to say the least, atypical.

Canada, a member of the British Commonwealth, entered the Great War in 1914 alongside its mother country. For the duration of the conflict, and for a time beyond, the Canadian government classified immigrants with citizenship in the Austro-Hungarian Empire—one of the powers opposing Britain and her allies—as "aliens of enemy nationality." This designation permitted the government to compel thousands of Ukrainians in Canada to register with the authorities. The government even interned about five thousand Ukrainians—mostly men, but some women and children, too—at camps and work sites, which did not close until the war had been over for two years. This dark chapter in Canadian history is surely comparable to the shameful internment of Japanese Americans during World War II.

The hostile atmosphere in Canada convinced John and Effie to move to the US, even though Effie was close to delivering their baby. But they ran into difficulty crossing the border. "The Gavreluks came to Canada first," notes Helen Livingston, Nellie Gavreluk's best friend. "And then there was some kind of difficulty getting into the States. They were held over, I think for three days, in prison. Nell was born while her parents were in prison."

I don't know all of my grandfather's work history after he reentered the US, but I do recall his saying that he'd worked as a lumberjack in northern Michigan. When he told me this story, he hugged himself as

Aunt Nell (l.) and Helen Livingston

though he could still feel the cold that had chilled his bones and the grueling labor that had made them ache.

Better work at better pay was to be had in a brand-new industry, and so, eventually, like thousands of others, he came to Detroit looking for a job in an automobile factory. In 1914 Henry Ford announced an unheard-of wage—five dollars a day—doubling the pay of workers in his employ. Practicing what became known as "welfare capitalism," i.e., looking after the welfare of one's labor force, Ford also shortened the work week. These practices affected the entire auto industry, and other manufacturing sectors as well—his improvements attracted workers, so other companies had to follow suit or lose their employees. Henry Ford was a vicious foe of labor unions, as well as a virulent anti-Semite. But he was a crafty entrepreneur.

John found a job at the Ford plant in Highland Park, Michigan, a small town almost entirely encircled by Detroit. He settled with his young family among the thousands of Polish and Ukrainian immigrants in the adjacent, and likewise surrounded, town of Hamtramck. After a few years at Ford, my grandfather switched his employment to Dodge Main, in Hamtramck. He worked as a fireman, charged with putting out fires within this sprawling complex that employed thirty thousand workers—forty thousand during World War II. I have in my home a copy of his work book, entitled "Bailey's Handbook for Stationary, Marine and Diesel Engineers and Firemen." Published in 1921, it's a universal compendium of questions and answers for people in his line

My maternal grandparents and family: John and
Effie Gavreluk with their children, Nell (l.) and Irene (Mother)

of work; he was required to carry it with him on the job. It's a complicated, technical volume that would challenge the best engineers. Obviously, Grandpa needed to understand it to do his job; evidently, his reading skills had improved to the point at which he could read and comprehend at least the basics of this manual. Eventually his literacy in English improved enough for him to pass the citizenship test and read the newspaper.

When they settled in Hamtramck, Effie and John were, in a way, returning to the Old Country. They bought a "worker's home" for a single family on Lehman Street—a long walk or short streetcar ride from Dodge Main—in an area where the primary languages were Polish and Ukrainian. Food, song, dance, and worship all reflected the lands the town's brave immigrants had left behind. Community concerts would feature Chopin and Tchaikovsky. Grandpa loved to eat at the workingman's cooperative restaurant, a gathering place for Socialists. While I don't know that my grandfather was an avowed Socialist, I do know that he loved the food and the company.

Swept Sidewalks and Manicured Lawns: Hamtramck

"Living in Hamtramck was an experience I wouldn't trade for anything," recalls Martha Mulkoff, my mother's best friend. "It was a neighborhood of people from Poland, Ukraine, Russia. All very ethnic in their ways. Most everything revolved around the church." To understand my family's story, and my own, one must understand Hamtramck. It is not only a place; for those of us who lived there, it became an idea. It was a culture that defined who we were and where we came from. It was a place we took immense pride in. Above all, it was then, and remains today, *authentic*.

The city was built upon strong values: hard work, family, deep religious beliefs, and a sense of social justice. And it was a place where people played as hard as they worked, with numerous bars along Joseph Campau, as well as social clubs, like the Polish National Alliance Hall on Conant, where on weekends folks danced the polka and sang late into the night. Greg Kowalski's excellent history, *Hamtramck: The Driven City*, captures the town's feeling of growth and vibrancy, its self-image as a community on the move. But it was more than that. To its residents—immigrants from the troubled countries of Poland, Ukraine, and Russia, as well as African Americans who had fled the toil and terror of the Jim Crow South—little Hamtramck represented refuge, opportunity, and hope for a better social and economic future.

Founded in the wake of the American Revolution, during its first century Hamtramck was known as a dusty farming community on the edge of Detroit. The town's namesake, Jean Francois Hamtramck, a native of Quebec, disliked the British enough to join the cause of our revolutionaries when war broke out in 1775. He distinguished himself during the war, rising to the rank of colonel. At war's end he built a house on the western bank of the Detroit River. A few years before he died in 1803, the area north and east of what is now downtown Detroit was named after him.

The expanding city of Detroit would eventually surround Hamtramck Township, but in the early nineteenth century Hamtramck was huge, including what later became known as Detroit's East Side. Hamtramck extended from the Detroit River north to 8 Mile Road, the county line, and from Woodward Avenue east through what became the Grosse Pointes. Yes, Grosse Pointe—the original jurisdiction, which developed into a set of five cities—was once part of Hamtramck. Over the years I have had great fun teasing people who hail from Grosse Pointe—friends and enemies alike—that their posh hometown once carried the working-class moniker of Hamtramck.

The cities around Hamtramck, however, began expanding their borders, and their tax base, as more and more migrants settled. In 1922, Hamtramck incorporated into a city, avoiding being completely subsumed by the bigger Detroit and the wealthier Grosse Pointes. The population of Hamtramck was growing rapidly. In 1901 the town contained 252 houses. By 1914, that number had increased eightfold, to 2,061, and by 1920 it almost tripled again, to 5,730. The majority of Hamtramck residents were Polish immigrants drawn by the jobs at Dodge Main and, to a lesser extent, at the Ford plant in Highland Park. Poles believed in owning their own homes, and they could do so in Hamtramck because the houses were small. The residents took great pride in their homes. They swept the sidewalks and the streets in front. They decorated their yards with flowers and kept their small patches of lawn manicured.

Hamtramck was a town united not only by where people came from but also by what they did every day. "You knew almost everyone," remembers Helen Livingston. "It was friendly there. Just about everyone was Catholic, the majority either Polish or Ukrainian—although there were some Russians, too. People were either immigrants or the children of immigrants. All the merchants spoke Polish or Ukrainian. The Dodge Motor Company was there, and that's where a lot of the men worked. It was a working-class town. All blue-collar."

The pay at Dodge Main was good, but the conditions were horrific. "The work was repetitive to the point of being mind-numbing," writes Greg Kowalski. Summer temperatures "would climb over 100 degrees. And in the foundry, it was even worse, as workers baked in the oven-like heat. . . . Local bar owners recall how workers would stop in at 7 a.m. and drink enough to dull their senses for the morning so they could withstand the conditions in the plant. Then it was back to the bar at lunch, or after their shift to unwind."[2]

Conditions like these throughout the auto industry led to unionization. The United Automobile Workers organized the Big Three—General Motors, Chrysler, and Ford—during the 1930s and early '40s and soon grew into a powerful political and economic force throughout the country. Hamtramck became a passionately pro-union town.

2 Greg Kowalski, *Hamtramck: The Driven City* (Charleston: Arcadia, 2002), 34–35.

If unions were central to meeting the material requirements of the people of Hamtramck, the church tended to their spiritual and educational needs. In the late nineteenth century, the Polish Catholics of Detroit's East Side, unhappy with German Catholic domination of their religious affairs, broke away to form their own institutions. Respecting the Poles' desire for parishes of their own, the Archdiocese of Detroit established St. Albertus Church and then Sweetest Heart of Mary on the East Side, not far from Hamtramck. St. Stanislaus, just south of Hamtramck, followed in 1898. Nine years later the parish of St. Florian, patron saint of firefighters, was created in Hamtramck. Soon, with Hamtramck's Polish population exploding, two more parishes, Our Lady Queen of Apostles and St. Ladislaus, were formed within town limits. Each of these new Hamtramck parishes built a church and a school. The growing Ukrainian community wasn't left out—the archdiocese founded Immaculate Conception Ukrainian Catholic Church, also with its own school.

Not everyone in town was Catholic. Corinthian Baptist Church, founded in 1917, Macedonia Baptist Church, and St. Peter Zion African Methodist Episcopalian Church all served the city's African Americans. A synagogue operated from 1908 to 1925, first on the grounds of the Beth-Olem Cemetery and later on Wyandotte Street.

Today Hamtramck is a city of twenty-two thousand and is growing once again. It remains a city of refuge and hope for new groups of immigrants. According to the 2010 census, only 14.5 percent of the population is of Polish origin, compared to 90 percent in 1970, and Ukrainians account for only 3 percent. The African American community is holding strong at about 20 percent. The dramatic change has come with the influx of people from Bosnia, Albania, Bangladesh, Yemen, and other Arab countries. The old Eastern European Christian culture is not gone, but a new, Islamic culture has moved in. Babushkas with colored kerchiefs now walk side by side with women wearing the Islamic hijab—even some covered head to toe in a burka. Mosques have been established, both in Hamtramck and just outside its borders. On

Conant Avenue, Polish and Ukrainian are still heard, but Arabic is common as well, as residents visit an array of Bengali shops and Yemeni restaurants. In all, over thirty languages are spoken in Hamtramck, and residents practice not only Islam and Christianity but also Hinduism.

But even though the religion, language, food, music, and clothing have changed, what endures in Hamtramck are the same solid values and powerful longing for refuge that defined the town a century ago, when the Boniors and Gavreluks made it their home. Hamtramck, the place and the idea, is still alive and well.

FLOWERS AT HER COLLAR: EFFIE

My maternal grandmother has always been a mystery to me. Nancy and I know little about her, for little was spoken of her. The absence of an oral history in our family, about Effie and about others, has meant that our ancestors slipped away with the basic facts of their lives unknown to their descendants.

I'm not even sure where she was born. She had a brother, Peter, who boarded with my grandparents on Lehman Street before he married. Another brother, Albert, lived near Toronto; he visited us often in Hamtramck, pulling up at the house on a large, noisy motorcycle. Several times he offered me a ride on the back of the bike, but my mother would not hear of it. Peter and Albert both spoke English fluently, without an accent, and talked a mile a minute. So my guess is that Effie and her brothers were all raised in Canada, not Ukraine.

I know that she was a beautiful woman who was drawn to fashion. In two formal photographs taken in studios in Hamtramck, she sits with her family. The first, from about 1922 or '23, is shot in front of an art deco setting. Grandpa is standing, dressed in a dark, tailored, three-piece suit, with a white shirt and a dark tie. He looks like he could be the CEO of General Motors; his bearing is confident but not arrogant. My aunt Nellie, age three or four, sits on a bench in front of my grandfather. Her hair is curled, with a white bow tilted to the right side. She's wearing a white dress with frills on the short sleeves and a hem that covers her knees. On her feet are anklets and white shoes. Her open hands are placed comfortably on her thighs—like her father, she looks serious but relaxed. Effie sits next to her daughter, but with her legs bent, out of view, over the back side of the bench. Seen in profile, she wears a dark formal dress with a see-through left sleeve and a brooch pinned at the neck. One dark, formal leather shoe with a two-and-a-half-inch heel shows beneath the bench. Her body is protective of Nell even though mother and daughter barely touch. Her dark hair slopes over the left side of forehead and is crowned, in the Ukrainian tradition, by a braid that winds around her head. Effie's face is beautiful and calm. While the picture of this young family does not show happiness or joy, it does evoke stability and serenity.

The second photo, shot four years later at the Eross Studio on Joseph Campau in Hamtramck, has a more formal setting. John and Effie are seated in white wicker chairs. Nell, now seven or eight, stands between them, almost at attention, while three-year-old Irene, my mother, leans on Effie's left thigh. Irene's right leg is relaxed, with a bend at the knee, and there is an inquisitive look on her cute little face. Both girls sport pageboy haircuts, with bangs; they're wearing tan stockings and what appear to be matching dark dresses, with two pockets in front and a small Ukrainian sunflower design on the shoulders. Nellie's got on dark brown boots with many eyelets; Irene is wearing Mary Janes.

My grandfather wears a dark three-piece suit, a formal white shirt with starched cuffs, a small black bow tie, black socks, and black business shoes. There is a slight smile on his face. He looks handsome and happy.

Effie wears a long-sleeve dress that covers her knees and runs up to her neck. What seems to be a Ukrainian floral design rings her collar and falls in a line down the middle of her dress to her waist, and is repeated on her forearms. White stockings cover her legs, which are

Nell with John and Effie Gavreluk

The family four years later, with a new addition, my mother

crossed at the ankle. Her shoes are similar to those of Irene, whom she cradles with her left arm and hand. Compared to the previous photograph, Effie looks as though she's added weight to her face. Her short dark hair again is combed over the left side of her forehead, with a barrette holding it away from her left eye. There is no softness or beauty to her expression; rather, she appears tense, almost angry. Her elder daughter mirrors her stern visage—an expression out of character for Nellie, whose demeanor, as I remember it, was usually full of joy. What was going on that day?

Whatever happened in the Gavreluk family leading up to that session in the photography studio, I can see from both pictures that Effie had style, in both her clothing and her hair. Her flair for fashion was a gift she handed down to her daughters. "Irene and I were really into clothes," recalls Martha Mulkoff. "She was always into high fashion, as much as you could be at age eighteen or nineteen. That was very important to her." That sense of style was inherited by Nancy and then by Nancy's daughter, Eva. Both of them modeled clothing during their

Knockouts: My sister, Nancy, and my niece, Eva, mid-1990s

youths—like Effie and Irene, they were real knockouts. Tracing this touch of glamour back across four generations of women—from my niece to my sister to my mother to my grandmother—is gratifying to me. It draws a positive connection, and a creative link, to the past.

Effie will always be the beautiful young mother she was in those photographs, for she never got the chance to grow old. In the late 1920s, she contracted tuberculosis. "Effie spent most of her time in a sanitarium," says Helen Livingston, who recalls Effie as a lovely, friendly woman. "But on occasion she would come home and stay—maybe a week, maybe less—with the family." I've researched TB sanitariums that operated in southeastern Michigan during the 1920s and '30s; I found one in Howell and another in Northville. Perhaps she stayed at one of them. With travel what it was at that time, I imagine that Effie's family could make only infrequent visits to see her. I don't recall my mother or Aunt Nell ever talking about visiting their mother.

One intriguing clue to my grandmother's character and history came a few years ago from a Ukrainian-American activist. "Your grandmother was a suffragette," this woman told me. "She was involved in the movement." I have no other evidence of my grandmother's work in the cause of women's suffrage. However, the events of the period support the possibility. In 1916, the Canadian provinces of Alberta, Manitoba, and Saskatchewan, all home to large populations of Ukrainian immigrants, gave women the right to vote. Soon afterward, the Ukrainian National Republic extended suffrage to women. In 1918, the year Effie and John left Canada, Michigan passed a constitutional amendment granting the vote to that state's women. And two years later, the Nineteenth Amendment to the US Constitution was ratified, making female suffrage the rule throughout the nation. Yes, it's certainly plausible that my grandmother was involved in the battle for equity before her illness struck.

I was told by my family that Effie died because rheumatic fever had damaged her heart valve. But we know she had TB, too, so I can't be certain of her cause of death. I do know my mother was about eight years old when my grandmother died, dating her passing to around 1931. Effie Gavreluk, mother of two young daughters, couldn't have been older than thirty-five.

There are so many questions I wish I'd asked my grandmother: How did you and Grandpa meet? What made you happy? What made you sad? What kind of education did you have? What was it like to give birth in a prison? I wish I'd asked Grandpa about her; I'm sad now that I wasn't more curious about Effie when I had a chance to get some answers. Her death must have been a crushing blow to Grandpa. And there was more heartbreak to come.

During my youth, I heard John Gavreluk described as "a hard-hearted soul," "a stern guy," "a son of a gun." Those words did describe his exterior. He found it almost impossible to show love for us, verbally or physically. He never hugged, kissed, or showed any outward sign of affection, but we somehow knew he loved us. When Jeff was in grade school and walked home every day for lunch, Grandpa would have the meal ready—hot dogs, soup, sandwiches. He cared for us. He watched us. Perhaps his reserve was attributable in large part both to his not being the object of affection during his childhood and to his deficiency in communication. What's more, his work in the auto plants damaged his hearing. My brother, Jeff, who is ten years my junior, spent a lot of time with Grandpa during the latter years of his life. "He was hard of hearing," Jeff recalls, "and boy, when Huntley and Brinkley came on, he'd be sitting there with his hand cupped to his ear. He was a yeller and seemed perpetually miserable. He had a good heart, but he just didn't know how to show it." I agree with my brother's description of Grandpa—both his apparent misery and his heart. Later, when I would take my grandfather shopping, or to picnics and concerts, he would introduce me to his friends with great pride. Nancy, typically, shows the greatest insight into the man, noting the tragic course of his life. "In our home," she says, "it was my grandfather who lost his wife, and then his two daughters." Irene, like her mother, died in her thirties; Nellie passed away a dozen years later, at the age of fifty-four. "I'm sure he had tremendous pain from those losses. I don't know if I recognized it enough when I was younger. Oh, I knew about it, but even now, since I haven't gone through something like that, I can't imagine what it was like for him."

PIROGI OR CREPES?: A QUESTION OF NATIONALITY

"Bonior. That's French, isn't it?"

I've been asked this question more times than I can count. The possibility that my name is French has always confused me. My father, his parents, and numerous other relatives on that side all spoke fluent Polish. Our entire everyday culture revolved around Polish customs and traditions in food, the arts, and religious observance. Yet my last name did look and sound French. What was I to make of it?

Members of my family could not give me an answer. They insisted that both my father's parents, whom I knew as JaJa and Busia—traditional Polish equivalents to Grandpa and Grandma—were born in Poland and that our last name had had not been shortened in America, as long Polish names often were. Our name was never Boniorski or Boniorewicz.

In the 1980s, before there was an Internet, I began to search for the meaning and history of my name. Whenever I traveled, I looked for it in phone directories. I hit the jackpot in Chicago, where the phone book listed a good dozen. I began cold-calling down the list. An elderly gentleman with my last name answered the phone at his home in Chicago Heights. He thought the Boniors were French nobles who migrated to Poland after the French Revolution.

I accepted this story until a college president from Michigan set me straight.

In about 1995, Thaddeus "Ted" Radzlowski, who headed St. Mary's College (Orchard Lake), in Oakland County, introduced me at a speech

I was giving on Capitol Hill to the American Association of Presidents of Independent Colleges and Universities. Hearing that I was Polish, Dr. Radzlowski, a scholar of Poland, had researched our family name. It was not French, he told me, but fully Polish. It is derived from *St. Boniface,* he said, a Polish saint from the northern parts of Poland and Prussia. *Bonior* literally means "a deep pool in a mountain stream"; used figuratively, it describes someone who is a deep thinker but reticent—connoting roughly the same meaning imparted by the English expression "Still waters run deep." I was surprised but joyful to hear this information, and thankful to Dr. Radzlowski for his research. Shortly afterward, my friend Stan Kemp told me that he'd seen a military statue of a Bonior in Warsaw. Years later, in Krakow, I found numerous Boniors—perhaps related to me, for Bonior is not a common name in Poland—who were doctors or taught at Jagiellonian University. I wasn't French after all.

Krakow, birthplace of my paternal grandmother, was the second stop on our 2011 trip to Eastern Europe; we went there from Stetseva. Our Ukrainian travel agent in New Jersey needed help planning our visit to Krakow, so she contacted a travel agency there. The agent she wound up speaking to was . . . Agnieszka Bonior! Aga, who speaks excellent English, served as our guide during the four days we spent in her city. She couldn't have been more welcoming and knowledgeable. She helped us dig up some of our family's history, and she gave us a sense of Krakow's rich past and vibrant present, taking us to Cloth Hall, St. Mary's Church, Jagiellonian University, and Wawel Castle and Cathedral, as well as walking us through various residential neighborhoods, including Kazimirez (the Jewish quarter) and the Schindler Factory Museum. Trying to locate people named Pustelnik—my grandmother's maiden name—I checked the Krakow phone book, but none were listed.

Our next stop was Auschwitz-Birkenau, the Nazi death camp some thirty miles outside Krakow.

As I had been when visiting the killing fields in Cambodia, I was overwhelmed by the brutality of this place. I felt empty and hopeless as we walked around the site and learned of its history from the sensitive and thoughtful teacher we'd hired as our guide. According to the United States Holocaust Memorial Museum in Washington, at least 960,000 Jews were murdered at this camp, along with approximately 74,000 non-Jewish Poles—some Boniors, I learned, were among them—plus thousands more: Roma, Soviet prisoners of war, and others.

The enormity of the crimes in twentieth-century Europe, and the massive scale of the upheaval and violence that engulfed the continent during two long wars, underscored for me why its poor and minorities were willing to uproot themselves to seek refuge on the other side of the globe. Not only did my grandparents face a daily grind of poverty in Ukraine and Poland but they also had to reckon with the region's political and social instability. The United States and Canada represented their chance for a more prosperous life—and a more peaceful one, as well.

A BIT OF MISCHIEF:
JAJA

Frank Bonior, whom I knew as JaJa (pronounced with a hard *J*: JAH-jah), was born in Poland on May 14, 1882. I regret that I know virtually nothing more of his early history. In what town was he born? How large was his family? When did he emigrate? When did he meet my grand-mother? How much education did he have? Speaking through my father as interpreter, I would ask JaJa these questions over the years, but I received no satisfactory answers. They didn't want to talk about the Old Country; that was the past, he would always tell me.

What I do know is that in 1912 in St. Louis, Missouri, he married Frances Pustelnik, my grandmother, whom we called Busia (BOO-sha). I have their wedding picture. Frank is sitting, resting his left arm on a small table decorated with a vase of flowers, his right arm on his right thigh. He has a neat mustache and curly hair. His face looks serious, with eyes that are wide and expressive. He's wearing a high white collar and white bow tie, a vest with a watch chain, striped pants, and a boutonniere on the left lapel of his black jacket.

No more than five feet tall, Frances is wearing a white wedding gown decorated with white cloves. A laurel of flowers adorns her hair, and she carries a bouquet in her right hand. She is standing to my grandfather's right, slightly behind him, with her left hand on his shoulder. She, too, appears serious, with expressive eyes. The overall effect of her appearance is a suggestion of confidence, as though she is bringing JaJa down to size. It's the only time I ever saw her stand up to her husband.

Busia and JaJa on their wedding day

Between five feet ten and six feet tall, trim in stature, Frank Bonior worked as a manual laborer. When I knew him, he had a handlebar mustache, which he waxed—the look of it fascinated me. He smoked a pipe—I loved its sweet aroma, deeming it far superior to the stale smell of my dad's Lucky Strikes.

I don't know the facts of his arrival in the United States, so I need to surmise. I assume that he arrived by ship from Poland and was cleared through Ellis Island. I imagine that he set off right away for St. Louis, where there was an established Polish community. I suppose that he came to the States with his brother Joseph. And I figure that their (or just his) destination in St. Louis might have been St. Stanislaus Kostka parish, the center of the city's Polish life.

I know more about what came next. Within a few years after marrying, Frank and Frances were parents of two boys, John and Joseph, both born in St. Louis. The family soon followed other members of the extended Bonior clan to Chicago, where, in 1918, Frances gave birth to Marie. Now a family of five, they moved again, drawn, as were the Gavreluks, to Detroit's booming auto industry. They settled in Hamtramck, on Moran Street, in a small wooden house just three blocks from Our Lady Queen of Apostles Church, on Conant Street. The medium-size brick church would be the center of their religious and social life. In 1922, Frances gave birth to her fourth and last child, Edward John, my father. Actually, he was her fourth and last *surviving* child—another two died in infancy.

Frank got a job at Palmer-Bee, an auto-related manufacturer in Detroit. After years of working there, however, he had an accident on the factory floor and broke his back. The injury cost him his job—just as the Great Depression was setting in. The family found itself in dire straits. The Bonior boys had all studied printing at Hamtramck High School, so when Palmer-Bee fired JaJa, my uncle John quit school to set up a printing shop in the garage at the back of the house. John, Joe, and Ed hustled business from the church and from neighborhood shops and offices. The brothers also set type and did layout, while my aunt Marie served as proofreader. Uncle John was everyone's hero, sacrificing school to put the business together so the family could survive. When JaJa's back healed, he "ran production"; in other words, he fed the press and ran a folding machine, jobs that did not require knowledge of the English language. Busia did her part by taking in laundry. Plus, my father had a side business: hustling "numbers" in the neighborhood. He worked for Stan Kemp's father. Dad sold the numbers wholesale to people in the neighborhoods, and they in turn retailed the numbers up and down the street. My father would collect the proceeds, and when the drawings were held, he would pay out the winners. It was a tough time, but the family cobbled together enough income to make ends (barely) meet.

The print shop became a special place to my sister and me. Like the church, it owned its own aroma, a mixture of ink and solvents—my sister and I remember it well. We remember the distinctive sound of the place, too, starting with the clank and chug of the two handfed presses. Often my uncles and my older cousins would sit in the shop having a drink. They'd laugh and tease, they'd argue about politics. I'd stare in awe as I listened to the verbal jousting over the rhythmic beat of the machinery. Most of this back-and-forth was in Polish, showing me just how expressive my family could be in a language that was familiar to them. I wished I could join in.

When Dad would take me over to his parents' house, we'd sit in the kitchen for lunch. JaJa and Busia delighted at hearing my father tell stories about their grandchildren. JaJa was a stern man most of the time, but he had a large laugh, and when he smiled, he lit up a room. On holidays—Christmas and Easter—he'd engage in a bit of mischief. He'd set up a shot glass, full of whiskey, in front of everybody's place setting. And I mean everybody's—the children's included. JaJa expected each grandchild to take a sip from the glass, or at least to wet his or her lips with the liquor. The littlest ones, of course, hated it, and wiggled and squirmed in their mothers' arms while the poison touched their tender mouths. JaJa reveled in the chaos of the spectacle. But even though he tormented us with this ritual, he loved giving his grandkids hugs and kisses, although most of us were afraid of his waxed handlebar mustache.

The house on Moran was modest, with less than a thousand square feet of living space. On the main floor was the living room, with two stuffed chairs along a wall; on the floor between them stood a radio, enclosed in a large, wooden cabinet. Above the chairs were two pictures, one of the Blessed Virgin Mary, the other of the Sacred Heart of Jesus. On the opposite wall was a sofa, with just enough floor space between it and the chairs to walk through the living room to the front door, which led to a small, roofed porch barely large enough to hold a pair of chairs. I like to imagine my grandparents before I was born, sitting in the stuffed chairs in the living room listening to broadcasts in Polish or, with translation by their children, to FDR's fireside chats or Edward R. Murrow's reporting on the Second World War. I can picture JaJa sitting on the porch smoking his bowl of cherry-flavored tobacco while Busia, sitting next to him, holds a rosary laced among her arthritic fingers.

At the end of the living room, opposite the front door, was a small open area. This space was probably designed to be a dining room, but instead it contained two heavy desks and served as an office for the printing business. Off one side of this room were two bedrooms, one for my grandparents, the other for their four children. Off the other was the kitchen, where the family ate its meals. The kitchen had its own magical scent—a blend of *kapusta* (sauerkraut, sometimes with mushrooms mixed in), strong coffee, and whatever else might be on the stove. Maybe Busia would have a huge pot of soup simmering, perhaps with a ham hock inside.

I enjoyed sitting in that kitchen watching my father interact with his parents in Polish, even though I understood little of the conversation. Starting when I was about eight, Busia would give me "coffee," although the cup was at least half full of milk, or *mlecko*, as I was taught to say in Polish. Sitting at the kitchen table, I learned to speak the basic phrases I've used ever since, sharing them with my children and grandchildren. My favorite is *Daj mi buzi*, which means "give me a kiss."

Off the kitchen was a bathroom with no shower, and from the bathroom a set of winding stairs led to the attic. The stairs were a sacred place: My cousin Ed, who was raised by my grandparents, kept his toys, games, and collection of baseball cards on them. On the opposite side of the kitchen was a door that led to what we called the "cold porch," an enclosed but unheated room that Busia used for storing food, especially for family gatherings. Beneath all of this was an open basement, which was full of wonderful things. Primary among them was a large table, where all my grandmother's freshly baked apples pies would sit before she served them on Christmas and Easter. There was also a small cellar where, most of the time, potatoes were stored. Before big holiday gatherings, however, something much more delectable would sit there: cases of pop. My favorite flavors were black cherry and rock & rye, a cherry-vanilla concoction that its maker, Michigan bottler Faygo, calls a "complex and intriguing drink." Occasionally I would find a *cream* soda: Heaven!

Special Gifts:
Busia

Born in Krakow on June 16, 1889, Frances Pustelnik was a small woman with a big heart. Her life revolved around her home, her family, and the church. Neither she nor JaJa spoke English, but they were saved by Hamtramck, where Polish was sufficient for all the needs of daily life. Almost all of their neighbors spoke Polish. Most storeowners spoke Polish, as did their clerks. Priests spoke Polish. A daily newspaper, the *Hamtramck Citizen*, was in Polish. There were Polish radio broadcasts, which originated at the Senate Café and Bar on Joseph Campau in the north end of town. And the five movie theaters in Hamtramck, all within walking distance from the house on Moran, often showed Polish films. JaJa and Busia got along just fine without the English language.

In my memory, Busia usually wore a simple house dress. She never stinted on the warm smiles and loving hugs for Nancy and me. Often, before our visit with her and JaJa would end, she would quietly take us into the children's bedroom, where my cousin Ed now slept, and squeeze a dime or quarter into our hands. She'd raise a finger to her lips to signal that this gift was a secret—and JaJa was not to know. I cherished the bond we created with these clandestine exchanges. Despite the language barrier, we understood perfectly not only her instruction to keep mum about the money but also something much more important: We were special to her.

She was no stranger to heartache. How those two dead babies must have weighed upon her over the years. When her husband lay dying with colon cancer in their bedroom in 1959, she would cover my ears so that I would not hear my grandfather cry out in pain. JaJa was the first relative whose death I experienced. For all the sadness she must have been feeling at the impending loss of her companion of nearly half a century, Busia and her abiding love were there for Nancy and me, protecting us, helping us through that difficult time.

Busia always carried her rosary beads, often praying the rosary to Mary, I'm sure. But if she used them as worry beads, no one would have blamed her. Her life was not easy. When I knew my paternal grandparents, they were not poor, but the family was on the cusp of poverty during the Depression, after JaJa broke his back and could not work. There was no safety net back then.

She died August 3, 1967. Just before she passed, I returned from college and went with my father to visit her at St. Francis Hospital in Hamtramck. Nowadays, hospitals usually administer oxygen via tubes and masks, but at that time patients in respiratory distress would commonly be placed in an oxygen tent. There was Busia, lying in bed underneath a clear plastic canopy. This seventy-eight-year-old woman was fighting for every breath. Dad and I stood side by side watching her, helpless to ease her suffering or even to communicate by touch. Dad, the youngest of this kind woman's children, had tears in his eyes.

Busia lived to see her children get married and have families of their own, giving her and JaJa eleven grandchildren. She watched the older ones go off to college. She saw her children start and own successful businesses. She even saw her youngest child elected mayor of a new city, East Detroit. Like other females in our family, she was the understanding, gentle adult who smoothed the jagged edges of a strict, often joyless home.

We all loved her for that.

HOT OPEN ROAST BEEF SANDWICHES: DAD

Edward John Bonior was big from the moment he took his first breath: Legend has it that he weighed in at eleven pounds at birth—or was it fourteen?—setting a new hospital record. He would grow into a tall, handsome man who would overshadow a room full of people by his mere presence.

Born on Washington's birthday in 1922—2/22/22—he would find his way into politics and public service, and he would hang onto the number *2* like a boy carrying a rabbit's foot on a chain. When he was born, Hamtramck still had a trace of rural life—across the street from the home on Moran was a small plot of land with a milk cow. It was a good time, the Roaring Twenties. They would roar right into the Great Depression, when you went to bed and woke up thinking of nothing more sportive than survival.

As the "baby of the family," Edward John Bonior was much loved by his parents and siblings. JaJa could be stern, sometimes mean, but Busia was always there to dispense an extra dose of tenderness. If Dad ran into trouble in the neighborhood, his brothers and sister—John, Joe, and Marie—were there to protect him.

After the Depression hit, Dad and his pals would go down to the Grand Trunk and Western railroad tracks near the facility of the Mistele Coal Company. They'd hop the coal cars and toss off chunks to take home for heat. He further refined his throwing skills during a landmark labor dispute. In 1937 the workers at Hamtramck's Dodge Main staged a sit-down strike that lasted for seventeen days; until that point, it was the longest sit-down strike in American history. With the gates to the factory closed and the striking workers camped out inside the walled factory complex, my father would pitch sandwiches over the walls to the hungry men inside.

These lessons in survival and social justice were underscored by the lessons his parents taught him at home and by the Catholic training he received at Our Lady Queen of Apostles. Throughout his life he would find quiet ways to show his empathy for the poor and for children. He liked underdogs and enjoyed helping them.

Playing baseball on Hamtramck's empty lots and fields, he soon found that he was blessed with natural athletic talent. As he got older, he had the size to go with it, reaching his full adult height—six feet four—while still a student at Hamtramck High School. He instinctively knew that his size gave him an advantage in life, whether in his everyday dealings with people or in his athletic adventures. He played on the high school baseball, football, and basketball teams. Martha Mulkoff recalls his days on the hardwood as the squad's star center. "We used to follow him around because he was such a good player," she says. "He had these wonderful long legs. And he was good. Well, I can't remember how good he was—but he sure looked good." At that time, for at least some of his high school career, the rules called for a jump ball at mid-court after every field goal. Dad dominated those tosses, and likewise was a rebounding machine. Years later his younger son, Jeffrey, would rule the boards at Notre Dame High School. Dad's basketball skills would earn him a scholarship to the Detroit Institute of Technology. The school emphasized engineering and the sciences, and was at one time affiliated with the Massachusetts Institute of Technology.

As good as he was at basketball, what my father really excelled at was throwing a baseball. He started playing catch with me by the time I was five or six. As I got older, he would run through his full repertoire of pitches as we threw a ball back and forth on the sidewalk in front of our house. He had amazing speed on his fastball and could snap off a wicked, diving curve—his arm must have gained strength from all those lumps of coal and sandwiches he'd tossed. His knuckleball fluttered all over the place—it was a real challenge to catch. Having caught Dad, it came as no surprise when I later learned that the St. Louis Browns had been interested in him. When the Browns came to Detroit to play the Tigers, Dad would put on a Browns uniform and pitch batting practice to the team before games in Briggs Stadium. But those dreams were cut short by the war. Dad never got a chance to play professional ball, but through baseball he left me with special memories. Fathers and sons playing catch create a special bond, well described by John Sexton in *Baseball as a Road to God*: "The ball goes back and forth hypnotically, as life outside the arch slowly fades away and only the ball and the partner remain; sometimes there is conversation, often no words are required. Just quiet intimacy interrupted only by the pop of the ball colliding with leather."[3]

In high school, Dad studied a trade: printing. Printing then was what computers are today, a popular course of study, which, if mastered, could furnish you with a nice living. He also showed an uncommon interest in government and politics. "Whenever the big bands were in town," Martha remembers, "we all wanted to go dance, and have our Coke and potato chips. But Ed wanted to go to the city council meetings. He used to say, 'You might learn something, Martha.'" Years later, when he sought elective office himself, Dad would draw on what he'd learned at those sessions.

Meetings of the Hamtramck City Council were as entertaining as they were edifying, enlivened by a number of fascinating personalities. One was Mary Zuk, the first woman on the council and a Socialist to boot. And then there was Doc Ten—Dr. Rudolph Tenerowicz—the family practitioner who served as mayor and then congressman before going to prison on corruption charges. Once he got out of prison, his

3 John Sexton, with Thomas Oliphant and Peter J. Schwartz, *Baseball as a Road to God: Seeing Beyond the Game* (New York: Gotham Books, 2013), 185–186.

criminal record was no obstacle to restarting his political career: By popular demand he ran again for mayor—and won.

Dad cared about the public welfare, and, in office, was a conscientious public servant. But there was another side to his personality. He was a hustler. He loved a good time and he enjoyed finding ways to make that good time happen. His turf as a numbers runner was mostly in Hamtramck. As the Depression began to take hold, people would make a modest investment in a lottery—at that time private and illegal, unlike today's state-run system—in hope of shattering their feelings of despair. One day Dad hit the jackpot himself. He gave a portion of his winnings to his family, then bought a big, brand-new car. There was enough left to treat several of his high school football teammates to an evening in downtown Detroit, where the boys and their hormones visited a so-called "boarding house" stocked with women practicing the world's oldest profession.

My father always enjoyed playing the ponies and betting on football games. I recall vividly sitting in his lap, when I was six or seven, watching Texas Christian University play football on television. In his hand Dad held a gambling "card"—a piece of paper you could buy that listed all the week's big college games and their point spreads. If you beat the spread on five games, you won money. I was never quite sure whether my father merely played these cards or was part of the crowd running the operation. I suspect, although I have no proof, that he printed these cards in his shop. Besides, the cards were a purely wholesome diversion: I've forgotten the exact wording, but on the bottom there was always a disclaimer to the effect that the cards were "for informational use only."

After he graduated from high school, Dad gave college a try, but he lasted only a semester at the Detroit Institute of Technology. He kept working in the print shop; then, a few years after he graduated from high school, war called him. Thoughts of a career in basketball or baseball, printing or politics, were put on hold. However, when a pretty Ukrainian girl caught his eye, he was not about to put *that* part of his future on hold.

After his induction, the army sent Dad to Texas for basic training. Allied troops had just landed on the beaches of Normandy; casualties in Europe were heavy, as men continued to die in the Pacific. It must have dawned on Dad that he might not return from the war, or might not return whole. Although he never shared these thoughts with me, my guess is that, pondering his mortality, he realized that he wanted a wife and family, and wanted to make sure he got things started before shipping out.

My father with his parents during the war,
in back of the house on Moran

He went AWOL (absent without leave), hitchhiking from the Lone Star State back to Hamtramck in order to marry his sweetheart. Ed Bonior and Irene Gavreluk eloped, tying the knot in Toledo, Ohio. The blushing bridegroom then returned to the army and his punishment, which I assume he served out in Texas. His next stop was Fort Carson, Colorado, where he was sent by the army to receive training as a medic at nearby Fitzsimmons Army Hospital, in Aurora. On January 3, 1945, he sailed on the SS *Brazil*, bound for Le Havre, France, with the 123rd Evacuation Hospital unit. He would serve in the outfit's field hospital, the first stop for servicemen wounded in battle.

As so often is the case with returning war veterans, Dad shared little with his family about his time at war. I saw no evidence that the horrors he saw affected his behavior after the war. Nevertheless, it's no secret that bottling up such traumatic memories is not healthy. Nowadays we call the sad result of this silence post-traumatic stress disorder, or PTSD. During World War I, the diagnosis was "shell shock"; in World War II, it was "battle fatigue." Much more is known about PTSD now than at the time Dad came home from overseas, but even then, psychiatric and psychological professionals were working on bringing this affliction out of the shadows. Soon after the war ended, in 1946, John Huston produced and directed a documentary on the subject called *Let There Be Light*. Pentagon brass deemed the film too controversial—it would hinder recruitment was the excuse given—and embargoed it. It wasn't released until 1980, when Secretary of the Army Clifford Alexander made it public at the behest of Jack Valenti, head of the Motion Picture Association of America, as well as Hollywood producer Ray Stark and then–Vice President Walter Mondale.

Near the end of his life, Dad finally shared with my brother an experience he'd kept inside for over fifty years. As Jeff tells it, our father arrived in Le Havre sick as hell from the ocean voyage. From the ship, he boarded a truck that was to take him to Camp Lucky Strike, where he would be based. On the way, however, the truck got word that the enemy had blown up a train at the train station, and Dad was called into action. Arriving at the station, he ran over to administer aid to an American soldier who lay by the mangled train. As Dad cradled the soldier's head in his arms, he saw that a third of it was gone. That was his welcome to Europe and the war.

Dad was awarded two Bronze Stars and found his work as a medic rewarding and challenging. On several occasions he told me that he wished he'd been able to pursue a career in medicine. At the same time, however, what he saw in the field hospital made him determined, for the rest of his life, to stay as far away from doctors and hospitals as he could.

Dad's service opened his eyes not only to the horror of war but also to the larger world beyond Hamtramck—he was able to see much of France and Germany as the war wound down. But when the army discharged him in January 1946, he returned to his hometown, where his bride had already given birth to their first child: me. She and I were living with my grandfather John Gavreluk at the house on Lehman Street; my father joined us there. He got a job at Jordan Printing in downtown Detroit, bought his second car, a Plymouth, and began thinking about starting his own printing business. Meanwhile, the shop in the garage on Moran continued to operate, run by JaJa and Dad's two brothers, Uncle John and Uncle Joe. When he was around, my father pitched in, too.

In 1954, with help from his sister, my aunt Marie, he opened Eastland Printing, a small shop on Mt. Elliott near Nevada, a mile or so outside Hamtramck in what is now a devastated area of Detroit. Nancy, Jeff, and I all recall accompanying our father to the shop in the evenings and on weekends. We kept him company and did small jobs. I would operate the folding machine—it was safe, easy, and monotonous. For lunch, Dad would take me to a nearby small café where we would enjoy hot open roast beef sandwiches, with gravy and mashed potatoes. Jeff recalls working in the shop on Saturdays in later years, after our mother's death. After the work was done, Dad would close up the premises, then buy a bouquet of flowers. Father and son would then drive to the cemetery where our mother is buried and place the flowers on her grave. All three of us will always cherish the simple, tender moments we enjoyed with our father.

Dad never lost interest in politics, and in the mid-1950s he decided to run for elective office. He twice lost bids to join the city council in East Detroit, where we moved when I was eight. With the help of all his family and every friend he could muster, he was elected on his third try. Not many years thereafter he was elected mayor of East Detroit. His main goals as mayor were better sewer service and better recreation facilities. With the city growing exponentially, the sewer system could not hold the rains; the result was backed-up sewage in basements throughout the city. The town's growth also meant more youth, who needed places to go when school was out. Looking at surrounding cities that boasted pools or lakeside parks, Dad insisted that a city the size of East Detroit—fifty thousand residents—should have a swimming pool, so he got the town to build a large outdoor pool in Kennedy Park. He also made it a point of pride to respond personally to all citizen complaints, often visiting people's homes to discuss problems they had reported. But his commitment to constituent service was tested one morning at 3:00 a.m.

The ringing of the phone woke everybody up. Naturally a call at that hour sends up red flags; your immediate thoughts go to imagining some terrible event. *Who died? Who got hurt?* My father got out of bed, walked past my bedroom, and proceeded down the hall to the kitchen, where our phone hung on a wall. The call did not bring news of a tragedy or crisis—at least nothing anyone in the Bonior household would consider particularly alarming. Rather, an irate citizen of East Detroit wanted to give his mayor an earful because the streetlight on this citizen's corner was out. My father politely took down the man's name, phone number, and address and told him that he would have the DPW—Department of Public Works—fix the light that day. Dad hung up the phone and, grumbling, returned to bed. When he got to work later that morning, he had the DPW do the repair. The next night

I heard Dad's alarm go off in the middle of the night—at 3:00 a.m., in fact. He turned it off, got out of bed, and, as he had the previous night, headed into the kitchen. He picked up the phone and called the same irate citizen. "This is the mayor," he told the man. "I just want to find out if your streetlight is working." Then he hung up the phone.

I think I heard him chuckle as he padded back to bed.

As mayor, Dad was chosen by the city council to sit on the Macomb County Board of Supervisors, the county's legislative body, all of whose seventy-six members were appointed. After a couple of years his peers elected him to chair the board, making him, in effect, the county's mayor. The board soon made the job full-time, with a good salary; as a consequence, the printing business faded away. Dad accumulated a lot of power in a short time—a situation that began to alarm some in the county's old-guard power structure. When he came up for reelection as mayor of East Detroit, these opponents ran a city councilman against him, and won. Soon, Dad not only lost his chairmanship of the board of supervisors but was also stripped by the council of his seat on the board. We were all devastated. Dad struggled to find work, but at forty-five years of age, he was turned down right and left. He wondered out loud if he was finished.

I learned a lot from this experience:

1. Nothing is a sure thing. Life can change on a dime.

2. Unemployment can be catastrophic for a person and his family. After working his heart out for the community, Dad was crushed—not only by the citizens' apparent ingratitude but also by his inability to support his family. Without work, he felt his worth and dignity diminished. His confidence was gone. He felt defeated. When I became a legislator years later, with my family's example still fresh in my mind I would take a special interest in job creation and unemployment compensation.

3. I would always remember who did this to my father and our family, and I would find a way to pay them back. It took a while, but I did.

Just when you feel the gray skies above you will never clear, a rainbow appears. My family's rainbow was the Great Society. Congress had gotten to work enacting a number of President Johnson's groundbreaking social programs; after a year of unemployment, Dad was hired by Macomb County to head its branch of the Office of Economic Opportunity. He held the job for about fifteen years, and during that time he accomplished much on behalf of the county's citizens. He started the county's first Head Start and Meals on Wheels programs. He started programs for Legal Aid, credit counseling, and weatherization. He ran the Jobs Corps program and administered the Comprehensive Employment and Training Act. These job and training programs, directed by my father, succeeded way beyond expectations, putting thousands of citizens to work. He had a great staff, numbering as many as a hundred people. And he groomed individuals like Leo LaLonde, Frank Taylor Jr., John Bierbusse, Mike Busch, Linda McClatcher, and Ruth Lieberman, who all went on to great careers in their own right.

Decades later, my wife had a conversation with Ruthie Stevenson, an African American leader in Mount Clemens, then our hometown. Ruthie said to Judy, "We like David, but the reason African Americans vote for him is his father. We loved Ed." My father and his deputy, Ivan Harris, worked hard to train and find jobs for members of Macomb County's black community, in which the need was so pronounced. The two men made a difference in many lives.

Dad loved this famous quote from Hubert Humphrey: "It was once said that the moral test of government is how that government treats those who are in the dawn of life, the children; those who are in the twilight of life, the elderly; and those who are in the shadows of life, the sick, the needy, and the handicapped." When I went to Congress, it was my father's example that led me to become a staunch protector

Dad at the Office of Economic Opportunity

of programs to help and protect vulnerable people, and an advocate for expansion of such programs in time of need. Seeing all that my father accomplished, I understood how government could make people's lives more productive and hopeful.

Dad had a tough exterior, but underneath that veneer he was full of compassion for people who were struggling. There are stories of his taking kids off the street to go see the Tigers play, or buying a TV for a family that couldn't afford one, or seeing that clothing made its way to a family down on its luck. But his biggest contribution to his fellow citizens was simply doing the job he was paid to do—and doing it well: making sure that children got a "head start"; that the old and infirm enjoyed a decent meal every day, plus the few minutes of companionship also brought by a visit from "meals on wheels"; and that people out of work got job training, and the stipend that went with it, so that a father or mother could upgrade his or her skills and regain the dignity that comes with meaningful, steady employment.

JUST A SWEET PERSON:
MOTHER

My mother, Irene, born August 1, 1923, was the antithesis of my father in many ways. He was six four; she was five four. He was tough, with streaks of meanness; she was easygoing and nurturing. He rarely smiled; her face regularly lit up with delight. He was driven to succeed in politics; she wanted only to raise her children. But they had much in common, too. Both made their family a priority and worked hard to make a good home for all of us. Both loved to party and enjoyed the company of close friends. Both were religious but did not wear their faith on their sleeves. Both were average to above-average in high school but harbored no desire to go to college. And even though they didn't keep books in the house, both understood the importance of a good education, always preaching that schooling was the key to a good job and a stable life.

Mother would make best friends with Martha Kozak (who would marry Arthur Mulkoff), who lived two blocks away on Jacob Street. Both girls attended Playfair School, the neighborhood public elementary school. "We were buddies forever," Martha remembers. "From Playfair we went to Copernicus Junior High School and then to Hamtramck High School. We graduated together. All during that time, we had a very, very close friendship." Martha's family owned cinemas in Hamtramck, so Mother spent lots of time at the movies with her best friend. Perhaps her exposure to Hollywood heightened her interest in glamour and fashion. "Irene was a beautiful, beautiful girl," recalls Helen Livingston. "She looked just like her mother. What can I say about her? She was just a sweet person, a sweet girl."

When their mother died, twelve-year-old Nellie helped eight-year-old Irene deal with the loss, teaching her the joy of living. John, now a single parent, was in many ways a good father: He provided for his family, was proud of his daughters, and imbued them with good values and good manners. Affection, however, was not in his emotional toolkit. Laughter and affection, however, were constant features of my mother's

life—they were gifts Nellie gave her. Nellie also taught Mother Ukrainian cooking, especially the family favorites—pirogi, stuffed cabbage,
and a special treat, city chicken, a kabob of chicken, pork, and sometimes veal, breaded, skewered, and baked. Nellie was someone Irene
could emulate, a female role model she needed after their mother's
death. Having Nell, Martha, and Helen meant that Mother was surrounded by caring and fun-loving friends. All four girls were generous
and energetic, full of warmth, good humor, and a determination to
enjoy life, no matter what it threw their way. The companionship of
those days had a powerful, positive influence on Mother.

Irene Gavreluk grew up to become a stunning beauty—over the
years a number of her male contemporaries have told me of her gorgeous looks and the desire of all the neighborhood guys to date her.
One of her classmates in high school was Lucien Nedzi, who went on
to represent Hamtramck, Warren, and the East Side of Detroit in Congress. Our service overlapped by four years. On the House floor one

Mother (r.) and Martha Mulkoff

day in 1979 he and I were sitting together, talking, and he began to reminisce about my mother. He didn't say as much, but the way he recalled her made me think that he might have had a crush on her.

According to Martha, high school social life in the late '30s and early '40s was similar to the way it is today—young people didn't so much "date" as hang out with a natural group of friends. But Mother was secretly taken with the star athlete, the dashing man about town who drove a shiny new car. I say "secretly" because Martha, her best friend, was taken by surprise when it became public that my father and mother were falling in love.

After high school, Mother and Martha would take the Baker Street streetcar to downtown Detroit, where Mother worked in a bank. While Martha had her sights on a career in education—she became a school teacher and principal—my mother's idea of a future was to get married, have children, and be a homemaker. Away from work she enjoyed the pop culture of her time—she loved to sing along with recordings of Frank Sinatra, to dance to the sound of Glenn Miller and other big

My parents cutting their wedding cake

Mother and me

bands. She took in the latest films and shopped for the latest fashions. I don't know how much time, as she attended high school during the Depression, she spent pondering the possibility that her father might lose his job at Dodge Main. I don't know how worried she was, a few years later, about the war in Europe and Asia. I do know that as the Depression dissolved into war, and factories geared up to produce military materiel, economic fears lessened among the citizens of Hamtramck. Nevertheless, the citizens who lived through the Depression never forgot it, and the economic anxiety born of that period never left them.

When Dad left for France, Mother was five months pregnant with me. She missed her new husband—they'd been married only a short time—but she didn't lack for people who cared about her. Not only Nellie, Helen, and Martha but also another half dozen close high school girlfriends all formed a circle of love and care for her, and for me, as they waited for the war to be won and for their men to return safely home.

CHAPTER 3

Lehman Street between Joseph Campau and Gallagher

Hamtramck, Michigan, My First Home

FIVE OF US, WITH MY GRANDFATHER: MY FAMILY OF ORIGIN

Not a lot of discussion took place in our house, especially among the men. I wouldn't say that my mother was someone who was really talkative, although she could talk. She was not reticent. My father, however, was. I don't know for sure, but I think he just didn't have confidence in his ability to communicate well. He was a smart guy, and a tough guy, and in his political career, which was long, he gave many speeches. But I don't remember that. I remember that around the house, he just didn't speak much.

My paternal grandparents, Busia and JaJa, spoke no English—I don't know if I ever heard either of them speak a word of it. My maternal grandfather, John Gavreluk, who lived with us, spoke a little better, but he still didn't have much to say.

So around the dinner table there was not much conversation, although when I spilled my milk or wouldn't eat what I was supposed to eat—*then* there was communication. What discussion there was, was often about labor. My father and my grandfather, a retired auto worker, would talk about the United Auto Workers, about union contracts, about why it was important to be a union member. This was in the early 1950s, when the auto industry was strong and productivity was growing

Dad holding me at Belle Isle Park

exponentially. It was always a battle to get the workers their fair share of the proceeds; the UAW was a powerful force in seeking it. While there was tension between the two men of my household, they agreed on this subject.

Unions were simply part of the atmosphere in Hamtramck. Most of the people we knew had somebody in their family working at Dodge Main, the huge plant where my grandfather had worked for thirty years. Or if not at Dodge Main, then at the Ford plant in Highland Park.

As Martha Mulkoff recalls, "Everybody in Hamtramck belonged to the union. That was what you did. The young boys were almost guaranteed that they would have a job in the factory. And if you got a job in the factory, you were union. There was no question about that.

Unions in Hamtramck were synonymous with patriotism: You were either a union member, or you were a little bit lacking in what it takes to be an American. That's how strong it was."

This way of thinking is what, above all, I took to Congress from Hamtramck: Working-class values. Knowledge and appreciation of how hard people work. Fair compensation for honest work. Unions. Neighborhood. Community.

My views on class and labor began with those discussions I would hear at the table between my father and my grandfather. They were infrequent, but they occurred.

And I remembered them.

Still overseas when I was born, my father didn't meet me until I was a year old. But even at a distance he somehow managed to see that I was named for his hero, Dwight David Eisenhower. Later, my father wanted Ike to run for president as a Democrat. He didn't, but I was born already, so that was that.

The naming turned out to be appropriate, for I was born on the first anniversary of D-Day, the Allied invasion of Normandy. It was drizzly outside St. Joseph Mercy Hospital the morning of June 6, 1945, as my mother, supported by Nellie and by Helen Livingston, was giving birth to her first child. Built in 1922 on East Grand Boulevard in Detroit just a few blocks south of Hamtramck, in the neighborhood known as Poletown, St. Joe was leveled in 1981 to make room for a new General Motors plant. That day, however, it was functioning fine, as I emerged at a healthy seven pounds, eight ounces.

From the hospital I was taken home to 3029 Lehman, where I quickly became the darling of my mother and her circle of close girlfriends. "We took turns," says Martha. "We really coveted getting a chance to rock him. He was the first baby in our group, so we were really, really giving. He got a lot of attention from six surrogate mothers."

On one occasion, Martha's eagerness to take care of me, and to help my mother get some time on her own, clashed with my grandfather's

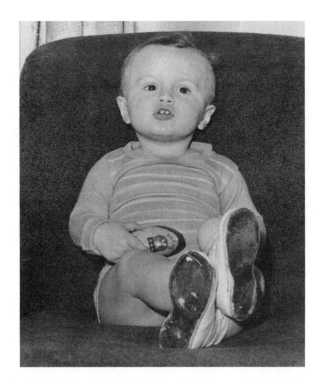

*On my first birthday, June 6, 1946, a ball in my left hand, and in my
right, a wooden shoe Dad had brought home from Belgium*

old-world ideas about child-rearing. As Martha explains it, "Like all
young mothers, Irene was homebound. She would call and say, 'Do you
think you could come over and stay with David?' I was happy to. Irene
would go shopping for herself, which she loved to do, and I would hold
David in my arms and sing to him. It was a good-sized house, and I
would walk around singing all the modern songs. Everything that I
could think of—Frank Sinatra songs, others. Big band music. One time
Irene's father came in and told me that maybe I should tone it down a
little bit. I guess I wasn't being such a good influence. I can understand
that now, but at the time I did not understand what he was talking
about. I thought the songs were perfectly beautiful. All the latest songs.
A bit of boogie-woogie."

Earliest memories can be deceptive. Do I really remember sliding on the freshly waxed hallway floor before slipping backwards and splitting my head open? Or is this just exaggerated lore I've heard repeated at family gatherings? I'm more certain of other memories. I know that at age five my tonsils were removed. I clearly recall the ether mask coming down over my face and the aroma that accompanied it. And I can still savor the anticipation of all the ice cream promised as a reward after the operation. The surgery took place at St. Francis Hospital in Hamtramck. When the hospital closed, the municipal authorities turned it into the city hall.

"I don't remember David as ever being any problem at all," says Martha. "He was always good." Maybe Martha doesn't remember my

First steps, at Belle Isle

being a problem, but I do—one day, anyway, when I was five. My mother was excited about new white curtains she and my father had just purchased and hung over the windows that looked over the front porch and into the street. For some unknown reason I took a pair of scissors and cut a hole smack in the middle of these brand-new drapes. I can still see the sad and bewildered look on her face. There must have been a reason for my attacking this beautiful addition to our home, but to this day I can't explain it. I was terrified that when my father came home from work I would get a deserved spanking.

Did I? I can't remember.

Our home on Lehman was a typical workman's house: wood-frame, on a thirty-by-seventy-foot lot. The houses on our block were close together—it seemed that no more than ten feet separated one from the next. Many of the structures in Hamtramck were two-family dwellings, but we were fortunate to have the whole house—two stories and a full

The house on Lehman

basement—to ourselves: five of us, with my grandfather, once Nancy arrived two years after me. Steps led up from the sidewalk to the ample, yellow-brick, covered front porch and the main floor. The entranceway from the porch led to the living room and to the stairs, which led to the second floor, where the three bedrooms were located.

The living room was furnished with a sofa and two stuffed chairs, all bordered with six-inch tassels that tickled the rug. A lovely wood coffee table sat in front of the sofa. On it was set a black ceramic jaguar, as well as a twelve-inch-long chrome model of a fighter airplane that was really a cigarette lighter—you spun the propeller to get your light. Next to the lighter was a ceramic box of cigarettes—no doubt a common coffee-table piece in the 1950s. As a small boy I was always tempted to start the lighter. I never did, but I loved to gaze at the shiny black jaguar and dream of danger.

The living room opened up to the dining room, where we never ate. Six chairs matched the handsome mahogany table, which was always covered with a pad and cloth so it would not be scratched. Against the wall was a buffet in which we stored some precious flatware and other ceramics that my father had brought back from Germany. I recall using the table as a house, playing under it with toy soldiers, cars, and fire trucks.

The dining room opened to the parlor through lead-glass French doors, which I thought the most elegant feature in the house. The parlor is where I took refuge in play and make-believe and where our Scots pine Christmas trees were meticulously decorated, mostly by Mom, during the holiday season. And it was where, on another couch, I would perch on my knees and gaze out the windows into our backyard, wishing the rain would stop so I could go out and play.

The hallway leading upstairs and to the kitchen ran along the wall that separated the living room and dining room. I cannot remember if we had a half bath off the kitchen, as was the case with many homes in Hamtramck. Many had been built between 1915 and 1930 with no bathrooms—just outhouses in the back. Over the next fifteen years, as

Two years old

indoor plumbing took hold for the average working family, many households converted their pantries to small bathrooms.

Our kitchen was large enough to accommodate a metal table, where we ate our meals. One day I saw my mother standing over the kitchen sink with a knife in her hand, crying. I was alarmed until she explained to me that she was peeling onions.

A door from the kitchen led to a covered open porch with two steps that took you to the backyard. A cherished memory of my mother occurred by the porch. She and her sister, Aunt Nell, were sitting on the steps enjoying each other's company while Nancy and I played near them in the yard. I overheard the two women talking about tap dancing—they'd probably seen tap dancers on a recent edition of the Ed Sullivan variety show. I walked over to where they were sitting and proudly announced that I could tap dance. I proceeded to demonstrate, breaking into a wild show of foot shuffling and arm waving. Mother and my aunt thought I was hilarious. They fell into uncontrollable laughter that only encouraged me to keep it up. That I could bring them so much joy being a silly six-year-old dancer warmed my heart then and created a gentle memory of the two sisters together, happy and full of joy, that warms my heart now.

The bathroom upstairs featured a tub but no shower. My parents' bedroom overlooked, through a single dormer, the street in the front of the house. Nancy and I occupied the bedroom in the back, over the parlor, overlooking the yard. And Grandpa had the middle bedroom, which was strictly *verboten* to Nancy and me.

A stern man, Grandpa kept the two of us out of the basement for a couple of years. That was where the "boogeyman" lived, or so he said. Evidently he liked to scare us—in a good-natured way, or so he must have thought. But what do a six- and a four-year-old know about the reality of a dark place that was, in fact, nothing more than a coal bin? Nancy and I were petrified of the boogeyman.

Mom with Nancy and me in the dining room

Grandpa Gavreluk, looking serious, as usual

So much so that we both had dreams of being chased by him. My dreams had me fleeing as he chased me up the basement stairs. He never caught me, but it was tough climbing those steps with the monster nipping at my heels. "Grandpa did scare us," recalls Nancy. "He had those Eastern European—kind of old Ukrainian, Romanian—bizarre ways. When I think of his life—he left Europe at eighteen. He had an education only up to third or fourth grade, so he must have worked in the fields and had a pretty primitive life. Probably a lot of those primitive ways were with him, and he passed them on to us."

By the time I was six, however—about the time I started to harbor doubts about the existence of Santa Claus—I had developed the courage to confront the demon in the coal bin. I carefully descended the stairs into the basement and slowly approached the opening where a pile of coal lay in a small bin on the kitchen side of the house. I peeked in, prepared to hightail it back up the steps to the safety of the kitchen and my mother's loving arms. When no one appeared, I carefully entered the pitch black.

Nothing but coal.

Once the terror lifted, I could spend time in the basement—and there was a lot to see. A large coal-fired boiler sat in the middle of the floor—I would watch the red-hot coals through openings in the small door. About ten feet away from the boiler was a washbasin; I would watch as my mother would scrub the men's dirty clothing, from the auto and print shops, on an old-fashioned scrub board, then run the garments through the rollers of the ringer that you cranked by hand. The other end of the basement contained a small storage room where our family stored odds and ends, treasures (to a six-year-old) like oil cans, balls of string, tools, nuts and bolts, and a pile of small boards that I would use to make crude little boats. There were even guitars and ukuleles—apparently left by a boarder years earlier when the family had rented out a room, as nobody in the family was musical. The door to this room was always open, always inviting me to explore and create. I loved those old guitars and ukuleles, and those old oil cans.

THE CADILLAC OF BICYCLES: MY TRAVELS AROUND THE NEIGHBORHOOD

In our bedroom, Nancy had her dolls and other playthings, and I had an inflated plastic clown that doubled as a punching bag. When hit, the clown, which was weighted at its base, would spring back to its upright position, ready once again to absorb all the punishment my

Nancy and me in the backyard

energized six-year-old body could deliver. My sister and I would play guessing games in bed, which eventually would result in a warning from our parents that it was time to sleep. If our game that night was "name that tune," we'd then switch to humming the songs instead of singing them, in order to keep the grown-ups from hearing us.

Covering the two twin beds in our room were Mackinaw blankets with red, yellow, and green stripes at each end. And atop the blankets were Howdy Doody bedspreads. *Howdy Doody* was the rave television show for children that ran from 1947 to 1960. Howdy was a puppet, usually garbed in circus or Western frontier clothes. Live in the studio was the "peanut gallery"—about a hundred screaming kids warning Howdy of shenanigans about to be performed behind his back by Clarabell the Clown. Our first TV, encased in mahogany wood that matched the dining room table—my parents loved mahogany—arrived in our home with great joy and excitement when I was six. I loved cartoons, many times rising before dawn to turn it on and fiddle with the rabbit-ear antenna, staring at the test pattern until broadcasting commenced. I was waiting for my Farmer Brown cartoons, which were always accompanied by classical music. Often on those early TVs the picture would suddenly "jump," then start rotating up or down. I was immensely frustrated as I turned the knob that was supposed to settle the picture: If you turned it too far, the picture would reverse itself and turn the opposite way.

There were two other shows I never missed. One was *Lash of the West*, a short-lived Western whose title character, Lash La Rue, used a whip instead of a gun. Maybe this show is what initiated not only my distaste for guns but also my journey toward serving as Democratic whip in Congress.

The other was *Adventures of Superman*. I have fond memories of jumping up and down on my parents' bed and its boggy mattress, pretending I could fly. The idea of Superman had a firm grasp on my imagination—at one point I really believed I could fly and was obsessed with trying. I would drape a large towel—my cape—around my shoulders and bounce many times on that sagging mattress before, with a great leap of faith, I would launch myself into the air. After many heavy landings, I finally grew weary and figured out that it was not to be.

This realization was even more devastating to me than figuring out that there was no Santa. Even now, I still have occasional dreams in which I'm flying. And I love it.

The Poles have a well-deserved reputation for hard work and cleanliness—our block was spotless. Large, majestic trees, some of them Dutch elms, canopied the streets of Hamtramck, forming huge arches that gave the neighborhood the feel of a cathedral. Years later Dutch elm disease struck Detroit and Hamtramck hard, destroying most of the trees. The blight dramatically changed the look of the neighborhoods, robbing them of their calming spirit. Some urbanologists point to Dutch elm disease as one factor that contributed to the collapse of some Detroit neighborhoods.

Perhaps twenty-five houses were crammed into each side of Lehman on our block between Joseph Campau and Gallagher streets. Since nearly everyone was Polish, it was common to hear the language up and down the street. People were often referred to by the Polish version of their first names. For instance, Stanley was Stash; Walter, Wad; and David, Dawid or, as my father would call me, Davedco.

One of my most vivid memories of our street comes from a late-summer day when I was playing inside and heard through the window screens the cry of "rag man, rag man" and the clip-clop of horse hooves on the pavement. I ran out to the porch, and there on the street was a horse-drawn wagon piled with old clothing and rags. The rag man's visit, I learned, was a ritual in Hamtramck. Another horse-drawn wagon would make its way through our neighborhood to the cry of "ice man, ice man." The wagon indeed carried ice, covered with a black tarp. The ice had been cut into blocks to be sold and placed in wooden iceboxes, still common in our community, even though by the early '50s, refrigeration had come to Hamtramck. The ice was harvested from Lake St. Clair in the winter, then stored and covered with canvas or sawdust before peddlers carved it and sold it in the neighborhoods.

Our backyard was our play area until my father and my uncle Andy, Nellie's husband, built a cinder-block garage there. Now I'm not sure of the new structure's purpose: Either my dad was following in his father's footsteps by setting up a small print shop, with a hand-fed press, or he and my uncle, a precision toolmaker, were creating a small tool-and-die shop. But what I am—and was—sure of is that it ate up half our yard.

Behind the garage was an alley, where we stored the garbage cans. One might find discarded items up and down the length of the alley, as well as barking dogs and pigeons flying home to their coops. This place seemed to be no more than a step or two above the coal bin as a spooky location to be avoided by children.

Dr. Rudolph Tenerowicz had his medical office at the end of the block, near Joseph Campau. Doc Ten would discard his medical waste in a garbage bin in the alley. Well, one of the neighborhood kids discovered that syringes made nifty squirt guns, so we would rummage around in all that medical waste, searching for them. I'm not even certain we cleaned the things before filling them with water and shooting at each other. Heavens knows what stuff we were getting ourselves into. It gives me the creeps today just to think about it. Ugh!!

In a garage at the other end of the alley was Modern Seat Covers, where two or three guys worked redoing car seats in leather or vinyl. On my seventh birthday my parents gave me the best present one could imagine: I was now the proud owner of a Schwinn Black Panther, the Cadillac of bicycles. It was not long before I discarded my training wheels and was tearing around the block. A favorite stop was Modern Seat Covers. The guys there took a liking to me—they must have enjoyed the diversion from their work—and would give me strips of vinyl to stuff into my handlebars. Even if I got no strips on a particular day, I enjoyed stopping there just to smell the leather and vinyl.

Kitty-corner from Modern Seat Covers was Johnson Creamery. My source of income as a seven-year-old was foraging for empty pop bottles and cans and redeeming them at the corner markets for a penny or two each. When my bankroll reached critical mass, about twenty-five cents, I would cross Holbrook and Gallagher streets and enter the creamery. Propping myself up on a swiveling stool at the soda fountain counter, I would order a vanilla milk shake. The best part was the extra shake that the soda jerk would set down, next to your glass, in the cold metal container he'd put under the mixer to make the shake. It was a two-for-one deal. Who could resist that?

Around the corner on Joseph Campau was a shoe repair store with a sign in its window that boasted of the establishment's "First Class Work." With half a dozen elevated padded chairs for shoeshines and a couple of cobblers working on their machines, the inside buzzed with activity. The sound of rags snapping, and the smell of wax and leather, would hit you as soon as you walked through the door.

Next was the Peoples State Bank, an ornate two-story building with offices above the public area on the first floor. Across Campau was a butcher shop, a bakery with those scrumptious "angel wing" pastries I would beg my mother for, and a number of clothing stores. Down the middle of Joseph Campau ran the Baker Street streetcar line. Detroit and Hamtramck had fabulous rail service back then. Not too many years later, with the development of the suburbs and the attendant reliance on the automobile, Detroit, which owned the lines, would sell all the streetcars to Mexico City, Mexico, where they lasted another fifty years. What a terrible mistake.

The streetcar system was easy to use, efficient, clean, inexpensive, and communal. People loved taking the streetcar. Years later, during my early years in Congress, I had a chance to help revive mass transit in the Detroit area, but instead I refused to support the project. Looking back, I wish I'd drawn on these positive memories and worked to re-create a system that would tie communities together and help rebuild Detroit.

It was a local merchant who accounted for my first political campaign—I was six years old. On the corner of Lehman and Joseph Campau was a Better Made potato chip store, and next to it was a storefront that hosted a political campaign headquarters—I'm not sure, but it might have been for Doc Ten's return to Congress. Well, if there was one thing that rivaled a vanilla shake for my affections, it was a bag of fresh Better Made potato chips. To my pleasant surprise, I learned that if I passed out campaign flyers in the neighborhood, I would be rewarded with chips and red pop.

I was on board.

Big League Dreams: Finding Happiness with a Ball in My Hand

Beginning when I was only a few years old, I gravitated toward anything that resembled a ball. I threw balls, I caught balls, I kicked balls. I was always happiest with a ball in my hand. A joke in our family is that in my coffin will be a football, baseball, and basketball—and that I'd better lose some weight if I'm to fit in there, as well.

My son and my daughter were the same way, and so are nearly all our grandchildren. They just take to a ball. They love a ball.

I still light up when I see a ball.

I was born with not just natural athletic abilities but also an inner competitiveness. I could run fast and throw far—faster and farther than most of the other kids—and was coordinated in my motor skills, so that I easily picked up the skill to hit a baseball or make a jump shot. The immediate reward of lofting a ball to the outfield or seeing my shot swish through the net gave me great joy, so much so that at night I would dream pleasant dreams of doing these wonderful things.

In the early '50s, sports were just beginning to be popular on television. Visualizing myself someday playing before large, cheering crowds therefore became an essential piece of my waking dreams. This image was an affirmation of what my innate skills made possible. My father's history as an accomplished athlete, as well as his height, also lent hope that I might have a future playing sports professionally. All this I slowly began to absorb the way a child with musical talent might dream of someday performing at Carnegie Hall. Because I was shy as a child and teenager, I sought refuge, and found it, in both sports and religion. Just as it was easy for me to talk and pray to an invisible Jesus and feel the inner peace of connecting with Him, so it was easy to throw a rubber ball in the alley against the brick wall behind the furniture store and imagine I was pitching in the World Series at Briggs Stadium. Sports and religion were retreats into my inner self.

I was an adventurous kid who liked to roam the neighborhood. One of my favorite routes was to cross the street in front of my house, go through the neighbor's yard, then head into the alley that separated Lehman and Hanley streets. On the other side of the alley were Hanley Field and the Tau Beta Community House.

At Hanley Field I would watch the older kids play softball. Hanging

In Tiger uniform, age five or six

around behind home plate, I hoped I would get picked to even the sides. My longing gaze at the leaders of these games eventually wore them down, so after a while I was allowed to play right field—*deep* right field. One day I saw two high school kids throwing a football. One of them— his last name was Snow—was the quarterback at St. Florian High School. I had watched quarterbacks throw on TV, but seeing it live and up close, I was awed by the beauty of the ball leaving his hand and spiraling through the air.

Tau Beta was like a YMCA, offering arts, crafts, a little reading room, and a gym. It brought joy and created community in Hamtramck for many years, and was the site of my first basketball experience. I would occasionally wander from Hanley Field across the street into Tau Beta, and one day I discovered the gym and a basketball resting on the cement floor. I spent a good part of that afternoon trying to make a shot into the ten-foot-high basket. I eventually did and was hooked. The idea that you could throw this thing up to the basket, and it would go in—I just fell in love with basketball from this moment on. Wandering over to the gym became a regular habit of mine at six and seven years old. Eventually a man showed me how to use my legs to propel the ball up to the basket. One success built on another. I was on my way.

When I was five and six I would go to Hamtramck Park with my aunt Nell to watch her son, my older cousin Jerry, play Little League baseball. I was enthralled by the idea that I could wear a real uniform—just like the Detroit Tigers! How I wished I could join the boys on the field, but I would have to wait another year before I could play in a league: the Pee Wee Division. We got shirts and hats and hit the ball off a tee.

Playing catch with my father and softball with the neighborhood kids set me up to excel—at shortstop—in my first organized sports endeavor. By the time I was old enough to play Little League, we'd moved to East Detroit, but in high school I played American Legion baseball at Hamtramck Field, next to Hanley. I was filled with nostalgia as I returned to the venues of my early youth. Even then I had an acute feeling of time and place.

On the way to the ball field was a store; I stopped in regularly. I remember the first time I ever saw a sixteen-ounce bottle of pop—it was called Sweet 16. It came in either orange or strawberry flavor, and its sweetness seemed to last forever. What a bargain!

My mother wanted to know where I was, but as a little guy I was pretty much free to run around. One day when I was seven all my wandering—and all my dreams—nearly came to an end. I was playing on the other side of Lehman and went chasing after a ball into the street. I was running fast, not paying attention, when out of the corner of my eye I saw a car coming. As the driver slammed on the brakes, I instinctively slid onto the pavement to stop my momentum. When both the car and I had stopped, I found my left thigh touching the right front wheel. Nobody was hurt, but I was scared to death—and I bet the driver was, too. I can count a number of close calls over the course of my life, and often think how damned lucky I've been.

I was a little daredevilish in trying things, not cognizant of my environment because I was so involved in whatever I was doing at the time.

Maybe it's genetic. One day, just after I'd entered Congress, I came home from Capitol Hill to the house in Virginia we'd just bought. Before I went inside, I heard a voice—it belonged to my son, Andy, then about four or five—but I couldn't figure out where it was coming from. I said, "Andy?"

"Yeah, Dad."

I looked up and there he was, sitting in a tree, maybe thirty or forty feet off the ground. I started panicking—if he fell, who knew how seriously he might be injured? I called his mother to come outside. We considered calling the fire department, but we didn't. We coaxed him down.

I was terrified. He wasn't.

And now he's got a son just like that.

Becoming One with God: Catechism and Communion at St. Florian Church

Our home was, basically, devoid of books—there might have been some volumes of nursery rhymes around, and perhaps some other rudimentary books. My first-grade reader, *Fun with Dick and Jane*, was pretty much the extent of my literary world at the time, and it wasn't until

My son, Andy, and his son, Vance

seventh or eighth grade that I would read my first real book, *The Good Bad Boy*. But my father and grandfather read the newspapers every day—the *Detroit Free Press*, a morning paper, and the *Detroit News*, which came out in the afternoon. And my parents emphasized the importance of school and a good education.

My first school was Dickenson. I don't remember the classroom, but I do know how happy I was running around with my kindergarten classmates on the asphalt-covered playground. Decades later, I was surprised to see a picture of my class: Of thirty or forty students, all were black except for me and maybe three other kids. I attended our local public elementary school, a mere four blocks from our home, yet I don't recall seeing any of these African American kids while I played in the neighborhood. Clearly our neighborhoods were segregated by race.

My next school was Playfair, also a public school, which my mother
had attended. I loved the name—it fit my religious sense of justice,
which was beginning to grow within me. Somehow I was chosen to represent my first-grade class on the student council. One afternoon all
class representatives were told to report to a classroom for a school council meeting. When we got there, we found that the teacher in charge
was upset over something—I can't remember what—that had happened
earlier that day. She wrote some sentences on the blackboard, then
instructed us to copy them ten times, adding that we could not leave
the room until we had finished this punishment. I panicked—I didn't
know how to write. With tears streaming down my face, I protested my
plight and soon was returned to my class. I was thrilled a couple of
months later when my parents enrolled me, for second grade, in St. Florian School.

St. Florian, on Poland Street, was and is a gorgeous church, the
biggest in Hamtramck, built in Gothic Revival style in 1905. It looks
like a cathedral—it's cavernous inside, seating twelve hundred. The
school adjoined the church.

We would start our day at morning Mass. The teachers were Felician
nuns, from a Franciscan order that originated in Poland in the nineteenth century and took its name from St. Felix of Cantalice, a six-
teenth-century Italian Franciscan monk especially devoted to children.
In this country, the Felician Sisters have ministered mostly to Polish-
American communities.

I enjoyed walking between home and school every day. On the way
home after school, I often made a stop—at the candy store on Holbrook, where I would buy a licorice stick or candy dots on a roll of
paper. On the way *to* school in the morning, I also might make a stop—
in the empty weed-filled lot next to the store, where I would catch
grasshoppers. Storing them in empty, small juice cartons, I'd take them
to school, where I had great fun releasing them in class. I had a bit of
naughty in me, which even now will occasionally surface.

Class size was large, necessitating good order and behavior—which

I did not always help preserve. My grades were average—Bs and Cs. There might have been an occasional A, but there might also have been a poor grade for my conduct. At one point my third-grade teacher called my mother and father in to tell them that I was disturbing the class by making the other kids laugh. To this day I don't recall what it was all about—could it have been the grasshoppers?—but I do recall that my father made clear to me that he wanted it stopped. It was.

For the most part, that kind of behavior was out of character for me. I must have been in need of attention. And I sure got it from my parents.

Although . . . I can imagine my dad thinking my misbehavior was cool. Because he had a bit of naughty in him, too.

At St. Florian we were administered a strong dose of religion—it's what my parents were paying for on top of reading, writing, and arithmetic. We learned about heaven and hell, including what they looked like, and that the pope was infallible. We learned that other religions were inferior and that admission to heaven might not be attainable if you were not baptized and not a Catholic—especially if you were among the "pagan" babies of China, India, and Africa. We memorized the Acts of Faith, Hope, and Love and recited them out loud as a class and individually. We were taught the Stations of the Cross, the Holy Days of Obligation, and the Holy Rosary. Perhaps most important, we learned the Act of Contrition, which we would need to take part in the sacraments of Confession and Holy Communion. The lessons were dogmatic, with no room for individual expression in prayer. We learned the texts by rote and had to repeat them that way. However, all the teaching was aimed at equipping us to develop a personal relationship with Jesus. Once we achieved that connection, we could have our creative conversation with Him.

The catechism was wrapped in the "bells and smells" of the traditional church ceremonies. The candles, incense, and music mixed to create a "heavenly" state of bliss that set the stage for Mass, High Mass, novenas, and other religious events.

The culmination of this early training was our First Holy Communion. In order to receive the body and blood of Christ, a person must reach seven years old, defined by the Church as the "age of reason," the age at which one could know right from wrong.

Confession took place in a box with three compartments: two—one on either side—were for congregants; if both were occupied, one penitent waited his or her turn while the other confessed. The penitent kneeled facing a screen that opened to a center compartment, in which the priest sat at a ninety-degree angle to you. In the mysterious dark of the confessional, as the priest spoke to you in hushed tones, it could be difficult to make out who the priest was, although you often knew in advance which priest was presiding in which confessional. It was not unusual for sinners to " shop" for a friendlier, more forgiving priest to hear their confessions.

Your first confession went something like this: "Bless me father, for I have sinned. This is my first confession." (Later you'd say, "My last confession was X weeks ago.") Then you would reveal your sins and the approximate number of times you committed each one.

Entering the confessional that first time was not difficult because you had rehearsed all the lines and had to deal mostly with disobeying your parents or lying. The process became a bit more traumatizing later, when sexual issues entered your teenage life.

The reward for undergoing confession was a sweet one: receiving Christ at communion. You were then one with God. This was heady stuff for anyone, let alone a boy in second grade. I completely bought it—especially the direct link to God, the ability to talk to Him.

On the Sunday of our First Communion, our class was all dressed up: the boys in suits, white shirts, and ties; the girls in white First Communion dresses, which looked like wedding gowns. As celestial music filled the church, we children, hands together, fingers pointing to heaven, filed out of our pews and up to the altar. There stood the priest, before whom we stuck out our tongues to receive our reward.

I was enraptured.

At home after church I was the guest of honor at a big family gathering. Everybody shared a meal, and the adults gave me gifts—many of them monetary, the extra-special ones in the form of silver dollars. I received perhaps eighty dollars that day—a staggering sum. Of course, I had to surrender it to my parents, who no doubt had good use for it.

All my cousins and aunts and uncles and grandparents were there, and I was the reason for this celebration.

It was a great day.

First Communion

CHAPTER 4

To God, the Joy of My Youth

School, Sports, and Religion in East Detroit

GREEN LAWNS AND DRIVEWAYS: OUR MOVE TO THE SUBURBS

Hamtramck made perfect sense to me. The population's common religion, heritage, passion for labor unions, devotion to family, and love of the Detroit Tigers kept our community together. The war was over, the economy red-hot. It was a wonderful time.

But new spaces beckoned. In the 1950s, as Detroit's population burgeoned to 1.8 million, young war veterans and their families were restless for greener pastures—larger homes, front lawns, and backyards, as well as driveways to accommodate the automobiles that made the move to the suburbs possible. Many of my parents' friends had already joined the parade out of the city, and in early 1953 we followed. Our destination was a new three-bedroom ranch house in Macomb County, on Ego Avenue in East Detroit, just three blocks north of 8 Mile Road, which marked Detroit's upper boundary.

Together my parents and my grandfather Gavreluk paid eighteen thousand dollars for the house in a brand-new subdivision next to Ridgemont golf course, which itself would soon yield to another new subdivision. Thousands of workers were busy building hundreds of new homes all around us— there were no parks, but we kids had a ball playing king of the hill on the huge piles of clay formed when new basements were excavated. Plus, my sister and I had a gigantic new backyard

*Our family in front of the new house in East Detroit,
with Jeff, age two or three*

to enjoy: eighty by eighty feet, five times the size of our yard on Lehman. What else could a kid want?

Character, for one thing. For all the space and comfort we found in East Detroit, there was no history, or so it seemed to me. But at least there were sidewalks, not always the case in the suburbs. And if I no longer heard cries of "ragman" and "iceman" accompanied by the sound of horses' hooves, I did look forward to the evening musical serenade heralding the arrival of the Good Humor ice cream truck, as well as to regular visits by Red, the Awrey Bakery bread man in his bakery truck, and the Sealtest milk truck. Soon some of the people who had been part of our daily lives in Hamtramck moved out to become part of our daily lives in East Detroit. Helen and Roy Livingston and their young family, arriving five months after we did, settled into a home like ours at the other end of the block. Aunt Nell and Uncle Andy followed, taking up residence at the other end of town. We no longer made our lives in the comfort of an all-Polish neighborhood, but we did have a rightful

Nancy and me, at Eastertime, in front of the new house and its two-car garage

place in a congenial ethnic assortment: Poles, Italians, Irish, and Germans. No African Americans lived among us; it would take another fifty years before East Detroit was integrated in any significant way.

The families were proud of their new homes. Jobs were plentiful, and, thanks to unions, the pay and benefits were excellent. For these new suburbanites—people used to cramped quarters and a constant struggle to make ends meet—East Detroit was a living dream.

As new as East Detroit seemed to me in comparison to good old Hamtramck, the place had a history dating back to the early 1800s. Its founders, English and Irish Protestant landowners, called it Orange Township—orange being the color associated with Irish Protestants, after their traditional hero, William of Orange—in hope of attracting new settlers like themselves. But Irish Catholics were arriving in Detroit, and when land in rural Macomb County was offered for a dollar an acre, they bought. Before long the Irish Catholics had enough numbers in town that they renamed it Erin.

Soon a village started to take shape in Erin Township, including a new commercial area with a school, a post office, a bank, a restaurant, a meat market, and a bakery. When the automobile appeared at the beginning of the twentieth century, bringing the town's first car dealership, the village commissioners embarked upon a program of infrastructure improvement. Again the city was renamed—in 1924 it was incorporated as Halfway, because it stood at the midpoint between the cities of Detroit and Mount Clemens, the county seat. In 1929, rapid population and infrastructure growth moved the city elders to change the name once more—to East Detroit, a designation that took advantage of the town's proximity to Detroit, one of the most dynamic, fastest-growing cities in the world.

SPEEDBALLS AND LIGHTNING RODS:
THE PARISH OF ST. VERONICA

When we arrived, most of East Detroit's German Protestants resided west of Gratiot Avenue, the city's main commercial thoroughfare and east-west divider. The newly arrived Catholic families, from Detroit, Hamtramck, and other urban areas, lived on the east side, in parishes like St. Basil, St. Angela, and St. Veronica.

Our family's religious, social, and athletic life centered on the church and school of St. Veronica parish, where the number of the faithful was increasing as fast as in any other parish in Michigan. The Sisters of St. Joseph taught grades one through eight, in classes of forty to fifty children, in a handsome school building constructed in 1926. As had their counterparts at St. Florian, the nuns at St. Veronica enforced strict order.

St. Veronica

Arriving in winter, in the middle of the school year, I was a curiosity to the established members of my third-grade class, as they were to me. But I blended in quickly—a process helped along by my success in math contests. Standing at the head of the class, our teacher would hold up a multiplication flash card, showing it to four students standing in separate aisles within the last row of desks. The first to respond correctly to a flash card would advance one row, after which the teacher would present another card, and so on. The object was to answer fast and accurately; the winner was the first child to reach the front of the room. While I was not a prize student in English, I was good at math. That facility, added to my competitive nature, enabled me to win the contest often. My two main rivals were Diane Cichon and Harold Ivankovich.

Here are some of my other classmates:

- Malcolm Batherson, one of my best friends, who was later killed in an auto accident after visiting me at the University of Iowa
- Pam Vitali, who had the most energy and best smile in school
- Creighton Petkovich, a fun kid who played football on our team
- Annette Strozeski, the smartest kid in class
- Joann Ulrich, my first girlfriend (we didn't get much beyond holding hands)
- Ralph Bammel, a nice guy who played on the grade-school football team and died young
- Chester Smigalski, who rode a motorbike
- Fred Twardowski, also on the football team, a good-looking guy who changed his name and became an actor
- Barbara Jabalee, a girl with a really nice, friendly personality
- Bonnie Peternel, whose house I would visit just to talk to her
- Ronnie DiMaria, who would hold pool parties at the swimming pool in her backyard—she was the only kid at school who had one
- Joe McNeil, Ronnie's boyfriend

School spirit was outstanding at St. Veronica, thanks in large part to the principal, Mother Vernard, our smart, caring, firm mother superior. A big school project was the annual paper drive. Mother Vernard divided all the children into two groups: the Speedballs and the Lightning Rods. Large empty truck trailers were brought to sit in the church parking lot; the job of the students was to collect as much used newspaper as we could to fill them. Every morning Mother Vernard would come on the school PA system to announce which group was ahead and then deliver a pep talk meant to inspire the students to ever greater passion in their pursuit of paper. It would be difficult to find a football coach who could deliver a better talk at halftime.

The drives had a serious purpose: to raise money for the school and parish by selling the paper for recycling. But for the students, the drives were just fun. We'd go door-to-door, and not only in our neighborhoods—many of us prevailed upon our parents to drive us so we could hit houses all over town. Once we'd scoured East Detroit, we would branch out to Roseville, St. Clair Shores, and parts of Detroit. Once the trailers were filled, they would be hauled away and replaced with empty ones. On Sundays parishioners brought papers to church. I recall vividly my ventures into the parish of Assumption Grotto, the church on 6 Mile and Gratiot. This large parish, peopled by German and Italian families, featured old working-class homes on well-kept streets. When I knocked on a door asking for old newspapers, I was often greeted with the distinctive aroma of simmering sauerkraut or tomato sauce, and the immigrant accent to go with it. I loved the old-world hominess of it all.

I made friends on our street. Chuck Myers, Ron Seigle, and Toby Jewett were a couple of years older than I was, but that didn't stop me from hanging out with them. Toby's younger brother, Doug, was part of the gang, too, as was Michael Rossi. I played baseball at St. Veronica with Mike, who ended up teaching at Detroit's Catholic Central High School. Mike and I were forever fixing old bats and balls. If our bat handles cracked, we would mend them with nails or, even better, screws, which we covered with black electrical tape. We used the same tape to repair baseballs whose stitches were unraveling. Nancy also quickly found playmates on our street—her best friend was Marsha Holly. Since this was a brand-new neighborhood, not an established community, all the kids were eager to make friends.

As I got older I branched out, riding my Schwinn to Kantner School to play shortstop in Little League. I lost my sports innocence on my tenth birthday when I committed three errors in one inning, costing our team the game. This was a first for me: I simply *did not make errors*. I was humbled, I was shattered. After the game, my dad and I went home for a small family birthday party of cake and ice cream, but I was so distraught that I hid in the basement. My father came downstairs, patted me on the shoulder, and let me sulk. Such understanding and compassion were unusual for him—usually he was hard on me, not sympathetic or encouraging. I will always remember this rare and tender moment.

Even on days when I hadn't made three errors, the basement served as a useful refuge from interaction with people. One day, when I was ten or eleven, I found something wonderful in the garbage that a neighbor had put out for collection: an old *World Almanac*, hardbound, with a red cover. Eight inches thick (or so it seemed), it was packed with statistics and facts and descriptions and lists. With this unwieldy volume I took my first journey into a book. I spent hours in the basement thumbing through this amazing store of information, feeding my natural curiosity—especially about places and geography. In short order I could recite the populations of the largest twenty cities in the US and the capitals of all fifty states.

Reading, which would become a lifelong passion of mine, began with three providers of the printed word: 1) this almanac, 2) *The Good Bad Boy*, the novel for Catholic youngsters I read in the eighth grade, and 3) the columns of Ralph McGill, a pro–civil rights editorialist in the *Atlanta Constitution* whom a high school teacher assigned us to read. These three sources made up a good mix of forms: statistics, literature, and advocacy journalism. And they treated subjects—geography, Catholicism, and justice—I would always care about.

Also in the trash around that time I found an old ten-inch TV set. I carried it to my basement hideaway and set it up—it worked! I sat in front of it for hours watching NBA games. I saw George Mikan, the league's first great "big man," play for the Minneapolis Lakers, and Bob Petit, a prolific scorer and rebounder, anchor the St. Louis Hawks. And then there were the stars of the three teams from New York State: Bob Davies of the Rochester Royals, Dolph Schayes of the Syracuse Nationals, and Richie Guerin of the New York Knicks. The Fort Wayne Pistons, soon to move to Detroit, had George "Bird" Yardley, a perennial all-star who was also the world's number-one ball hog: Once Bird got the ball, it never went to anyone else.

To this day I can still name the starting lineups for that era's Hawks and Boston Celtics. With these legends carved into my mind I would play make-believe games from one end of the basement to the other,

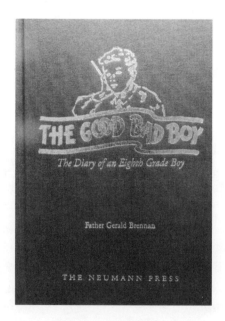

The Good Bad Boy

supplying breathless play-by-play as I "dribbled" a rolled-up pair of socks down the room and shot it at the "basket"—a small space between the top of the cinder-block foundation and the upstairs flooring.

> *Petit from ten feet. Too strong. Russell rips the ball off the back-board. Outlet to Cousy, who races ahead. Ten seconds left in regu-lation, Hawks by one. Quick pass to Sad Sam Jones on the left wing. Six seconds. Back to Cousy. Dribbles into the lane. Three seconds. Back out to Jones. Dribbles once, steps back for the jumper. Good! As time expires! Celtics win!*

I was in love with my fantasy world.

I was lucky to have gotten involved in scouting, which taught me not only new and wonderful skills like swimming, camping, mouth-to-mouth resuscitation, and knot-tying but also essential values. In both Cub and Boy Scouts we learned loyalty, preparedness, honesty, and serv-ice—not just by reciting mottos but by the way we interacted with each other and with our leaders, and by taking part in neighborhood cleanups and other community projects. Generous leaders like Margaret Corbin, Barbara Jewett, and Mr. Schoehner volunteered their time to make scouting enjoyable and worthwhile for the boys.

Like the team sports that would soon fill my life, scouting provided me with a uniform I wore with pride, showing that I belonged to some-thing larger than myself. I was able to climb a ladder of tasks: Earning your Wolf, Bear, and Lion badges took some work but was not so demanding that the achievements were unreachable. The successes instilled in us through our Cub pack, MC (probably for Macomb County) 11, helped all of us build confidence in ourselves, preparing us for the next steps not only in scouting but in life.

Scouting gave me my first exposure to swimming and other water sports. Our pack would travel on Saturday mornings to the St. Clair Community Center, on Fairview Street in the Lower East Side of

Detroit. Rules were strict. We had to take a full shower, with plenty of soap, then pass inspection before we were allowed into the heavily chlorinated pool. Often the lifeguard would find dirt around our ankles, so we'd march back to the showers to apply more soap before returning for re-inspection. More than anything I loved to jump into the pool's deep end, feel the exhilaration of touching the bottom, then propel myself up like a rocket to crack the surface of the water and gasp for air in what seemed like a resurrection. Once I could handle being underwater I discovered the joy of the diving board—jumping and diving off it became almost an obsession. We also played water polo and water dodgeball, both of which took plenty of stamina. When our hour at the pool was finished, I was exhausted.

But not so exhausted that I would deny myself shooting baskets on the court upstairs. I was always the first to leave the pool so I could throw on my clothes then fly up to the gym. Unlike the cement floor at Tau Beta, the floor here was made of wood. The feel and sound of dribbling the ball on that floor was almost as exciting as seeing the ball go through the hoop. Our five-year-old granddaughter, Alina Bonior, said it best one day when we were watching her brother, Vance, shoot baskets at a school gym: "I like coming here to listen to the ball bounce on the wood." Each week I could not wait to get back into that gym. By the time the parents and scoutmasters had rounded up the rest of the boys from the pool, I'd have had fifteen or twenty minutes to myself dribbling and shooting. Heaven for some might be clouds and angels. For me it was that basketball court with the wood floor.

As I got older, I would swim in the evenings at Denby High School in Detroit, and during summers I'd visit the outdoor pool at Heilmann Field. If the weather was right, friends and I would bike over to Lake St. Clair and swim at either Jefferson or Olson beach in the town of St. Clair Shores. With twin diving boards, these beaches provided fun in fresh water—although I wondered how "fresh" the water really was when I would sometimes swim past an assortment of slimy debris. I would learn later that sewage overflows polluted the water. That contamination remained a problem for decades.

Scouting also took me far beyond my accustomed environs. With my Boy Scout troop I took my first train trip, from Detroit to Toledo—it was just a quick turnaround, sixty miles there, sixty miles back. On another day, we visited the Military Inn on Detroit's far West Side to look at antique guns. Later I went camping at D-bar-A campground near Metamora, Michigan.

D-bar-A was my introduction to "the great outdoors." Hiking what seemed like a two-mile trail to swim in Trout Lake and sleeping on a cot in a tent were foreign to this city kid, and not without hardship: The trail to the lake was filled with mosquitoes, and nights in the tent were cold. But the evening campfires made up for the discomfort. Rituals of food and song and Indian lore brought us all close together as we watched the crackling and shooting flames.

Scouting even made me a bit of money. The Motor City Speedway, at 8 Mile and Schoenherr, used "scout ushers" at their events. Wearing my uniform, I'd show patrons to their places in the bleachers, wipe the seats with a rag, and hope for a tip. Sometimes I'd get a dime, sometimes even a quarter! Once folks were seated, I'd settle in to watch the races, which were called by Fred Wolf, a local radio and television personality. Amidst the roar of the engines we'd watch Iggy Katona chase Joy Fair around the oval, banked track in stock or midget cars. We looked forward to the evening's closing attraction: a "demolition derby," in which drivers would crash dilapidated stock cars into one another. The idea was to disable the other cars so that yours would be the last one running, earning you the victory. It was kind of like bumper cars in an amusement park, only with the satisfying sound of metal crunching metal and the thick stench of gasoline.

The engine noise from the races and the derby was so loud we could hear it on our block a mile and a half away. The days of the Speedway were numbered in this expanding suburban neighborhood, where quiet was the sound of choice.

WHOLE MILK AND BUTTER:
CHORES AND A BABY BROTHER

My father taught me how to work. When I was ten or eleven, as my mother's health began to decline, he assigned me a number of regular chores around the house, responsibilities that increased the weaker she got. If I didn't do a job properly, Dad would either explain it to me or show me what to do. In the kitchen my favorite chore was doing the dishes with Mom—she'd wash, I'd dry—as we listened to the top tunes on CKLW, a Canadian radio station out of Windsor. We heard a lot of Elvis Presley (including "All Shook Up"), some Jimmie Rodgers ("Honeycomb") and Sam Cook ("You Send Me"), and much more. It was a time for us to talk and sing and be together. I also learned to set the table and help prepare the meal. My mother was a skilled cook, whipping up delicious Ukrainian specialties like stuffed cabbage, pirogi, and city chicken, as well as superb renditions of just about anything else. If mashed potatoes were on the menu, my job was the mashing. Adding whole milk and butter—half a stick—I'd keep mashing until the concoction was 100 percent lump-free. A million calories? Sure, but who was counting?

I also swept the kitchen floor after meals and, once a week, washed and waxed both the kitchen floor and the steps down to the basement. Keeping the basement neat and clean was my job, too, so I swept it regularly. Down there the ironing board was set up—I pressed shirts and trousers for the family, and also polished everyone's shoes. Every week I washed the bathroom floor and, using an old toothbrush, scrubbed mold from the grouting between the tiles in the shower stall. I was charged with keeping the garage clean and orderly, as well, so I swept there regularly, too. I washed windows, and at the age of eleven I began to cut the lawn with our hand-push mower—front and back yards, horizontally then vertically. I enjoyed mowing but not what came next: hand-clipping the lawn's edges along the driveway and sidewalks. That part of the job would leave me with blisters and aching hands. The whole lawn-care process would take two hours out of a summer day. Eventually I started to cut neighbors' lawns, and wash their windows, for pocket money.

I took pride in the work I did and the tasks I accomplished. And I took pleasure in knowing I was helping my family, especially my mother, whose energy level was diminishing. When my sister got old enough, she was fabulous in picking up many of the household chores. Nancy was an amazing worker, steady and conscientious, willing to do pretty much everything asked of her. We both sensed that our mother's health was failing. Housework also provided me an opportunity to please my father, which, like most boys, I desperately wanted to do. Dad would inspect what I had done, and while he rarely complimented me on a job well done, he did come to accept my work as satisfactory.

When Nancy and I were eight and ten, respectively, our parents told us some exciting news: Our mother was going to have a baby!! I didn't know much about babies or how they were made, but I was delighted that we were going to have one. Jeffrey John Bonior was born at Holy Cross Hospital on the East Side of Detroit on January 19, 1956. As far as I now know, he was healthy and cute as could be. He grew up to be a beautiful child and a handsome man. He and my sister got most of our family's good looks, which came largely from our mother, a true beauty.

Back in the '50s, children were not allowed in the hospital as visitors, so in order to see our mother and our new brother, Nancy and I stood in the parking lot of Holy Cross Hospital and waved as Mom appeared with Jeffrey at the window four floors up. I don't remember how long they remained in the hospital, but at that time it was common for a healthy mother and baby to stay a week before coming home. That length of stay is unheard of today.

Jeffery brought great joy into our home, blessing us with a sweet presence that acted as a brake on the ironclad discipline of my father and grandfather. Our mother was always the softer and gentler person in the marriage, and with Jeff she seemed even more so. I had fun with Jeff, but as I spent more and more time playing sports, I spent less and less time playing with my kid brother. And by the time he was eight, I was at the University of Iowa.

I regret the time I missed with him. And I regret that, later on, I did not become a better mentor to him.

"VOTE FOR MY DAD": GETTING INTERESTED IN POLITICS

While I made my first venture into the world of politics as a purely mercenary five-year-old, distributing fliers for treats, thanks to my father I began to receive a real education in politics and government at an early age. After we got our first television I would sit on Dad's lap in the living room as he watched *Meet the Press*—Nancy remembers doing the same. Of course, I didn't understand the content, but I knew that he liked the show and thought it important.

The grandest time of all was watching the Democratic and Republican national conventions with my father, mother, and grandfather. Each gathering was broadcast for hours and hours, over four nights, and we watched practically all of it. Today everything is cut and dried going into the conventions, with little excitement or suspense—the presidential nominee has already been chosen and every minute of the proceedings is scripted and stage-managed. But in the 1950s, the conventions of both parties hosted real contests, with the outcomes in doubt until the delegates cast their votes. I sat in front of the TV, pencil and paper in hand, keeping track of the delegates pledged to each candidate. It was great fun.

It was also great sport, and I think that's what drew me to it initially. Politics was competitive, and so was I. I still didn't envision myself entering this business as an adult. It felt like the Friday night fights Grandpa and I would watch, when both my parents were out for the evening, on the *Gillette Cavalcade of Sports*. The heavyweights, like Rocky Marciano and Floyd Patterson, put on quite a show, but I found the lighter boxers, like Carmen Basilio, Gene Fullmer, and Sugar Ray Robinson, the most impressive pound for pound. Just as I'd score the conventions, I'd score the fights, allotting points to each fighter after every round.

A few years after arriving in East Detroit, my father tried his luck at running for city council. Because of our town's explosive growth, there was much that needed attending to. Sewer systems were inadequate, causing basements to flood with raw sewage during heavy rains. Schools were crowded, and the new housing developments lacked recreational facilities for all the children moving in. He recognized the problems and wanted to solve them.

Dad lost his first race for the council, then the second, although he came closer that try. The third time was the charm. The victory must have been a dream come true for him.

Despite setbacks, Dad didn't give up—a lesson I would apply to my own political fortunes years later. When I lost my first race to be House Democratic whip, I resolved to run again and reminded everyone who would listen that Babe Ruth had struck out 1,330 times. Well, my father struck out twice. Dad might not have made the Hall of Fame, as the Babe did, but he put together a worthy political career, serving the citizens of his community with four years on the council, then four years as mayor.

In each of my father's races I went door-to-door, handing out his literature, asking folks to "vote for my dad." I helped put lawn signs together and assisted him as he churned out fliers at his print shop on Mt. Elliott. Dad rented space for the shop in a building his sister owned. Side by side with her business, Camporee, which manufactured and sold camping supplies, the print shop had a small office in front. To the rear was the work area, which contained two hand presses, a folding machine along the rear wall, printer trays full of type, two tables to set up the type, and a shelf to store paper.

When Election Day came, I usually worked most of the day at a polling site passing out either a piece of literature or some object, maybe a ruler or pencil, with my dad's name on it. Those polling sites were where I learned about local politics. A lot went on there: Most candidates had supporters working each site; election officials would repeatedly warn them to stand at least a hundred feet from the voting booths. Candidates themselves would stop by throughout the day to greet supporters, shake hands, and even talk with their opponents' workers. People argued about issues, they teased each other. Every so often a car would arrive with drinks, sandwiches, and snacks for a particular campaign's personnel. Most voters would be courteous as we asked them to support our candidates, but occasionally a voter would unleash a tirade. More than once I was on the receiving end of such diatribes. "They're all a bunch of crooks!" was a line that became familiar to me. That sentiment never seems to die, although the exact words may differ. Recently I saw a bumper sticker that read, Don't Vote, It Just Encourages Them.

When I was twelve, my horizons expanded as my father assigned me to work a poll on behalf of a candidate for the Michigan House of Representatives. While I was not crazy about the guy, the experience piqued my interest: I wanted to know more about what a state representative did. Not long after Election Day I had a chance to go to Lansing and see the legislature in session. I was enthralled by the grandeur of the state capitol and fascinated by its history, particularly that of the House chamber. *These people have serious, important jobs*, I thought to myself as I watched them debate.

I liked everything about that day in Lansing. I began to think, for the first time, that this was something I might want to become part of.

When I entered St. Veronica in early 1954, I knew one thing above all about the school: Just two months earlier it had played for the Catholic Youth Organization (CYO) grade-school football championship. It had lost—to Royal Oak Shrine, 26–12—but the fact that my new school had vied for the title was a big deal. As far as I was concerned, success on the gridiron defined the culture of St. Veronica—both the school and the parish. CYO sports started in sixth grade. I knew I was not far away. CYO would play a huge role in my life over the next decade.

The Metro Detroit CYO grade-school sports program had gotten started in 1942. It caught on quickly: In 1959, when I played, the football league "had grown to 104 teams, the biggest little loop in the state," as the *Free Press* noted. Eight teams made up our division: St. Jude, St. Raymond, St. Veronica, St. Joan of Arc, Guardian Angel, Assumption Grotto, St. John Berchman, and St. Matthew. I can provide this information now because I still have the scrapbook I kept as a kid.

When I was twelve or so, one of the nuns, observing my interest in sports, gave me my first novel to read. *The Good Bad Boy: The Diary of an Eighth Grade Boy,* by Father Gerald Brennan, tells the story of a Catholic eighth grader who played CYO basketball. I loved this book because it paralleled my own grade-school life. Game by game I followed the ups and downs in the life of this promising teen athlete with the unlikely name of Pompey Briggs. Written as a daily diary, the book takes the reader through the Catholic calendar of religious events and feast days as Pompey struggles to remain "good"—true to the Catholic way of life—while sometimes succumbing to "bad" impulses, like manipulating girlfriends and feeling jealousy when one of them is admired by another boy. As an adult I tried for decades to find this book, a classic among male parochial school graduates of my generation. Thanks to the Internet, I finally succeeded. "You will laugh and reminisce as you read this entertaining and very special book," states one online Catholic bookseller. "Grade school boys will love and cherish it, as will all young Catholics. . . . A great teacher of Catholicity."

As a fourth-, fifth-, and sixth-grader, I idolized the older boys who starred on our football, basketball, and baseball teams. From my classroom window I would watch them practice and would dream about playing when my turn came. In 1956, when I was in sixth grade, my role model was the star of the St. Veronica football team—its halfback, Harold Quenneville. Harold ended up going to Sacred Heart Seminary after the eighth grade, a choice that, I'm sure, influenced my decision to follow him there.

Three other boys I looked up to were Gary Lytle, Terry Templin, and John Goff—all two years older than John's brother Mike and I. Younger though we were, Mike and I tried to outperform the big boys in game after game of three-on-three half-court basketball—the five of us playing, plus whoever else was around—in the Goffs' driveway. We played in all kinds of weather. Snow? Ice? The mercury down to single digits? None of it got us off that driveway. And while Mike and I never won, the games sharpened our skills and competiveness. Mike, Gary, and I remain friends to this day.

A RIDE IN A POLICE CAR: MOTHER'S HEART ATTACK

After dinner on a cold, late February evening in 1958, my mother and father left Jeff at home with my grandfather John and accompanied Nancy and me to see a basketball game at the new East Detroit High School gymnasium. It was a Class A play-off contest, Class A denoting the toughest competition among the area's largest schools. East Detroit was facing Austin Catholic.

I am not sure that this game meant anything to my sister, but I know it meant a lot to me. In addition to the neighborhood school idols I looked up to, on the court that night would be Dave DeBusschere, the local superathlete who that year would lead his Austin Catholic Friars to the state championship. I was only a twelve-year-old seventh-grader, but DeBusschere's reputation in southeast Michigan was huge. At six feet six, he would go on to lead the University of Detroit Titans to national fame. An All-American, he was drafted into the NBA by the Pistons but would achieve his greatest fame as a star forward with the New York Knicks, playing with Willis Reid, Bill Bradley, Dick Barnett, Walt Frazier, and Earl Monroe on the way to world championships in 1970 and '73. With the Pistons, at only twenty-four years of age, DeBusschere did a stint as a player-coach. And, remarkably, he pitched for the Chicago White Sox in 1962 and '63, compiling a 2.90 earned run average over 102 innings. Many CYO boys like myself looked up to this magnificent athlete as our model. So going to see him play for the first time was for me a huge deal.

When we arrived, there was a long line outside to get into the gym, which seated thirty-five hundred to four thousand. Dad left the three of us waiting in line as he went to pick up our tickets from a friend at the box office. While he was gone, my mother started to gasp for breath in the cold night air. Nancy and I were stunned at the sight. Because of the large crowd, there were numerous police officers nearby, and they came over to assist. I heard someone say the words "heart attack" as a large crowd gathered around us, then made room for the police.

Mother was on the ground fighting for her life. A police car arrived; Nancy sat in the front seat while I sat in the back with Mother as we sped down Gratiot Avenue the mile and a half to Saratoga Hospital. When Dad returned from the box office, we were gone. Informed what had happened, he rushed to the hospital to join his family.

Nancy, ten at the time, remembers trying to hide under the dashboard, terrified not only by our mother's condition but also by the siren, the flashing lights, and the speed at which we were traveling. I cannot recall what I was doing in the backseat with Mother. Was I holding her hand? Was I talking to her?

At the hospital, Mother was placed in an oxygen tent while we all waited in the emergency waiting room, not knowing if she was going to make it. For the first time I realized that she might die; the thought was sad and sobering. The doctors were able to stabilize her; of course, they kept her for tests and recuperation.

Whoever called her condition a heart attack outside the gym was correct. At that time, medicine had not yet made significant advances in treating heart disease, so when a layperson heard the phrase "heart attack," death seemed to be near. Even though Nancy and I knew, prior to this night, that our mother's health was marginal, we had not been considering that we might soon lose her. Now we were. Now the possibility of her death was real. I am not sure that I dealt with it well.

Mother eventually came home, under a cloud of uncertainty about her health and what should be done about it. Her activity in and around the house decreased even more, as visits to doctors' offices increased. I felt that another layer of dread and anxiety had descended on our home. As did most families, we had our lives to live, but now we led them understanding the serious nature of our mother's illness. Her sickness was real, it was not just "in her head," as one doctor had told my father prior to the attack. Before this incident, our home was already a serious place, with little humor to leaven everyday labors. The atmosphere became even more sober afterward. And then came her surgery.

It felt as if we were all helpless to make Mother's life better.

My sister and I did what we could, taking on more responsibilities around the house. What with my crowded schedule of afterschool sports practice, however, most of the extra load fell on Nancy. My sister was (and still is) a saint. Her performance of chores during this period was nothing short of Herculean.

But no matter how much extra effort we put into making the household run, our added diligence at sweeping the floor or taking out the trash or doing the laundry would not heal the weak heart that seemed destined to take our mother away from us. That realization weighed heavily on me and, I think, on others in the house, too. We found relief in tending to Jeff, grateful for the distraction and humor and delight that only a two-year-old can provide. If only momentarily, he took our minds off of Mom. We were glad to have our baby brother, an affirmation of life amidst the gloom of approaching death.

A Double at Briggs Stadium:
Succeeding In, and Learning From, Sports

Sports were big at St. Veronica. A high-priority activity. Our football team had three coaches. Our sixty-member marching band strutted in sharp uniforms to the baton of its conductor, Larry Egan, the music teacher at nearby Notre Dame High School. The games were played on Sunday evenings, under the lights at Memorial Field, located at the corner of Flower and East 10 Mile Road. The Marching 60 would entertain the crowd before the game and at halftime with snappy tunes and intricate formations.

St. Veronica had an active Dads' Club. This group, as well as the Knights of Columbus and the Ushers Club at church, would be key elements as my father assembled his political coalition. The Dads' Club raised money to support the athletic program—to pay for the lights on the field and buy uniforms for the various teams and for the band. It was an impressive operation.

My father became good friends with Frank Taylor, a teacher and the head coach for varsity football, basketball, and baseball. Frank's wife had died in childbirth; with the help of his mother, Ida, he raised his child, Frank Jr. Brought up in the Lower East Side parish of St. Rose, Frank Taylor was an exceptionally good coach—a capable teacher of skills, a thoughtful strategist, and a powerful motivator. His teams enjoyed enormous success, but that success didn't come easily for the players. Even though he was still only in his midthirties, Frank came from the old school. Tough and rough, he would often bring a boy to tears with his demands and harangues. His beliefs matched those of Eddie Robinson, the Hall of Fame Grambling football coach. "Football teaches the lesson of life," said Robinson. "It cultivates in the athlete the ability to pay the price. No struggle, no strength. No fight, no fortitude. No crisis, no courage. No suffering, no sympathy. No pain, no patience."[1]

---

1 Samuel G. Freedman, *Breaking the Line: The Season in Black College Football That Transformed the Sport and Changed the Course of Civil Rights* (New York: Simon & Schuster, 2013), 20.

Me with Frank Taylor, my coach and our family friend,
at my St. Veronica graduation

I have always had mixed feelings about Coach Taylor. Off the field
he was great to the kids. He would even take some of us to his cottage
on Harsens Island or on a vacation tour in northern Michigan. He
helped run my dad's campaigns and was at our house often—and was
perfectly friendly there. But on the athletic field, and even in the classroom—he taught a number of eighth-grade subjects—he was General
Patton. There was no denying the results: The endless drills and harsh
discipline produced championship after championship in all three sports
he coached.

With 104 teams spread all over Metro Detroit, our league drew cov-
erage from the *Free Press* and the *News*, along with the widely read
Michigan Catholic. Playing quarterback on the football team in 1959,
I got a kick out of seeing my name in print after a victory.

"St. Veronica turned back its foremost challenger in the Northeast with a 20–6 conquest of St. Jude. Dave Bonior scampered eight and 65 yards for touchdowns."

"St. Veronica kept rolling with a 33–0 verdict over St. John Berchman. Dave Bonior pitched touchdown passes to Randy Lamprides (35 yards) and Gary Jacklyn (55 yards)."

"St. Veronica had to hustle to stretch its winning streak to six by turning back St. Joan of Arc 21–13. Dave Bonior passed to Randy Lamprides for two TD's."

That kind of press was heady stuff for an eighth grader. Our football team won nine games in a row that season before losing on Thanksgiving morning to a group of all-stars from the other teams in our division. Many of the players in that game went on to play college football; a couple ended up in the NFL.

Quarterback, eighth grade, for St. Veronica

My success in football was followed by triumphs in basketball and baseball. In these sports, the school, with the support of the Dads' Club, was able to field boys' sixth-grade teams—serving more or less as a junior varsity for the seventh- and eighth-grade teams—as well as a girls' basketball team. Nancy was an aggressive and determined player for that team, especially on defense. I was shocked by her competitiveness and amazed by her intensity.

My best friend in grade school, Mike Goff, was too big to play CYO football—maybe six feet tall in eighth grade and weighing in at well over the league's 135-pound limit. But that restriction did not apply to basketball. We starred together on the team that ended up co-champs with St. Joan of Arc. I received my first trophy when we won the De La Salle High School tournament in Detroit. I played guard, fashioning myself after Bob Cousy, stealing the ball and hitting one-handed push shots from fifteen feet. Mike, our George Mikan, was dominant under the boards.

After basketball ended, Coach Taylor started right into baseball, holding practice in the cold and wind of a Michigan March. I shudder remembering how my hands stung at batting practice in the forty-degree chill—the coach forbade the use of batting gloves. And then there was sliding practice on our not-too-smooth St. Veronica infield—we all ended up with big red strawberries on our hips. Fielding drills brought challenges, too. Usually stationed at third base or shortstop, I got to know firsthand the accuracy of Coach Taylor's reputation for hitting the hardest infield practice in creation. The ball would come screaming at me, especially when I played third and had to react, basically, on instinct—there's a reason why the position is called the "hot corner." The coach's theory was that hard-hit grounders, while intimidating, were the only way to teach a fielder to stay down on the ball. Again, I can't argue with the results that followed from his exacting approach. Gary Jacklyn, Randy Lamprides (the best young athlete I remember ever playing with), Mike O'Brien, and I formed a tight infield that made almost no errors. With a quality battery most games—

Bill Klinger catching, John Bruzinski or Eugene Stys pitching—
we ended up CYO champs of the East Side. Our reward was playing
the league championship game, against Sts. Peter and Paul, at Briggs
Stadium. To play where the Detroit Tigers played—what an awesome
treat! For years all of us had dreamed of playing there, and now it was
happening.

I played an errorless game at second base and went two for five at
the plate. My biggest thrill was a one-hop double off the wall in right
center. How I have savored that memory these fifty-five years. Despite
my personal good game, we lost after Mike Goff, our centerfielder,

*Two ballplayers:
me, in eighth
grade, with Jeff*

misjudged a fly ball, allowing three unearned runs to score. I felt bad for Mike. It turned out to be the last game we played together as teammates.

That summer our school had a Dads' Club outing on Bob Lo Island, in Lake Erie. Half a century later I still cherish the recognition I received at the awards ceremony held there. It won't mean anything to anyone when I pass, but this honor gave me tremendous confidence. I would build my life around the confidence I gained from athletic competition, and around the other lessons these games of my youth taught me. Playing sports every day instilled discipline and persistence in me. Sports taught me to get up and fight when the game was not going my way. It taught me to win graciously and to lose with class. It showed me how to value my body, and to understand how my body and mind work together. And it prepared me for life in an American culture that was immersed in athletics.

I still have the small bronze cup given to me that day on Bob Lo Island. The inscription reads:

ATHLETE
OF
YEAR
1958–59
DAVID BONIOR

DRAWN TO THE PRIESTHOOD:
MY INCREASING INVOLVEMENT
WITH THE CHURCH

I have left religion for last because, for a time in my adolescence, religion won out over politics and sports. While today fourteen might seem a ridiculous age at which to embark upon one's adult career, the 1950s were different.

The constant stream of religious instruction that had begun in St. Florian only intensified at St. Veronica. Each school day would start in the church, with Mass, which lasted about forty-five minutes. Because one needed to fast to receive Holy Communion, we would all wait until the beginning of our first class to eat breakfast, which we brought with us. The breakfast my mother packed for me usually consisted of a hard-boiled egg, two pieces of toast sandwiched together with jelly, and an orange drink that was advertised as juice.

Because our class would sometimes sing in the choir at morning Mass, we spent time during the day learning the proper Latin musical responses as well as the hymns sung during communion and at the end of Mass. We learned to chant and sing "Ave Maria." But we also had fun with music—occasionally the nuns would have us sing nonecclesiastical tunes like "Row, Row, Row Your Boat" and other rounds. And between Thanksgiving and the sixth of January, the Feast of the Epiphany, we sang all the wonderful Christmas carols.

In fifth grade, my devotion to the Catholic faith took a giant step forward: I accepted an invitation to "try out" to be an altar boy. I had for years watched the boys dressed in cassock and surplice as they assisted the priest on the altar. I was still smitten by the "bells and smells" of the Church, but the attraction was now something more, tied up with the centerpiece of the Mass, the transubstantiation, the moment when the bread and wine of the Eucharist are transformed into the body and blood of Christ. I was exhilarated by the miracle of it and intrigued by the mystery of it.

And now I had a chance to be closer to that miracle and that mystery.

The candidates for altar boy—or "acolyte"—had much to learn: We had to memorize the Latin response to the priest's prayers at Mass and master the precise choreography of each part of the ceremony. Altar boys also had to prepare the items used: Prior to the Mass we filled the crucibles with wine that was kept in the sacristy. The strong, sweet aroma of the wine was a strange wake-up to us at 6:00 a.m., the time of the day's first Mass. We also lit the altar candles. Sometimes that job was more complicated than it had to be, thanks to a trick the boys from the previous Mass might play on us. Using, as we always did, an altar stick to extinguish the candles at the end of Mass, they would smash the stick down hard, burying the wick under the hot melted wax. Because the candles were high up on the altar, we couldn't see the condition of the wicks as we held up the wand—the candle lighter/snuffer—to light the candles. St. Veronica was a huge parish, with four masses on Sunday morning. If this was a 9:45 Sunday Mass, perhaps a thousand worshipers would be watching as two eleven- or twelve-year-olds would be unable to get the candles burning so that the service could begin. Snickering might fill the church; an unwelcome tension would bind the congregation together. Meanwhile the priest would be in the sacristy thinking that he had another Mass in an hour and a quarter and needed to get this one underway.

The nuns who were in charge of training the altar boys made a terrible mistake in pairing me initially with Leon LeClair, another fifth-grader with no experience. One Sunday morning we were assigned to our pastor, Father Hoover, a gruff, short man. We were so intimidated by him and the situation that he wound up having to instruct us, at several points during the Mass, where to position ourselves—movements that were supposed to be second nature for altar boys. Our performance was so dismal that the exasperated priest raised hell with the nuns afterward. What the good sisters should have done, at least for our first few tries, was pair each of us with a more practiced boy.

But eventually I got the hang of it.

Serving Mass became a regular and indispensable fiber woven throughout the fabric of my life, affording me both spiritual comfort and temporal stature.

On weekdays I would rise at 5:00 a.m. and trudge to church. The quiet of the morning seemed to be all ours—Catholic children are taught they are protected by their own guardian angel; he was my partner in these mystical duties. Inside the sacristy I donned my cassock and began my ordered rituals. First I would light the altar candles, then I would fill the crucibles with water and red wine so dark and pungent that I was reminded of my place, as a child, in this most solemn of religious expressions. With our hands palmed together and our fingers pointing to the heavens, the priest and I together entered the altar from the sacristy. The half dozen elderly parishioners would slowly rise out of respect, wanting ever so much to be close to their Maker as their own time drew near. High in the choir loft in the rear of the church, Mrs. Lenhardt would play the organ and sing, in her angelic morning voice, which would fall like soft snow over the mostly empty pews.

Standing at the foot of the altar the priest would cross himself, reciting in Latin, "In nomine Patris, et Filii, et Spiritus Sancti. Amen. Introibo ad altare Dei." *In the name of the Father and of the Son and of the Holy Ghost. Amen. I will go to the altar of God.* Kneeling beside the priest, I would respond in my newly acquired language, "Ad Deum qui laetificat juventutem meam." *To God, the joy of my youth.*

And so it would continue for the whole Mass—the priest praising and I answering, both of us in Latin during the time before the Second Vatican Council changed the language of the Mass to the vernacular. The climax of the service was the transubstantiation. So profound was this moment that I felt privileged to ring the altar bells as the celebrant lifted the host and then the chalice of wine high above his head for all to witness the miracle.

Certificate of altar boy service

The honor of serving Mass, with its rituals and responsibilities and new language, was a seminal experience for me. Assigned to a Sunday service, I would be seen by thousands of parishioners. Assisting at baptisms, weddings, and funerals, I was witness to the full cycle of life—the joy and grief, poignant and rich, embedded in the rituals of my faith.

From a safe place, windows opened to a bigger world. My understanding—of people and of myself—deepened. I found spiritual grounding and peace of mind. The Church would be both an anchor and a lighthouse in my life.

"Whereas Ed thought David would be a professional football player," recalls Martha Mulkoff, "Irene's dream was that David become a priest. She expressed that to me quietly, but with a lot of feeling. That was what was going to happen."

I don't deny Martha's recollection, but the fact is that I got little encouragement—or discouragement, for that matter—from either parent regarding my decision to enter the seminary. Yes, Nancy and I attended Catholic schools. Yes, we were active in our parish. But except on Christmas and Easter, we didn't say grace at meals, nor did we have religious pictures in the house. On the subject of religion, my parents were pretty much mute.

Still, Dad had a lot of religion in him. His parents, Busia and JaJa, were devout; only three pictures hung on their walls: Jesus and Mary in the living room, and Franklin Roosevelt in the office. Dad would go to Mass every Sunday—Mother went less frequently—although to some extent his attendance was a function of the political base he'd developed in the Ushers Club. Although he didn't try to sell religion to me or Nancy, he had religious habits: When we'd drive by a cemetery, he'd cross himself. On Palm Sunday he'd keep the fronds, making a cross from them which he'd keep on his dresser or in the living room for weeks. After my mother died, he kept a cross on his dresser. And although he could get angry, he never swore; he'd grown up on the streets and had served in the army, but, as far as I heard, his language was better than mine.

The idea of the priesthood didn't come to me from my family. I think it came from my exposure to my faith. I was fascinated by the mysteries and teachings.

I found myself drawn to Christ—the Christ in the portrait the nuns of St. Veronica painted. They glorified Him but also made Him so human: a boy who became a man, a forgiving person who did good works. And what a story: He started off in a manger, the son of a carpenter. I could relate to those origins—in my family and neighborhood we were printers and auto workers and carpenters. And He ministered to people, even those who were sinful, like Mary Magdalene. My interest in social justice has a lot to do with the Jesus the nuns of St. Veronica taught me to revere. Add to this concept of Christ the model the parish priests presented to me, mix in the reward for a life of devotion—eternal bliss—and a vocation for the priesthood seemed more and more the right path for me.

A famous priest also helped shape my consciousness. Every Tuesday our family would gather around the television to watch Bishop Fulton J. Sheen on his show, *Life Is Worth Living*. A renowned theologian and charismatic speaker, Bishop Sheen would wear a red skullcap and a cape, which he would maneuver dramatically as he looked into the camera and held forth on current events and moral questions. The first televangelist, he won an Emmy for Most Outstanding Television Personality. What I found appealing about him were his personal flair and his absolute belief in his own words.

Most of our parish priests were, I felt, also worthy of emulation. An exception was Father Thompson, who rarely smiled. When it was time for the altar boys to fill the chalice with water and wine, he had us use only a drop of water, and at the offertory, he drank generously from the cup. But the moment I most remember came one school morning. I was looking out our classroom window toward our new church building, which had just been completed across the street. The new church had a belfry tower, where pigeons liked to roost. This day, in the sight of God and before a school full of children, Father Thompson came charging out of the rectory holding a shotgun. He crossed the street, took aim at the bell tower, and began to blast away at the birds. I wasn't the only child watching this display—at least half the classrooms had a bank of windows looking in that direction. The nuns were stunned to say the least: Gun blasts and dead birds were not what they expected from their priest. I'm sure the neighbors were none too pleased, either. Father Thompson was not my idea of a role model.

But I admired two younger priests, Father Jerome E. Shanahan and Father Donald Devine. An Irishman with an outgoing personality, Father Shanahan loved to sing and socialize with his flock and was thought of as the best preacher among the four or five priests who celebrated Mass in the parish. A big booster of all our sports teams, he was also a car buff who parked his black Model T Ford in the rectory garage.

My parents knew him well—perhaps he stoked Mom's interest in my becoming a priest.

Compared to Father Shanahan, Father Devine had a quiet, contemplative demeanor. But he was no less happy—both men always seemed to have smiles on their faces. You had the feeling that Father Devine's joy came from prayer and the simple wonder of life. The parish leader of the altar boys, Father Devine one day rented a bus and, during school hours, drove perhaps forty of us to Wall Lake Amusement Park, where we rode the roller coaster and enjoyed playing hooky.

Our pastor at St. Veronica was Bishop Donovan, a tall man with an aristocratic bearing, whom I found to be thoughtful, if reserved. It was considered an honor for a parish to be led by a prelate—"high management," as we in our working-class community thought of him. He did not attend our church every Sunday—my sense was that he had many other duties in addition to his pastoral role at St. Veronica—but when he did celebrate Mass in his red prelate vestments, worshipers took pride in feeling that our parish was indeed special.

While I know that I had conversations with my parents about my future, I can't say that I recall the specifics of any of them, and I certainly don't remember their posing questions for me to contemplate as I pondered my choices. Perhaps that job was left to the parish priests. One meeting I had with a priest—Father Shanahan, I believe—took place in the rectory. The father told me that Sacred Heart Seminary, in Detroit, would admit me, but its rector had concerns over whether I could handle the academics required of a seminarian. I understood his doubts: My grades were mediocre and my study habits were minimal. But Father Shanahan's tone let me know that despite these real concerns, Sacred Heart was willing to give me a try. I'm only guessing here, but I imagine that each parish in Metro Detroit had a quota of seminary recruits they were responsible for filling. I might have been picked out early as a potential candidate.

In 1950s America it was common for Catholic families to give one of their children to the Church as a priest or nun. We were taught that, in spiritual terms, the Holy Order of the priesthood ranked one step above marriage. My attitude about committing my life to the Church was mixed. While I felt the allure of my faith, I wasn't eager either to give up my athletic career or to embrace celibacy. I loved sports and was starting to develop the sexual desires normal for a boy emerging from puberty. This was the first really big decision of my young life. I was torn.

In June 1959, upon my graduation from eighth grade and St. Veronica, I received a letter from Sisters Marcine and Marie de Montfort, SSJ (Sisters of St. Joseph). Aside from the salutation, it was a form letter—all the graduates got it. Nonetheless, it gave me much to think about.

Dear David,

Thank you for all you did to make this year so pleasant. May God take special care of you as you take the big step into high school. Maybe you will quickly forget Math rules, English diagrams, and Social Studies facts, but please do not forget the Catholic way of life we have shown you. Please grow up to put God first, to receive the sacraments at least once a month, to respect your parents, to work hard in school to prepare yourself well for a future job.

Have fun but keep close to God and Mary.

CHAPTER 5

An Empty Chair at a Banquet

My Mother's Death and My Years in High School

A SERIOUS PLACE:
SACRED HEART SEMINARY

The building housing Sacred Heart Seminary, on Detroit's West Side, explodes with holiness, from the stunning stained-glass windows in the chapel, to the elegant oak paneling in the hallways, to the distinctive glazed tiles, made by Detroit's renowned Pewabic Pottery studio, that cover many walls and floors. The stately structure, built in the Gothic Revival style, opened its doors in 1924, six years after the seminary's founding by the Diocese of Detroit. Today listed in the National Register of Historic Places, it's located at the western edge of the historic Boston Edison neighborhood.

For me the word "Sacred" in its name is apt. Sacred Heart Seminary, where I started high school, was a serious place to learn and pray.

It's where you went to become a priest.

I liked the idea of becoming a priest. Prayer fit me. I found inner peace preparing to do "God's work." But I did have doubts. Doubts about whether I was academically talented enough to learn all the Latin being thrown at me. (Even today, half a century later, I have nightmares about not being able to find my Latin class at the University of Iowa.) Doubts about living a life of celibacy. And doubts about whether I could endure a lifetime without really knowing how good an athlete I might have been.

Sacred Heart Seminary

Doubts about my faith, however, had not yet grabbed my attention. They would in college, but for now my strong commitment to the faith of my upbringing sustained me throughout all my struggles. Chet Raymo, an insightful philosopher of nature and religion, summed up my situation when he wrote, "By looking for God in our ignorance, we can make him in our own image, call him Father, speak to him as friend, claim a personal relationship, count on his intervention in our lives. It is a consoling thought to think that the creator of the universe—those hundreds of billions of galaxies—has me, yes *me*, as the apple of his eye."[1]

Sacred Heart Seminary operated at two levels—high school and college. Our freshman high school class contained about 120 students—all male, of course, since the priesthood is not open to women—from all the Detroit-area parishes. About half the students at the high school boarded there, while the other half, which included me, commuted

1 John Sexton, with Thomas Oliphant and Peter J. Schwartz, *Baseball as a Road to God: Seeing Beyond the Game* (New York: Gotham Books, 2013), 124–125.

daily from their homes. There were three students from St. Veronica. We carpooled together—I sat in the backseat while seniors Joe Silveri and Harold Quenneville drove the forty-five minutes each way.

A day at the seminary started with short prayers, and there was an additional visit to the chapel for Mass at 11:30. Otherwise, however, the school day was not much different from that at any other college-preparatory high school. We all operated on a tight schedule of classes and activities—even tighter for those of us who commuted. We carried a full complement of classes, most of them taught by priests. My curriculum was composed of algebra, English, history (taught by Father Shauermann), Latin (Father Ozage), and religion (Father Prohaska). Leading the school was its rector, Monsignor Albert Matyn.

The personal and academic discipline was rigid. If you got out of line in any way, you were given demerits, which were tallied on a small card you carried on your person at all times, presumably to remind you of your need to control your behavior. Too many demerits and out the door you went. The rule I found most onerous was the prohibition on talking outside of class. The idea of not talking all day was too much even for (mostly quiet) me. So after lunch—which we ate in silence—I found myself sneaking into the weight room, off the gym floor, where my new friend John Carlin and I would share our thoughts about this new experience we were having.

I was a mediocre student. I had no foundation in study habits. And with a literary background that, aside from my interest in *The Good Bad Boy*, consisted mainly of scanning box scores in the newspapers, my reading comprehension was poor. When asked to recite passages in Father Shauermann's history class, I would panic and stumble, invariably disappointing him and embarrassing myself. No one took me under his wing, no one brought me along. The system was just too rigid—I felt lost and I was. Perhaps the seminary's concerns over my academic readiness—the concerns Father Shanahan had warned me of before I left St. Veronica—were on target. At the end of my first semester I got my grades: two Bs, two Cs, and a D in algebra.

There was no joy to be found in the classroom, so I found it elsewhere.

After class there was intramural flag football. I excelled at quarterback, leading our scruffy little team to a first-place finish. I'd found success at *something* in this place! But a question was constantly on my mind: Could I find as much success playing regular football at a regular high school? It bothered me that I might never know the answer.

My favorite sport was basketball, and I was fortunate that Sacred Heart had an interscholastic team. I tried out and ended up starting at guard, averaging 13 points a game. Brian Cronin, a senior, and I, a freshman, carried the team. Playing smaller parish schools like St. Theresa and Holy Redeemer, we ended the season with just a .500 record. But the fact that I could start and excel gave my confidence a huge boost and earned me the attention of both my fellow students and the faculty. However, our coach, Mr. Koval, who was also my algebra teacher, cut me no slack away from the gym. I understood the Xs and Os on the locker-room blackboard far better than I did the numbers and symbols on the blackboard in his classroom.

When the weather was good I would be among a small band of students, maybe seven or eight, who walked a path along the interior perimeter saying the rosary. These promenades occurred in midafternoon, at about the same time students from one of the largest public schools in the city, Central High, would pass by on their way home. The girls, knowing of our commitment to celibacy, would sometimes taunt us with sexually suggestive language and gestures from the other side of the black iron fence that separated us. Some of their teasing was humorous, some downright appealing. It was hard to concentrate on my Hail Mary's and Glory Be's.

The girls of Central High were directing my focus onto just one of the sacrifices I would be making were I to stay in the seminary. My doubts about my presence there were growing from month to month, and as the school year dragged on, I struggled to decide whether to continue or leave. I prayed hard for guidance. I shared my concern with my parents, who did not try to push me one way or the other. I confided my doubts to my classmate John Carlin, who was also entertaining the idea of leaving. I shared my thoughts with my friend Mike Goff, now at St. Ambrose. This was by far the most difficult decision I'd had to make in my young life.

Word of my dilemma got out—perhaps via Mike, perhaps not—to the athletic director at St. Ambrose, Father Weisner, who began actively trying to recruit me to his school. A small coed institution, St. Ambrose was nonetheless a powerhouse in Michigan high school football. Many of my friends from grade school were enrolled there and playing on the football team. Father Weisner's entreaties to me caused a mini-scandal in the archdiocese. Priests were supposed to recruit *into* the seminary, not *out* of it. I was flattered by all the attention, but I also wished it would go away.

1960 champion sandlot team of fifteen-year-olds; I'm seated, third from left.

It was early summer when I informed my parents that I'd come to a decision: I wanted to leave the seminary and join Mike at St. Ambrose. I felt great relief at having the decision behind me. Years later I would learn that fewer than a handful of seminarians in my class actually became priests. The idea of grooming fourteen-year-old boys for the priesthood was a failure. We were not ready to make decisions of such life-changing magnitude. The numbers proved it.

My parents accepted the first half of my decision: my leaving the seminary. In fact, I secretly wondered if they were not themselves relieved that I'd chosen a more traditional path for myself—a life they were more familiar with. But my father's acceptance came with a declaration of his own: He was sending me to our neighborhood all-boys Catholic high school, Notre Dame. I was terribly disappointed—I'd had my heart set on reuniting with Mike and other grade school friends at St. Ambrose. But Dad's decision was firm, and it came with a good reason: His struggling printing business had Notre Dame as a customer. The good Marist father who ran the school would expect Ed Bonior's son to enroll there. I tried to argue with my father's logic, but I knew I really couldn't. Our family livelihood was dependent on the business we got from Notre Dame.

I was trapped, and that was that.

Before school began in September, I had a summer's worth of work to do. I decided to make some money by caddying at Hillcrest Country Club, in Clinton Township. Each morning I'd walk a mile to Gratiot Avenue, then hitchhike ten miles to the golf course. At fourteen, which made me one of the youngest caddies, I was rarely chosen to carry a bag. I'd sit and wait in the caddy shack as all the other boys' names were called; most often I'd be the only kid left without employment. I soon tired of this discouraging drill and decided to become a golf entrepreneur.

The course had two treacherous water holes, sixteen and seventeen, featuring the Clinton River and a meandering creek, respectively. For half the summer I'd watched golfers plunk shots into the river or creek and thought, *There must be a small fortune in balls down in that water.* I abandoned my post in the caddy shack and began to wade into the water hazards, feeling with my feet for balls resting in the muck at the bottom. Each day I would pull out a bagful, then clean them up for resale to golfers finishing the eighteenth hole. Or maybe I'd catch customers in the club's parking lot. Occasionally, after I'd sold half a dozen balls, the buyer would shake his head, laugh, and say something like, "I could swear I hit that ball into the river not twenty minutes ago."

My other job was selling copies of the early Sunday editions of Detroit's three major daily newspapers on a street corner on Saturday nights. "Get your *News, Times,* and *Free Press,*" I would sing out from 6:00 p.m. to 2:00 a.m. Sunday morning. My corner was Gratiot and Outer Drive, across from the Detroit City Airport and the Davidson police station, and two blocks from the football field at De La Salle High School. It was quite a prize to get this corner—I got it thanks to Gil Templin, a newspaper distributor whose son Terry, two years older than I, was a star athlete at St. Veronica and Notre Dame. Mr. Templin was a great guy—after I started at Notre Dame, he would pick me up in the morning and drive me to school with Terry and Terry's sister Karen. Hawking papers, I'd haul fifteen dollars in tips each week. The kids with regular newspaper routes in their neighborhoods would work every day of the week folding and distributing, and on Saturday they had to go around collecting. Working just one night a week, I took home the same pay they did. My business had a number of built-in advantages: Instead of my traveling to customers each day of the week, customers came to me. They bought the larger—and more expensive— Sunday paper. I sold all three papers, whereas a daily route meant delivering only one: either the *Detroit News* or the *Detroit Free Press,* with the *Detroit Times* not even an option. I did a lot of business when the cops changed shifts at eleven and when the bars closed at one. Many people were interested in the results from Saturday's horse races. And there was business from the fans attending the Saturday night football games at De La Salle. (I was especially taken with the sweet, perfumed scent of the young coeds who passed by, to and from the games.) At 2:00 a.m. my father and mother would pick me up. We'd go home, sit in the kitchen, and count up my big bag of quarters.

I loved counting those quarters. But even more, I loved standing on the corner and singing out, at the top of my lungs, "Get your *Neeewwwwssss, Tiiiimmmmessss,* and *Freeeee Preeeesss.*"

WORTH THE MONEY: NOTRE DAME HIGH SCHOOL

The seminary was a *serious* place. Notre Dame was serious as well, but leavened with a prep school exuberance and playfulness. For the most part the teachers were dedicated and excellent, letting our parents feel they were getting their money's worth at two hundred dollars a year. There were over two hundred students in my class, about a thousand in the school. ND, in the city of Harper Woods, was located directly across Kelly Road from the city of Detroit. And while ND, a college-preparatory school, was all boys, the environs did not lack for girls. Our campus included three other high schools, all adjoined to one another. Regina, the Catholic girls' school my sister attended, was next door to ND, no more than thirty yards away. On the other side of Regina was another religious high school, Lutheran East, which was coeducational. And bordering the rear side of all three was the local public high school, Harper Woods High. Together the four schools served about three thousand students.

My favorite teacher was Conrad Vachon, who taught English and French. Mr. Vachon was tough, but he was also theatrical, with a good sense of humor. Some students feared him, because he was demanding and sharp-witted. But we all could see that he really cared about our education. He took an interest in me and might well have recognized my propensity for siding with the underdog—it was he who steered me to the columns of Ralph McGill. Reading McGill's dispatches from the

Rare photo of me studying, junior or senior year of high school

South, which were syndicated in the *Detroit News*, I began to learn about the growing civil rights movement. Mr. Vachon also introduced me to English literature, assigning the class Thomas Hardy's *Return of the Native*. He insisted that we all see the film *Lust for Life*, the story of Vincent van Gogh. My education was getting broader and more interesting. My grades improved, landing me on the honor roll every quarter my sophomore year.

Because of state rules for high school athletes, I entered ND ineligible to play sports for one semester. Practice, however, was not forbidden, so I trained with the junior varsity football team. And thanks to our coach, Bob Kefgen, I was able to get my first union card—in, improbably, the Screen Actors Guild. Coach Kefgen took eleven members of his team, dressed in full football regalia, to Cranbrook, a stunning nearby campus that contained an exclusive private school, a museum, an arts academy, and a scientific research facility. A production crew was onsite, filming a commercial for Ford. The action of the spot was eight of us squeezing into a new van. There was also a shot of me throwing a football next to the vehicle. For my small-screen debut I was paid eighty dollars—a princely sum at the time. Looking back, I wonder if the payment broke any rules for high school athletes.

My first union experience was a winner. Our ad played on the television show *Wagon Train*, which starred Ward Bond. At home, as we waited for the show to air, someone would yell, "Commercial!!" and everyone would come running into the living room to see me on TV.

A DEATH IN THE FAMILY: MY MOTHER'S PASSING

It was Friday, November 18, 1960, and my mother was scheduled for a test at Harper Hospital before traveling to New York City with my father on a trip that would combine his business with a little pleasure for both of them. We thought nothing of the medical test. We were just excited that Mother would be accompanying Dad on his trip to the Big Apple.

For me, Friday meant the end of the school week. What's more, I was delighted to be among the forty thousand fans at Briggs Stadium that evening to see St. Ambrose play Cooley High School for the city football championship. Mike Goff was playing; I was thrilled for him. St. Ambrose won, culminating a wonderful night. After the game I got a ride with John Carlin back to his house, which was near 7 Mile Road. My thirty-minute walk home took me past fifteen street corners, each lit with a streetlamp. Fantasizing that someday I, too, would get a chance to play in the big game, under each lamp I would set a pose and watch my shadow. One pose might be a crouch, getting ready to plow through the line like the famous Heisman-winning running back Howard "Hopalong" Cassidy, the Ohio State star who carried the ball for the Lions during their glory years in the '50s. Another might be with my leg extended high in the air, as if I were punting a ball à la Lou

"The Toe" Groza. At each corner my shadow became my companion as I playfully choreographed my way home.

I reached Ego Avenue at about 11:30 p.m. When I turned the corner, I saw that numerous cars were parked along the curb near our house. We had a large picture window in the front of the house; I could see that inside, in the living room, were numerous relatives and friends.

Something was wrong.

I went around to the back door, my usual point of entry into the house. Before I got there, my father met me in the backyard. I could see on his face that he had something important to tell me. He looked at me and I stopped moving. "Your mother died," he said without hesitation. "Go inside and take it like a man." No comforting. No hug. No touching of any kind. No tears.

No explanation.

I walked into the house, through the kitchen, and into the living room. The room turned quiet; all eyes were on me, as I was the last family member to know. Dazed, I didn't say a word. I went straight to my room.

I sat on the side of my bed trying to comprehend what I had just heard. What I had just seen. I was no stranger to death—I'd served all those funeral masses as an altar boy. But this was our mother—who was so *young*. Father Devine entered my room. He told me how sorry he was. "Your mother is in heaven," he said. He talked about God's will and all the things a priest says at a time like this. His voice was quiet and tender—he was doing his best. I heard him, and I didn't. His soothing voice was like consoling background music, but my mind was focused on trying to comprehend this earth-shaking event, on starting to take in how painfully I would miss her, on feeling the intensity of my sadness at not having said good-bye to her. I felt bewildered and stunned. I felt sad, but shock overwhelmed everything else. She was going in only for a test, not for an operation. She and Dad were going on a trip. How could she have *died*?

Nancy learned the news before I did. "I was home with my grandfather," she recalls. "My father came home with Aunt Nellie and Uncle Andy, and they told us. It was heartbreaking. They told us right there, as soon as they walked in the door, because they were filled with so much emotion and grief. Nobody did any comforting. All I remember is everybody walking around crying, not knowing what to do."

Many people came to the wake, held at the funeral home, to pay their respects: relatives, friends, priests, nuns, political acquaintances of my dad's. My classmates came by, and I thanked them. I was depressed, but tears came only when Mike Goff put his hand on my shoulder. I broke down. It had taken three days, but his presence and touch got me there.

Jeff, not quite five years old, tried to make sense of the event as best he could. "At the funeral home," he recalls, "we had to go out the side door to go to the cemetery. She was lying in the open casket. My dad was holding me, and I said, 'C'mon, Mommy, we're leaving.' I didn't know what was going on."

Holy prayer card for Mother's funeral

Our father asked his sister, our aunt Marie, to accompany the family on a trip to New York—my guess is that it was the same business trip he'd intended to take with Mother. Dad felt that it would be good for all of us to get away as a family. He was determined to keep us together and to move us all forward. For us kids, this was our first trip out of Michigan. We traveled by car and stayed at the Waldorf Astoria, on Park Avenue; the exclusive accommodations told me that Dad must have been traveling on government business, because there was no way we could have afforded to stay there on our own. The trip was a kind idea, but we all would have been much better off just talking about Mom and about what had happened. The circumstances of her death remained opaque, and our feelings about it stayed locked inside each of us. Instead of talking, Dad took Nancy to see a show on Broadway, while Marie stayed with Jeff and I went by myself to see Elgin Baylor play basketball at Madison Square Garden. Afterward we all went out to eat at Mamma Leone's. We were running away from, instead of confronting, the tragedy that had just dramatically changed all of our lives.

In later years I wondered why my father broke the news of my mother's death to me the way he did. In a way, it makes sense—he was not a man who shared his emotions with others. I remember only one time when he told me that he loved me, and that was the day before he died. In his later years he might occasionally sign a birthday card "Love, Dad." It was special to see those words, which had been such a long time coming.

Perhaps Dad's cold emotional response to life—or, perhaps more accurately, his lack of emotional response—stemmed from his service in the army. Surviving World War II and being witness to so much death and destruction might have triggered an emotional shutdown— a shutdown he might have thought enabled him to maintain his mental equilibrium when in fact it did the opposite, eating away at him slowly for over half a century. Or maybe Dad's grief that chilly November night was so pronounced, so overwhelming, that he had only one way to tell me what happened: cold, short, and with a message to "buck up," to take it like a man—like he did, in other words.

I doubt that I will ever know the answer. I should have asked him in later years. But I did not. I was afraid to open up this part of our lives—and so, in that way, I was indeed my father's son.

The intent of the adults in taking us to New York City was to look forward, not backward to Mother's death. That rejection of the past seems to have been the attitude not only of my father and his sister but also of all my grandparents. The past represented the poverty and instability of Europe, the pain and sorrow of leaving home. In the Old World there was hunger, death, and destruction. But in the New World—in the future—there was hope. It was this family attitude that I think drove me to be interested in history. I hungered to know my own family's story. Indeed, the lack of information I received from my family about its past is one of the main reasons I am writing this book. Perhaps it's also why I glued myself to the TV when the *Victory at Sea* and *The Twentieth Century* documentary series were shown in the 1950s and '60s. It's certainly why I earned an MA in history that centered on Germany, Poland, and the Austro-Hungarian Empire. And it was why I always insisted on including a "history lesson" in the many speeches I gave even though political consultants and some staffers would say to me, "Nobody cares about the past."

I wish I knew all of my family better: my maternal grandmother, whom I never met; her husband, with whom I shared a home until I was eighteen; my father, whose hard outer shield was too much for me to penetrate; and my mother, who died decades too young.

At home after the trip to New York I felt a huge void. I'd had my mother for fifteen years. But seeing my brother daily reminded me that because he was only four years and nine months of age when she died, he might not remember her and the love she gave to him. My sister lost the only other female in our home. My grandfather, who had lost his wife when she was in her midthirties, had now lost his youngest daughter at about the same age. My father had lost his wife and the mother of his children. A thick pall of grief lay upon our house.

At night I dreamed about her returning to our family—I wanted it so much I almost could feel it happening. And while my sister, my father, and I were processing her loss at night, we would hear my grandfather's moans and nightmares. It was as though we were each going through our own nocturnal therapy sessions, each of us dealing with the loss alone, aware of the collective grief but unable to join forces to confront it. The sadness was everywhere: In our silence. On our faces. In our steps. The grief was strangling us slowly.

We could not survive this way. So those from the outside, recognizing our pain, came forward to help.

Aunt Nell and Uncle Andy spent a lot of time with Jeff and Nancy. My father's friends were there for him as they drew him deeper into politics and city affairs.

I could feel the concern of teachers and coaches, so I plunged back into school and sports.

That's what you do. You go forward.

A Hunger to Win: Playing for Coach Bazy

Back at ND, I made the varsity basketball team. Rated, along with nearby Catholic Central, among the top ten squads in the state, we went 18–2 for the year. Both teams had amazing talent. Our starting five were Gary Lytle (who went on to win a basketball scholarship to Michigan State), Danny DiNunzio (basketball scholarship to University of Michigan), Terry Templin, John Goff (Mike's brother), and Tom Corbett. I was not eligible to play until February, about halfway through the season. We tied for the conference championship with Catholic Central but lost in the quarterfinals of the state tournament to a faster team from Highland Park High. My claim to fame that season was being matched on defense against their all-state guard, Bobby Joe Hill, who scored 19 points against me. More significantly, he went on to lead Texas Western to the NCAA title in 1966. The first NCAA champion with an all-black starting lineup, the Texas Western Miners defeated an all-white University of Kentucky team, coached by Adolph Rupp, in the finals. The game was the subject of a terrific book, *And the Walls Came Tumbling Down*, as well as an inspiring film, *Glory Road*.

The following year, when I was a junior, was a big disappointment athletically. To begin with, it was becoming obvious to me that I would not be a strapping six feet four like my father. I was a hair shy of five feet eleven and weighed 175 pounds—and that would be all she wrote. Although I started at quarterback on a team predicted to win the conference championship, my performance came up short. In our annual Boys' Bowl Charity game against rival Catholic Central, played before seventeen thousand spectators, I was benched at halftime, and remained sitting for the rest of the season. We ended up with a disappointing 4–1–2 record, in third place behind Salesian and the conference champ, Catholic Central.

Basketball was even worse. Having lost every one of our starting five from the previous year, we were not expected to be any good, and we met those expectations. I injured my left knee halfway through the season, spending six weeks on crutches. The ligament was either torn or severely strained, causing the knee to blow up full of fluid, which had to be repeatedly drained. The doctors were undecided on whether to operate. Instead of the knife, I opted for shots of cortisone to reduce the swelling. I was then given a weighted boot that I used for exercises to strengthen the knee. The remainder of my basketball season was shot, as was my baseball season.

Reality was starting to set in: Perhaps my ticket to the future would not be printed on a ball. I was starting to give up hope that my athleticism might finance my way through college, and therefore to fear that I might not be able to afford a higher education. I was falling into a deep funk. I was bitter that I was not at St. Ambrose, where I believed life would have been a lot better. My grades plummeted, knocking me off the honor roll and back down to my mediocre Bs and Cs.

But then the sun came out.

Meeting to discuss the state of affairs in ND's athletic programs, the school's administration and the Dads' Club decided that they were not satisfied, and soon after, the principal dismissed the head coaches of both the football and basketball teams. The school replaced the two men with one, Walter Bazylewicz. "Bazy," as our new football and basketball head coach was known, had already amassed a highly successful record coaching high school sports. He was a winner—and a winner was what the ND family was looking for. Bazy, who had played on the line with my father at Hamtramck High, was old school. He was tough, he drove you hard, he could get all over your ass. He came with that reputation, and we players knew it. But there was a great hunger to win among all involved, and we were prepared to give the effort our all. That summer, Bazy asked the athletic department if he could meet with the leaders of the football team. The department assented, so Paul Verska, our all-state guard, George Arnold, our linebacker and cocaptain, and I met him for hamburgers and fries at Dunkenburger, a new fast-food restaurant near school. We let Bazy know that we were excited about playing for him; I think he was genuinely excited about his new challenge, too.

Because most of our starters from the previous season had graduated, none of the local sportswriters were picking our team to do well. But what the critics did not realize—nor did I—was the abundance of talent waiting for a turn, capable sophomores and juniors who had to that point compiled little in the way of records to measure them by. As for me, I had a lot to prove after last year's midseason benching. Bazy assigned his assistant coach, Mitch Marcinkowski—a fireman in Hamtramck—to work with me over the summer. I had a whole new offense to learn. So Mitch, one of the finest coaches I've ever had and one of the finest people I've ever known, drilled me on my footwork for the new plays and put me through my paces practicing roll-outs. I must have thrown two thousand balls that summer, some to my teammates, some through a tire I rigged up in my backyard. This season was do-or-die for me—it was my senior year, my last chance to secure a college athletic scholarship—so I was going to give it everything I had.

I continued the weight-training to strengthen my knee. Would the knee hold up? That was a big question in my mind, as well as in the minds of the coaches. They kept me out of contact at practice and told me that my job was simply to hand the ball off and to hit my passes, not to risk reinjuring my knee by attempting to run for big yardage. I was okay with that plan.

The season started with a big upset victory on the road against University of Detroit High School. I threw two touchdown passes, one to split end John McDonald, the other to halfback Bob Lantzy, in our 13–12 triumph. Bob, like Paul Verska, would go on to become one of the most successful coaches in the history of Michigan high school football.

The next game I threw two more TD passes in our victory against St. Joseph. After a scoreless first half against De La Salle, I marched our offense down the field, capping off the drive with a short TD toss to our all-state tight end, Joe Przybycki (who would receive a football scholarship to Michigan State and became a starting offensive tackle on the Spartans' 1965 National Championship team), that sealed our 7–0 win.

Our next game was the Boys' Bowl, site of my humiliation the year before. Eighteen thousand spectators poured into the University of Detroit's stadium to see what turned into a protracted defensive battle. The game was scoreless in the fourth quarter when we got the ball on our own 38-yard line with one minute left on the clock. I hit Przybycki for 18 yards. Next play, I came back to Lantzy for 26. I hit two more passes. With seconds remaining I hit wide end Dave Berari (who would be named all-city) for a touchdown. Then I passed to Lantzy for the extra point—only one, as our league's rules didn't allow for a two-point conversion. Our team won, and I had redeemed myself after last year's failure. Our 4–0 record put us on top of the Central Division.

I threw two more TDs against Detroit Cathedral in our win at Keyworth Stadium in Hamtramck, three blocks from where I grew up. Next I fired another pair of touchdowns against our East Side rival Austin Catholic as we stretched our winning streak to six. Our final division game was at home against Salesian, whose record was 5–0–1. Ten thousand cheering fans watched a fabulous performance by our defense, as Verska, Arnold & Co. shut out the vaunted Salesian offense. Before the game, Bazy told me I could finally run the ball, so I did, picking up first downs and once again feeling like a complete football player. I threw a touchdown pass to Dave Berari and an extra point to Przybycki. Our running backs, led by Randy Lamprides and sophomore Pat Fulford, ran wild. We won in a rout, 27–0, bringing the conference championship to ND.

Next stop, the Detroit Catholic championship game.

St. Ambrose would be our opponent, and so, in a strange twist of fate, I found myself competing against my friend Mike Goff—although how strange, and how fateful, the matchup was I wouldn't find out for years. A record twenty thousand fans came out to see the annual Soup Bowl, so named because proceeds went to the Capuchin Fathers, whose mission was to feed the hungry and house the homeless. Both teams were undefeated, both were ranked among Michigan's best. The stakes were sky high: The winner of this game, the Catholic champion, would then play the public school titleholder for the championship of the whole city.

We took a 13–12 lead into halftime. With my knee strong, I was feeling good about running the ball, and in the third quarter I ran an option play, breaking free along the sideline with nothing but daylight and the goal line in front of me. Not used to running, I carried the ball in my wrong hand. It needed to be tucked in under the arm closest to the sidelines, but I was openly swinging it toward the center of the field as I ran for the end zone. My carelessness led to disaster: From out of nowhere, Mike, playing safety, ran me down and stole the ball from me. It was as clean a pick as one could imagine; I hardly felt the ball leave my hand. He would intercept two of my passes, as well. By the time the final whistle sounded, it wasn't close: St. Ambrose had won, 33–13. We were crushed! And I felt terrible personally: I had let my team and my school down. I carried that feeling for thirty years, until one day Mike put it all in perspective for me.

I learned the significance of that game in Mike's life when he, his brother John, and our friend Gary Lytle joined me at the US Capitol for lunch in the House dining room. Mike's father was a bricklayer; his mother, a woman with the patience of a saint and the command of a platoon sergeant, was a busy housewife. Of course she was busy—she had *nine* children to look after. Growing up in this large, working-class family, Mike would never have been able to go off to college without a scholarship. Mike said that that game against us thirty years prior had been his best, and because of it he'd been given a "full ride"—a complete scholarship, room and board for four years—to the University of Buffalo. Thirty years of despair and guilt melted away inside of me, and for weeks afterward I would be moved to tears just thinking about Mike's story at lunch that day. His great plays, aided by my ineptitude, had helped him achieve a scholarship, a degree, and, eventually, a good life.

MY FUTURE ARRIVES: FINDING A SPOT IN THE BIG TEN

We barely had time to catch our breath after the gridiron season when Bazy called our first basketball practice. Prospects for the team were low: With a new coach, we had to learn a new system. I was the only senior on the starting five. New coach, new system, young team equals trouble. Bob Nevada, six feet five, and Bob Smith, six feet eight, although both inexperienced, gave us size up front. Bob Lantzy, quick as a cat, was our

THREE-LETTER ATHLETE, SENIOR YEAR
NOTRE DAME HIGH SCHOOL

Handing off

At the free throw line

Our team (I'm in the top row, third from left)

point guard, and Randy Lamprides and I played an isolated two-on-two game whenever our opponents played man-to-man defense. This system worked well, making us the surprise team in the conference. At the season's midpoint we were 5–3, beating the weaker teams but losing to U. of Detroit, Catholic Central, and our archrival, Austin.

The second half of the season saw us improve, with victories over the same powerhouse teams we'd lost to earlier. I averaged 15 points a game for the season—back when there were no three-point baskets to pad one's scoring—and was the team's captain. At season's end I was hitting long buzzer-beaters to win games or send them into overtime. It was an immensely satisfying year that included an overtime thriller against St. Peter Chanel, a top-ranked high school from neighboring Ohio, and a glorious triple-overtime triumph over Austin. We finished our season with a respectable 12–5 record.

While my mind was on basketball, it was also on my future. In my immodest estimation I was having an excellent senior year, one that merited my receiving a full ride to college to play either football or basketball.

High school graduation, June 1963

Each day, between the end of school and the start of basketball practice—without a gym in our building we practiced at the public high school later in the afternoon—I would hurry home to get the mail, checking for "letters of interest" from university sports programs. As I waited for my future to arrive in that mailbox, I was selected city and state All-Catholic for my season at quarterback. Slowly, the letters from football coaches began to arrive. Each day brought a new level of excitement as I pawed through the envelopes in the day's delivery, hungrily examining the return addresses for the name of a college. I felt more anticipation than when I was a child of six waiting to open my Christmas presents.

First came a letter from coach Bob Devaney at the University of Nebraska. Then one from Notre Dame in South Bend. Then Colorado State wrote. Almost every day for weeks there were letters from both large universities and small colleges. There was nothing, however, from either Michigan or Michigan State, our state's two Big Ten behemoths.

Returning to Notre Dame in 1998 to deliver graduation address, with students (l. to r.) Rick Suhrheinrich, unidentified, and Paul Soderberg. Rick and Paul worked in my campaigns.

Despite the silence coming from Ann Arbor and East Lansing, I still had my heart set on a Big Ten school. The Big Ten was the conference with the athletic prestige, the academic excellence, and, last but certainly not least, the girls—all the schools were coed. The only two members of the conference that showed an interest in me were Indiana and Iowa. Iowa recruited heavily from Michigan and, especially, the Detroit area. I had a couple of friends already there on football scholarships, and, fortunately for me, Bazy was friends with head football coach Jerry Burns, who had played high school ball at Catholic Central High School and the University of Michigan. Iowa had won the Big Ten football conference championship in both 1958 and 1960. It was definitely on my radar screen. And once things got going with Iowa, the idea of going to Indiana just faded away. The thought of a basketball scholarship faded away as well: I got only a handful of letters from coaches of that sport, all from small schools that couldn't compete in my mind with the majesty of the Big Ten.

In the spring of 1963 I received a letter inviting me to visit the campus in Iowa City. After flying there—my first time on an airplane—I bunked for the weekend in the dorm room of Iowa football player Mike Mullins, who was from East Detroit. I'd played F League baseball, which was similar to American Legion ball, with Mike a couple of years earlier. I loved the place. I was in awe of the campus and the athletic facilities. And the coeds! Oh, the coeds!

I was smitten.

I still had one spring left at Notre Dame. Having missed playing on school baseball teams during my first three years of high school—by spring of each year I'd been focused only on getting to the end of the school year—I was really looking forward to playing for Tom Kelly. Everybody loved Coach Kelly. He'd taken ND to the city championship two years earlier. Led by Gary Lytle and Mike Petrucci, the 1961 team beat everybody, winning the city title at Briggs Stadium.

We ended up with a disappointing 10–7 record, but I was honored to captain the team, and to start every game, usually at third base. However, the most heart-warming honor I ever received in sports came during my last baseball game—my last game, period—at ND. Coach Kelly started me at third base but, inexplicably, moved me to shortstop in the second inning. In the third inning I started to get the picture when he told me to play second base. He played me at a different position each inning, ending my day with a stint as catcher. His gesture meant the world to me. This was my good-bye to Notre Dame sports—what a gratifying way to go out.

At the athletic banquet at the end of the school year I was awarded MVP in both football and basketball. My father was there to see me receive those accolades, but I wished my mother could have been there, too. Without the love, understanding, and support of both my parents, my achievements would not have been possible.

Iowa's Jerry Burns was the affair's guest speaker. After the festivities had concluded, Burns, Bazy, Dad, and I sat down to talk. Burns said that all thirty-three of his football scholarships were already promised but that he wanted me at Iowa, would see that I received a scholarship

after my first semester, and would help me get a job to pay for that first term. This news was bittersweet. I could have gone elsewhere on a full ride, but I wanted the Big Ten, and this was my only option.

I rolled the dice and accepted the offer. I was to be a Hawkeye!

Banquet, 1963, with Jerry Burns sitting at left and Coach Bazy handing me the MVP awards for football and basketball

CHAPTER 6

Beginning to Grow Up

My Four Years at the University of Iowa

WALK-ON:
MY ARRIVAL

My first trip to the University of Iowa had been made by air and paid for by the school's athletic department, but *I* was paying for my next trip, so I chose the less expensive train, boarding at Michigan Central Station in Detroit. When we stopped in Chicago, a number of University of Iowa students, identifiable by their T-shirts, hopped on board. One seemed built for football—a strong, tall guy with a thick neck. Roger LaMont—all six feet two and 230 pounds of him—and I ended up sitting together, and we soon discovered that we had a lot in common. He was from Chicago's St. Rita's parish and was attending Iowa on a full-ride football scholarship. Sharing a religion, football, and working-class roots, we bonded easily. Since we two freshmen were both unsure what lay ahead for us, we stuck to talking about our high school experiences and, before we realized it, the four-hour ride from Chicago to Iowa City was over. My powerful new friend helped me with my two bags, and we shared a cab ride to the campus. He would remain a good friend throughout my years at Iowa.

When I entered my room in the Quadrangle dormitory, I was greeted first by a bag of golf clubs, then by the bag's owner. Jim Peterson, my new roommate, a rangy native of Clinton, Iowa, had ambitions of joining the Hawkeye golf team and later becoming a teacher. He was a gracious and lovely guy, the definition of "Iowa Nice," a term that would come into our political parlance to describe the people of that state. I could not have asked for a better roommate.

I became fast friends with a fellow Michigander, John Ficeli, a six feet two freshman football lineman from Grand Rapids. John's claim to fame was having fought Buster Mathis for the Michigan heavyweight Golden Gloves championship. Mathis beat him and went on to a successful and lucrative professional career, losing title fights against Muhammad Ali and Joe Frazier. Attending Iowa on a full football scholarship, John weighed 225 pounds, every ounce of it muscle, and eventually became the starting center on the varsity team. Italian through and through, John showed passion and energy for just about everything that came his way, displaying his emotion on his face and hands. His favorite singer was Roy Orbison and his favorite song was "Pretty Woman"—he would regularly regale us with his rendition. In the second semester of our freshman year, John left the Hillcrest dormitory to join Jim and me as a third roommate in Quadrangle. Both Jim and John soon honored me with invitations to meet their families in Clinton and Grand Rapids. After meeting their parents and roaming their neighborhoods, I understood how lucky I was to have them as roommates and friends. Many years later I would reciprocate, having each of their families visit our home in Washington.

Toward the end of the school year, as John and I studied in our rooms during spring finals week, I kept staring at two pairs of boxing gloves that hung over the railing of John's bed. I had teased him throughout the year that I could whip him in the ring—a preposterous boast, but I enjoyed getting under his skin. So one afternoon I challenged him to put on the gloves for a friendly sparring session on the lawn between the Hillcrest and Quadrangle dorms. Agreeing that we could use a break from the stress of studying, John consented.

Jim laced us up and out the door we went. It wasn't long before word got out that we were boxing on the lawn, and soon just about every window of the two dorms was open as study-weary students cheered us on. The fight was, to say the least, one-sided. John kept me

The Old Capitol, a University of Iowa landmark

at bay with his longer reach, jabbing me—toying with me—so I could not get inside him. I could not get close enough to throw punches that connected. He threw two right crosses, one of which I blocked. The one I didn't slammed into the side of my head. I kept dancing into his left jab until he suggested I move the other way. I eventually adopted a Floyd Patterson "peek-a-boo" posture, with both my gloves covering my face, which, while not cut, had turned red as a beet. I tried again to get inside John's punches only to be met with a barrage to my body that sent me reeling backward as the crowd of onlookers, now numbering in the hundreds, roared. I did not go down, but I knew I had had enough. "No more," I said, foreshadowing by sixteen years Roberto Durán's words as he surrendered his welterweight championship to

Sugar Ray Leonard: "*No más, no más*. No more box." John must have thought I was crazy to fight him, but he probably liked the idea that a quarterback—who on the football field let the linemen do the dirty work—would try. He could have killed me if he'd wanted to.

Roberto, I feel your pain.

In my first week at school, I registered, without much guidance, for Western Civilization (mandatory), Rhetoric (mandatory), Geology (better known as Earth Science), Political Science 101, and Sociology 101. I was anxious about this load. I did not want to flunk out of school; I did not want to embarrass my family, my friends, or myself. I kept telling myself that I'd had four years of college-preparatory courses in high school and that the other students did not look like Einsteins; if they could do it, so could I. It would be a while before I declared a major, but I knew I was interested in studying political science and sociology—if I could keep up.

My trepidation extended beyond the classroom to the gridiron. Because I was not on scholarship, the other freshmen on the team viewed me as a "walk-on." All scholarship athletes were lodged in Hillcrest; I was across the parking area in Quadrangle. On Sunday evenings all scholarship athletes ate free, with a list of approved names checked by the cashier in the cafeteria. My name was not on the list, so I had to not only pay cash but also do so in front of the scholarship boys I ate with. Some of the new players I met those first weeks of school rubbed it in, suggesting that they had heard stories of coaches promising scholarships then reneging once the athlete had arrived on campus. They made me feel that I'd been conned into coming to Iowa. I became nervous about what it all meant.

But even with these concerns racing around in my head, I was proud to be a Hawkeye. Dressing in our locker room underneath Kinnick Stadium for the first day of freshman practice sent chills up and down my spine. An Iowa legend, Niles Kinnick won the Heisman trophy in 1939 and was a consensus All-American at halfback. He was killed in 1943 in an accident while undergoing flight training for the U.S. Navy. At five feet eight and 167 pounds, he was tough and determined; I figured that if he could excel at his size, there might be hope for me at five feet ten, 180. His example, as well as the idea that sixty thousand fans would be cheering me on from the stands above where I was dressing, were enough inspiration for me those first few weeks of practice.

However, those fans wouldn't cheer for me this year. Freshman football included no games in the fall; the only game the freshmen played was at the end of spring practice, when they blended with the varsity for an intrasquad contest. Football this fall would be all about practicing and learning, impressing the coaches, and getting ready for a shot at the varsity the following year.

That first day of practice there were thirty-three freshman football players on scholarship and another twenty-five walk-ons. We all wore steel or aluminum cleats screwed onto the soles of our shoes. A chorus of clickety-clack could be heard as we trudged from the locker room onto the asphalt pavement that led to the practice field, about a hundred yards from the stadium's north end zone. We were eyeing each other nervously, trying to assess who our competition would be.

After calisthenics and wind sprints, the coaches broke us up by position. The receivers went to one corner of the field, the interior linemen to another, the linebackers and defensive backs to a third. The running backs went to the center of the field, and the quarterbacks set up near the receivers. Including me, there were fourteen QBs. This number did not surprise me, as just about every other freshman player I'd met to this point, aside from Roger and John, had played quarterback in high school. But the multitude at the position was unsettling nonetheless. At least three of the boys were on full ride: Dave Sorenson, Rich O'Hara, and the program's prized recruit, Dave Dirks, from Father Flanagan's Boys Town, a perennial power with a national reputation.

After the fourteen of us threw to one another for a while, we were joined by the receivers. My anxiety eased when I saw the difficulty the others were having throwing to a down-and-out sideline pattern. In this move, a receiver runs straight ten yards, plants a foot, and breaks off on a ninety-degree angle for the sideline. I breathed a sigh of relief when it became obvious that only Dirks and I could throw this pass with any strength and consistency. This route tests a QB's arm and accuracy. He has to throw the ball hard, leading the receiver, not throwing it behind him. If not thrown properly, the pass can be easily intercepted. I'd practiced this pattern in the summer, after work, with two alumni of Notre Dame High: Tom Boltz, six feet six, then a player for the New York Jets, and Vic Battani, a solid five feet nine all-state running back who had starred at the University of Detroit. At seven each evening, at the old Mack Park stadium on Detroit's East Side, I would take them up and down the field throwing down-and-out passes. That work paid off for me at Iowa.

After a few practices, the coaches moved some players to other positions. Sorenson became a defensive back, O'Hara a wide receiver. I stayed as a quarterback, listed behind Dirks at the position. I was okay with this. There was plenty of time to prove my worth to the coaches, which I could do from the number-two spot on the freshman QB depth chart, but not from number four or five. I got their attention by working hard; I was always first out on the field to practice my punting and throwing. I also made sure I was available after the official practice to give help to other players who needed it. I had an incentive to work harder than everyone else: I needed the scholarship many already had.

I can't say football was fun. It was a job. It was tough, dirty, and dangerous. Every day someone was getting hurt. Coaches yelled and screamed at us, driving us as if we were in boot camp. Aside from playing in the games themselves, there was not a lot I liked about the sport. I got much more joy and satisfaction from playing basketball and baseball, but football was my meal ticket. I took the job seriously.

Football ate up a large part of every day. Freshman practice lasted two hours—but that was hardly all of it. There was half an hour dressing and getting taped beforehand, and another thirty minutes cleaning up afterward. So for freshmen, 3:00 to 6:00 p.m., five days a week, was

Quarterback, Iowa Hawkeyes

football time—and that commitment was still two hours per day less than the varsity put in. For varsity, after practice there would be what was called a "training table" dinner, at which all who'd played in that day's scrimmages would wolf down generous helpings of Iowa beef and assorted other protein, then watch film of last week's game and of the team we'd be playing next. There might be a team meeting thrown in, as well.

My workday didn't end when practice ended—I had another job, a *job* job, to go to. Coach Burns had followed through on his promise to find employment for me; I worked at the Congress Inn, believe it or not, in neighboring Coralville, Iowa. After I showered and dressed, I headed for the highway and the two-mile walk to the inn. Three days during the week and both days on the weekend, I did an assortment of jobs that included prep in the kitchen, busing tables, vacuuming the dining-room rug after the dinner patrons left, and cleaning the restrooms.

The job turned out to be far more profitable than I could have imagined when I took it. It was a chance meeting in the restroom next to the bar that helped set me on the path to my scholarship.

It was about 9:00 p.m., midweek during the football season, and I was cleaning toilets when Coach Burns came into the men's room. Our eyes locked and he had a look that said, *I know who you are.* He didn't say anything to me but nodded in recognition. The head coach of a Big Ten football program doesn't have much to do with the freshmen grinding out practice, hoping for a shot at the varsity a year later. However, it was only four months earlier, at Notre Dame's athletic banquet, that we'd had our conversation. I had learned in the interim that Burns had been a QB at Catholic Central and ended up playing for the University of Michigan. Knowing those facts gave me the feeling that he could see his younger self in me. Now, by accident, I'd reentered his world instead of disappearing from it forever. He was an important man, and I was a lowly freshman from Detroit cleaning toilets. But there was a connection.

Freshman football concluded in November on a positive note. The coaches appreciated my work ethic and seemed pleased with my performance when we scrimmaged. My guess is that the freshman coaches submitted a good report on me to Burns and his senior staff.

As soon as freshman football ended, freshman basketball began. Rich O'Hara and I were the only football players on the team. Among the other players were four on full basketball rides. Our only game of the year was the annual varsity vs. freshmen game, which drew about ten thousand curious fans to the Field House. I was the sixth man, first off the bench. I played about half the game, guarding six feet four Jimmy Rodgers, who was good but no Bobby Joe Hill.

Despite my limited minutes in the game I performed well, playing tough defense and scoring 8 points. Two of them came off a steal and a coast-to-coast driving lay-up. I also hit three jump shots from a range of fifteen to twenty feet—some that might have qualified as a three-pointer had the rule been in effect back then. The varsity crushed us, but I felt that I had impressed the basketball coaches—and maybe one of the other coaches, too: I spotted Jerry Burns in the stands.

With trepidation I called the athletic department to get an appointment with Coach Burns. I wanted to ask him for the scholarship he'd promised me. I met with him a week later in his office. "Tell you what I'm going to do," he said. Then he paused, as if he was trying, then and there, to figure out what he was going to say next. That pause seemed like forever. Finally he said, "I'll put you on half a ride and we will see how you do in spring practice." This was bittersweet news. Bitter because I had been promised a full scholarship. Sweet because it meant I could afford to stay in school without cleaning toilets at the Congress Inn.

I had four months to live with his decision and to prepare myself for the spring workouts. I'd no longer be practicing with the freshmen; spring practice, which began in April, was strictly varsity.

There were four quarterbacks ahead of me on the depth chart in April: starter Gary Snook, backups Fred Riddle and Mickey Moses, and my classmate Dave Dirks. Looking at my status as the number-five QB, I was afraid I would not get my chance to perform. But fate was on my side.

Snook, hobbled by an injured leg, could not fully participate in spring football. Fred Riddle left the team to focus on applying to medical school. Mickey Moses was excused because he was a starter on the baseball team. And Dave Dirks had an injured knee ligament that limited his play. Soon thereafter he became academically ineligible and left school.

For three weeks, therefore, I was the starting varsity quarterback. I was playing on offense with John Niland (later a starting lineman for the Dallas Cowboys) and Karl Noonan (a wide receiver for the Miami Dolphins). On our final day of practice we played our annual spring intrasquad game before a crowd of twenty thousand in Kinnick Stadium. It was a gorgeous afternoon with a bright blue sky and no wind. I quarterbacked the Black team against the Gold team.

We were running a pro spread, drop-back offense that took advantage of Snook's height—six feet three—and strong arm. At five feet ten I preferred a roll-out sprint offense—at my height I had difficulty seeing over the linemen, ours and theirs, whose height was in the six feet two to six feet five range. I'd had to quickly adjust to the spread, getting used to throwing off my toes. I was surprised how quickly I made the shift in the three-week practice season.

Kinnick Stadium

On the first set of downs I broke the Black huddle and walked up to the line of scrimmage, our own 34. Spreading my hands into a V shape, I placed them under center and barked out the cadence, ready to receive a hard snap. At the instant the ball reached my hands, my left foot moved a step backward. I continued the motion, pivoting and extending an empty hand into the breadbasket of our running back, Dalton Kimball, who faked receiving the handoff. I kept moving, dropping back four steps, all the while bringing the ball to my ear in a ready passing position. I pump faked a throw to our tight end, Tony Giacobazzi, who was running an out pattern to the right sideline. Then I released the ball, hitting Noonan on a fly pattern up the same sideline. The tight spiral reached Karl in full stride. He brought it in like Willie Mays hauling in Vic Wertz's drive in the 1954 World Series. Karl cradled the football into his hands and raced the remaining yards into the end zone.

Bonior to Noonan. Touchdown!

Maury White, writing for the *Des Moines Register*, recapped the drive: "Bonior, trapped, twisted for a first down. Then he lofted a beautiful pass that Noonan took on the Gold 36, snatching it from two defenders, and continued for the 66-yard route unmolested." I've lived off this sweet memory for fifty years.

The rest of the day mirrored this first drive. I hit ten of fourteen passes—three for touchdowns—and had two good runs. John O'Donnell, the sports columnist for the Davenport daily newspaper, wrote of "Bonior, who with a little experience will play a lot of ball. He gained 190 yards over the heads of the second unit." A week after practice ended, Burns called me into his office to tell me I had earned a full scholarship.

I'd done it the hard way. And because I had, I earned a special level of respect from my friends and teammates.

I was on cloud nine.

SANDHOG:
WORKING SUMMERS IN MICHIGAN

The summer jobs I held during those years were lessons in demanding physical work. The summer before my freshman year had me working road construction in Macomb County. The most difficult task was handling the hydraulic jackhammer to break up buckled concrete. Your whole body vibrates when you operate one. It was heavy and loud, and it produced cement dust that irritated my eyes and lungs. I also patched potholes with hot asphalt I would shovel off the back of a truck. The tar smell would stay with me—in my mind and on my work clothes—for days.

The following summer I worked at a factory owned by R.C. Mahon, a steel-fabricating factory in Warren, Michigan, not far from our home in East Detroit. My job was to pull steel panels off an assembly line and line them with sheets of insulation that I slid inside the panels' curled edges. The insulation might have been fiberglass—my lungs again became irritated. The foreman was Ewan Batherson; his son Malcolm, whom I'd known since third grade, was one of my best friends. Outside the plant, Mr. Batherson was the nicest guy you would ever want to meet. Inside, however, he drove his workers hard, determined to meet the quota his bosses had set for him. I worked enough days at Mahon that I earned my United Steelworkers of America (USWA) union card to go along with my card from the Screen Actors Guild. The workers needed union protection in that plant because the company pressured them to produce more and more. And management was apt to abuse the workers by its interpretation of work rules negotiated in the union contract—things like the number of bathroom breaks or the ability of a worker to shut down the line because of an injury. You felt the tension on the factory floor. And the Mahon factory was far from the only one with this issue—disputes over work rules led to labor-management antagonism in factories across the country.

When the lunch whistle blew, some workers would sprint to the bar across the street. Waiting for them in front of their favorite stool would be a shot and a beer to help break the repetitive monotony of their work. Because the plant was union, the pay was good, but for a college student, doing this taxing job and seeing how the workers dealt with it underscored why an education was so important.

After my sophomore year, I worked as an attendant in the boys' section of a juvenile detention center in Macomb County. It was called the Youth Home, and it is where I made the contacts to get my job as a probation officer after I graduated from Iowa.

After my junior year, my father helped me get a job working as an inspector in underground sewer-tunnel construction. The crew of half a dozen "sandhogs," as the men who dug these holes are called, was tunneling forty feet below ground to build a five-foot-diameter cement sewer line. They would dig a length of tunnel, then erect steel forms for the huge concrete pipe to be created. My specific job was to make sure the space between the steel form and the clay earth measured exactly the right size—I think it was four inches, or perhaps six. A crew at street level would pour a concrete slurry through a hole drilled right above where we were working, and the slurry would fill the space around the form. After the concrete set and dried around the forms, we would peel them off and repeat the process as we tunneled farther.

The tunneling was done with a hydraulic hammer fitted with a spade shovel bit. Like the jackhammer I used on road construction— or should I say road *de*struction?—this hammer was heavy and noisy. As an inspector, my job was simple: measure with my ruler to make sure that the concrete pipe was of the proper thickness. However, the workplace environment was not so simple. It turned out that the construction crews were all African American and the inspectors all white. This imbalance made me uncomfortable, so after a couple of days I decided that I would not only inspect the pipe's thickness but also work on the tunneling crew. I took my turn, like everybody else in the "hole," digging and using the hydraulic shovel.

As none of the crew members could remember any inspector pitching in to do the real, tough work, I developed a good rapport with them. Another benefit was the impressive set of pectoral and biceps muscles I developed that summer. The experience was not easy by any means. The work was hard and dangerous—occasionally the portion of the hole being newly dug would collapse, forcing us to dive back into the safety of the steel forms. The work was noisy, too, for there was no outlet through which the roar of the equipment could escape. But l learned an important lesson that summer: the importance of people looking after one another, the value of teamwork.

Late each Friday afternoon, just before the week of work was to end, I'd bring down two six-packs of beer for the crew; we'd each drink a can before we walked through the concrete tunnel and then climbed the ladder forty feet up the shaft to the street surface. I liked being part of the team but hated being the inspector and overseer. It was exhausting work, but the job was much more rewarding when I participated in the grueling manual labor.

That summer taught me another valuable lesson—about gambling. The tunneling job was close to the Hazel Park horseracing track. Like father, like son: My dad was fond of playing the ponies, so was I. Mal Batherson, my Sacred Heart friend John Carlin, and I hung out at the track after work on those summer evenings, and, I'm embarrassed to say, I lost all of my summer earnings to betting. I learned, the hard way, that in the long run you can't win at gambling. The track, or the "house," always comes out ahead. It was not smart of me to gamble away so much hard-earned cash.

In addition to suffering through seeing my horses finish out of the money, I spent a good deal of my time at the track dodging Dad. He'd be at one end of the grandstand, I'd camp out at the other end to avoid running into him. He probably saw me but never said a word to me about it.

The hard labor I performed those summers was certainly not the way I wanted to spend the rest of my working life. But I was glad to have the jobs, because they taught me a lot. I gained an understanding of what my grandfathers did for a living day in and day out. I came to appreciate work and realized that all work has meaning. I decided that people who do tough jobs deserve both respect and just compensation—and, of course, the right to belong to a labor union. The idea that workers on jobs like these might not have that right was unthinkable back then. With a union came collective bargaining and all the benefits that built the broad American middle class.

In some ways the experience of those summer jobs was as important to me as the education I received in college classrooms. I would draw upon that experience, and on the feelings it engendered in me, for the rest of my life, especially during my time as a legislator. When we discussed worker safety in Lansing or Washington, I knew—personally—what was at stake.

A DANGEROUS GAME:
BACK TO THE GRIDIRON

In early August 1964, just off a great spring practice, I reported to football camp in Iowa City. Football was my sport now: Between academics and the demands of the gridiron, I would have no more time for other sports. My basketball career at Iowa was over, my baseball career never got started.

I was excited about the coming season. Snook and Moses were back at work, so I ended up the third-string QB behind them. I was surprised and elated when the coaches posted the charts showing who had made the traveling team and who would be included in the training table—my name appeared on both lists. Not only could I both play quarterback and punt but I also was a good example to show others that if you tried and hustled, there would be a reward.

Our first game was against Indiana in the Hoosiers' new stadium. We won that game and the next two before we traveled to Madison to play the Wisconsin Badgers at Camp Randall Stadium. We jumped off to an early lead but lost momentum in the second half. However, the score of the game meant little compared to what happened to a teammate. My classmate and friend Dave Moreland, a defensive back, went down after a violent collision with a Wisconsin running back. After being helped off the field, he sat down next to me on the bench. I saw the dent in Dave's helmet and the dazed look on his face. He did not know where he was, and he was scared. As his anxiety continued to build, I tried to calm him down, to assure him things were going to be okay. But I had no idea what a concussion was, didn't know he had one—in fact, I don't think I ever heard the word until years later—and certainly did not know how to help my friend. The coaches didn't offer him any special attention; they just left him sitting on the bench. People didn't realize how dangerous the game of football is to the brain. And today, when the perils are finally becoming known, players are bigger and faster, and the trauma to the head is more pronounced.

Dave was done for the game, and he was dazed for a day or two. But he did recover, and he played the rest of the season. He went on to graduate and to pursue a fruitful career as an art professor in Washington State. But the experience of sitting next to him that afternoon in Wisconsin has stuck in my mind all these years.

There's no getting around it: Football is a violent sport.

After the three-game winning streak to start the season, we lost the game to Wisconsin and then the remaining six on our schedule. We ended the year a disappointing 3–7.

The rest of my football career left me playing behind others: first Snook, then, in the class behind me, Ed Podolak. Both would play in the NFL, Snook for the St. Louis Cardinals and Podolak for the Kansas City Chiefs. Years later, when folks would ask what position I played, I'd answer, "Assback."

"What is *that?*" they would ask.

"I'd get up to go into the game and the coach would say, 'Bonior! Where do you think you're going?' I'd answer, 'I'm going into the game,

*Reunion of football team, c. 1987, standing (l. to r.): Me, Rich O'Hara,
Terry Mulligan, Dick Gibbs, Dave Moreland; kneeling (l. to r.):
Roger LaMont, Tom Ross, John Ficeli*

Coach.' To which the coach would say, 'Get your ass back on the bench!'"

My role my junior and senior year was to be the scout QB. I'd learn
our coming opponent's offensive plays and then run them against our
first-team defense in practice. I never got into a game, which I could
see made sense, because both Snook and Podolak had more talent than
I did. Podolak's talent wasn't just as a passer; when he turned pro, the
Chiefs turned him into a running back. He's still the second leading
all-time rusher in franchise history.

I accepted my role. I knew that I was not good enough to play. It
was enough for me that I made the team and the traveling team, got my
scholarship, and survived physically. There was a lot to be thankful for.

My best efforts on the scout team notwithstanding, we went 1–9

My letter jacket still fits after half a century.

my junior year, causing the college administration to can our entire coaching staff. A replacement crew came in, out of Utah. Among our new leaders was an assistant coach named George Sieffert, who went on to coach the San Francisco 49ers to two Super Bowl championships.

Senior year saw a 100 percent improvement; that is, we doubled our win total to finish at 2– 9, placing us at the bottom of the Big Ten. At our season-ending banquet, each senior was asked to say a few words. I ended my remarks with a literary reference: "As F. Scott Fitzgerald noted, 'On the debris of our despair we build our character.'"

The press loved the quote, thinking it not only summed up the lousy year but also offered hope for the future. Several Iowa sports columnist used it in their pieces.

However, there was a problem: While I got the quote right, I attributed it to the wrong author. I should have said Ralph Waldo Emerson (although I've recently learned that that attribution, while common, is questionable).

The most influential experience for me as a member of the Hawkeye football squad came away from the playing field. When I arrived at training camp my sophomore year, I was paired up to room, for the three weeks of camp, with Craig Nourse, a running back from Flint, Michigan. We both had quiet personalities; looking back, it's fair to say that we were uneasy living together in the same small dorm room. To start with, Craig was black, from a black school and a black neighborhood, while I was white, from a white school and a white neighborhood. Communication at the beginning was further dampened by our physical state once we reached the room: We were so fatigued from our days of double practice sessions that we collapsed in our beds as soon as we came through the door.

I tried to break the ice by asking Craig about his family, but all I got in return were short responses. I don't think he was being rude, just shy and uncomfortable—feelings I understood. I cracked through when I changed the direction of the conversation: I told him about *my* family. He responded in particular to the fact that my mother had died at such a young age. I sensed that hardship and loss were common themes over which we could bond. Slowly over the three weeks of camp Craig and I discovered what we liked about each other, and a friendship developed. Our conversations were about football, family, and our common homesickness for our communities back in Michigan.

Flint has been the hometown of many great football players. Craig, recently inducted into that town's football Hall of Fame, was one of them.

FORWARD OR BACKWARD?:
THE CIVIL RIGHTS MOVEMENT

On August 28, 1963, just as I was beginning my years as a college student, a quarter million people gathered in front of the Lincoln Memorial in our nation's capital to hold the largest civil rights demonstration in American history. Organized by Bayard Rustin, with help from a host of civil rights leaders, as well as labor leaders like A. Phillip Randolph and Walter Reuther, the March on Washington for Jobs and Freedom brought home to America's citizens the imperative to finally grant full citizenship to the descendants of the men and women brought here from Africa in slave ships. Marchers heard music from artists like Bob Dylan and Mahalia Jackson, and were inspired by many rousing speeches. Today the march is best remembered for the final speech, in which Martin Luther King Jr. talked of his dream. An important speech that is often forgotten is the one delivered by a young John Lewis, chairman of the Student Nonviolent Coordinating Committee (SNCC), who implored America to dig deeper, to go further on the road to justice. I had the honor of serving with John in the U.S. House of Representatives.

I was still in Michigan on the day of the march, getting ready to leave for Iowa. Dr. King had come to Detroit two months earlier, on June 23. He led a march of one hundred thousand people to Cobo Hall, the city's convention center; inside, he spoke before twenty-five thousand, using some of the same words about his dream that he would use in Washington. I was aware of King and the movement at this time. I followed them in the press. But I did not participate.

Civil rights and Vietnam were the two overriding issues in our nation and on our campuses during the 1960s—in fact, they were two of the most significant and consequential issues of my lifetime. At the core of both was the ideal of justice, and how far from that ideal stood the *reality* of justice. Seeing these issues take hold of the nation, and of my little corner of it in Iowa City, I began to understand that school was more than just a place to rack up a credential or play a sport. These two issues seeped into my soul and made me face the world as it really was.

School was becoming a place where I could learn about justice and harmony in a world where those goals were prized but difficult to achieve.

During my freshman year I was drawn to downtown Iowa City to see films—with four theaters bordering the campus, the opportunities and choices were plentiful. Film became an escape for me, taking me back to my childhood in Hamtramck when I would go to the movies at the Farnum Theatre at the end of our block on Joseph Campau Street. Film was my window into another world, the big, bustling, fascinating "out there." And theaters were dark places where I could watch movies without worrying about displaying my emotions.

One evening in Iowa City, I went by myself to see *One Potato, Two Potato*, starring a young Barbara Barrie. Filmed in black and white, it explored the difficulty of an interracial marriage. I was moved to tears by the poignancy of its message on racial injustice. It helped me begin to see and understand the specific issues and practices on which courageous civil rights activists were then focusing the nation's attention. From the lunch counter sit-ins to the heroic travels of the Freedom Riders to the bloody bridge crossing at Selma, the fight to end the appalling and degrading practices of the segregated South had reached a tipping point for our country. America was going to move; if you were paying any attention at all, you knew there was no standing pat. The question was: Would we move forward or backward?

The nation's campuses became an important community in the fight to end Jim Crow. Still, I was slow to fully enlist in the causes that would later mean so much to me. When I arrived at the university, my life revolved around school, work, and football; I had neither the time nor the money to engage in much else. Occasionally, when I was studying at the Student Union and needed a break, I'd go down to the lower floor and shoot pool. The pool hall became a sanctuary for me, a place where I could get my mind off the shifting tectonic plates from Geology class and the Norman conquest from Western Civilization. "Eight ball in the side pocket," I called out before a shot one night. When I straightened from gently striking my cue—I sank the shot, by the way—I looked up and saw Judy Strong through the glass partition. Tall, with long, wavy, dark brown hair falling into the hood of her gold-colored car coat, she was wearing black flats as her long, shapely legs strode purposefully into the River Room, the haven for social and political activists.

With John Lewis, c. 1993, at Edmund Pettis Bridge, Selma, Alabama

I was starting to develop a social consciousness but was not yet ready to join Judy, who was the president of the campus chapter of SNCC, and the other activists in the River Room. I would get to that awareness eventually, joining with Judy, John Lewis, and many others to work on vital issues of justice in the Congress. Judy recalls spending a memorable evening with John when he visited a meeting of the chapter held at an Iowa City church. That night John told his true stories of the civil rights movement: the sit-ins, the marches, the freedom rides, the bombings, the beatings, the fires, the lynchings, the jails. Soft-spoken and no more than twenty-four years old, he was already a hero. Judy had been an activist on campus trying to raise awareness, support, and money for movement efforts across the South. They were, at such young ages, special people; they still are today.

I have sometimes wondered: If I'd followed Judy into the River Room that evening, would my life have been any different? Perhaps, but was I ready then to sacrifice almost everything for the cause of racial justice? Probably not. I was certainly a candidate for recruitment. I believed in and relished the idea of fighting for a worthy cause. Even as a college student I realized that it took organization and leadership to get things accomplished politically. I'd learned that lesson in East Detroit. But my personality—my shyness and my inarticulateness— left me without confidence to take on these significant pieces of the world I was living in. John was the courageous and moral leader. And Judy was a strong and committed follower of John. It would take many years for me to grow up and finally catch up to them.[1]

1 Curiously, Judy's life and mine crossed again in 1986, when, after both of us had been divorced, we were single once more. We married in 1991.

Judy Strong (r., later Judy Bonior) with her roommate
Mary Love on campus in Iowa City

A Name on the Wall:
The War in Vietnam

During my junior year I saw a poster on campus announcing a meeting of the Young Democrats, to be held in Schaeffer Hall that night at 7:00 p.m. Feeling the need to become involved in something larger than myself, I decided to attend the gathering and join the Young Democrats. I arrived at Schaeffer Hall at 7:00 to find an empty room. *Strange*, I thought. *Could I have gotten the time or place wrong?* After ten minutes, four bearded guys walked into the room. Without a greeting or an introduction, their leader announced that the meeting would come to order. (I was sitting quietly, so I saw no need to call for "order.") The leader then launched into a diatribe against President Johnson and the war in Vietnam. After about ten minutes of ranting, he invited all present to take out our draft cards and burn them while he burned his. I sat dumbfounded as four cards went up in flames, which left lingering puffs of smoke hanging in the small lecture hall. I left my card in my wallet and kept silent. My chief concern was that they not burn the building down. While I was opposed to the war, I was not ready to set fire to my draft card—or to the building in which I took my classes.

They barely paid me any attention before they stormed out.

The students on campus hated the war and hated LBJ. From the meager turnout this night, it was clear that the number of Iowa students willing to be counted as Young Democrats—and thus associated with the party of the despised president—had dwindled to a handful, at best. And with the four guys walking out in protest, I wondered if I might be the only Young Democrat left at the University of Iowa.

Vietnam devoured a generation of young Americans and inflicted catastrophic death and destruction on the Vietnamese people. In 1963, the US had sixteen thousand troops in Vietnam. That number increased to almost two hundred thousand in 1965. By the time I was ready to graduate, in 1967, nearly half a million American service members were stationed in that country halfway around the world, and the number of them coming home dead or wounded had risen fast. To this point, opinion polls showed that a majority of the American people still supported the war. But the public's patience would be exhausted as more and more boys were drafted and as the perception of defeat or, at least, stalemate, set in after the Tet Offensive of early 1968. Vietnam was the first war to be broadcast on television. Images of battle and death and injury were refreshed daily in the living rooms of the nation, and the nation did not like what it was seeing.

During the course of the war, over twenty-five million men were of an age to serve in the military. Of that number almost nine million served, nearly a third of them in Vietnam. The rest were able to avoid service. College and medical deferments were big loopholes in the system, as were family circumstances and employment in defense-related industries. When most student deferments were done away with in 1969 in favor of a draft lottery, the young men whose birthdays were assigned high numbers were not called. In addition, each local draft board interpreted the regulations differently, so there was no uniformity from place to place in deciding whom to draft. For example, a draft board in Macomb County, Michigan, might decide that a social worker was not exempt, while a draft board in St. Louis, Missouri, might decide that he was. There were conscience exemptions as well, given out mainly to people with a religious objection not just to this war, but to all wars. And of course, tens of thousands of young men avoided the draft by leaving the country, most of them going to Canada.

The war and the draft were destabilizing, disruptive forces in the lives of millions of draft-age citizens and their families as young people altered their life paths in response to the prospect of conscription. Some young men stayed in school longer than they otherwise would have. Some pursued jobs they had no real interest in. Some married and had children before they were ready. Some left their hometowns. And, because college students enjoyed deferments unavailable to their contemporaries not in school, the draft underscored the class divide in America. Tensions and anxieties were running high.

During my junior and senior years, a number of antiwar protests were staged on campus, often pointed toward our ROTC (Reserve Officers' Training Corps) program. Students in ROTC—pronounced ROT-see by the protestors—received a stipend in exchange for undergoing training to become officers; once they graduated, they were commissioned and joined the military. In their uniforms, they stood out on campus. They trained in the Field House, where many of our athletes also practiced. The officers-to-be would perform marching drills not ten yards away from our basketball team shooting lay-ups.

One of my football teammates, Carl Harris, from Flint, Michigan, took part in ROTC and was commissioned a lieutenant in the army in 1967. Carl was a big man, but gentle; soft-spoken, with an easy way about him. In January 1968 he was killed in action. Years later, when I worked in Congress to bring the Vietnam Veterans Memorial to the National Mall, I would think of Carl and his wife, Charlotte. Today when visitors or friends are touring DC, I take them to the Wall and always look for Carl's name, on Panel 34E, Line 36. Sometimes I see people with paper and pencil rubbing over a name. I choke up every time I see this exercise in wrestling with the heartache of loss.

BEER AND CARDS: MY DORMITORY FRIENDS

In addition to my friendships with fellow Midwesterners John Ficeli, Roger LaMont, and Jim Peterson, I became buddies with a group of guys from the East Coast: Herb Mandel, from New York City, who fashioned himself a pool and card shark; Ted Brubacker, whom we called "Bru," from White Plains, New York, on a track scholarship; and Mike McMahon, from Tenafly, New Jersey, who liked to remind all of us that the pop singer Lesley Gore ("It's My Party" ["and I'll cry if I want to"]) was also from Tenafly. Freshman year, Mike and I broadcast the home Iowa football games on our dorm radio station, which was heard only in Hillcrest and Quadrangle Hill. He had gotten the job of doing the play-by-play and had asked me to join him because he thought it would be fun to have the color done by a real football player. I cringe today at the hackneyed and inane remarks I must have made on the air. I might have been a novice at sports broadcasting, but I knew one thing for certain: Because my scholarship was not yet secure, I was not about to level a whit of criticism at the coaching staff.

We hung out with another Easterner, Bob Dormer, from Morristown, New Jersey, blessed with a droll wit and the awe-inspiring ability to open his throat wide and empty a pitcher of beer in seconds—not a healthy or wise thing to do, but hey, we were freshmen in college and what did we know? Obviously, not much. Rounding out our dorm crew was another Midwesterner, Cal Kulman, a baseball player from Minnesota whose semi-Norwegian accent contrasted perfectly with the alien accents of the guys from New Jersey and New York.

The bunch of us spent far too much time playing two card games, pitch and hearts, in sessions that would last into the wee hours. Often when I got back from work at the Congress Inn there would be a card game going on while sports were blaring from the radio—a Cardinals-Dodgers game from L.A. on KMOX or some other sporting event emanating from the West Coast. In February that year we heard Muhammad Ali, then still named Cassius Clay, take the heavyweight title from Sonny Liston in Miami.

Our motley gang would venture out on the weekend—and weekends started on Thursday night—to drink beer and meet women. (We were almost always more successful at the beer part.) A number of bars downtown served the college community. There was Joe's Place, which catered to graduate students. Baseball players hung out in Donnelly's Pub. The "in crowd"—the elite of the Greek community—held court at The Airliner, across from the Pentacrest, the complex of buildings that make up the heart of the campus. But my favorite place was Little Bill's.

In Little Bill's you could find hippies, African Americans, Writers' Workshop types—the Iowa Writers' Workshop is famous for turning out talented crafters of literary fiction—bar and restaurant workers, university dropouts, and, occasionally, an intellectual football player like Bill Briggs. Unlike the Little Bill of the bar's name, this Bill, an African American who lived in New Jersey, was anything but: six feet three, 230 pounds. Nevertheless, he was quick and fast. A defensive lineman for the Hawkeyes, he was drafted into the NFL, playing a number of seasons for the Washington Redskins. At Iowa, Bill was drawn to social justice issues. At all times except the dead of winter you'd see him at Little Bill's in Bermuda shorts and sandals with straps that laced up over his calves. Smart, big, and strong, with those sandals he looked like a figure from the Old Testament.

I had a football scholarship, not a beer scholarship, so I needed to make a few bucks to enable me to visit Little Bill's on the weekend. For better or worse, my father's trait of hustling rubbed off on me. So during junior year I came up with the idea of creating fake identification documents for students. The drinking age was twenty-one then, and not all the bars carded their patrons. But some did, and I accommodated underage students who wanted the pleasure of drinking anywhere in town. It was a lucrative enterprise. For ten dollars I would produce a driver's license and a draft card. For the draft cards I gathered old ROTC manuals and cut out the official-looking Department of Defense insignia from the covers. For driver's licenses I specialized in copying them from Alaska and Idaho, locations remote enough that the bartenders checking the documents would not notice if every piece of the design was not exactly as produced by the authorities in Juneau and Boise.

I made enough on this scam to drink all the Pabst Blue Ribbon, Budweiser, and Schlitz I needed that year. The law never caught up with me, and I assume after half a century the statute of limitations has expired on my deviant behavior.

It has, right?

SCOFIELD, STEIGER, CIARDI: INTELLECTUAL PURSUITS

The previous pages to the contrary, my college years weren't all about gambling, sports, and drinking; I had a more dignified side. The fall of my sophomore year, after winning my full scholarship, I registered for a course of piano lessons. I might have been moved to take this step by the memory of staring at those guitars in our fruit cellar in Hamtramck. And there was all that "Motown Sound" I was surrounded by back home. I was not silly enough to dream that I could ever play like Stevie Wonder, but I did think playing the piano might be something nice to do other than sports.

I was serious about learning to play piano, and my instructor was serious about teaching me, but our good intentions were not enough to overcome certain obstacles. The piano I practiced on was in the dormitory lounge, which was located right off the dormitory cafeteria, so while I played, my "friends" took turns passing by and offering derogatory comments. It was totally humiliating. In addition, there was an extra charge for the lessons, ninety dollars, and the music department sent the bill to the athletic department, which went off the wall. Ninety dollars was a lot of money back then. After four lessons, the masters of my sporting life told me that my musical life needed to end. I dropped the course, bringing my brief career as a pianist to an abrupt close.

And I was just figuring out middle C.

Of course, I was assigned to read numerous books for my courses. But I was drawn more to the moving image than to the printed word, so throughout my time in Iowa I continued to frequent the town's cinemas. In addition to *One Potato, Two Potato,* I was particularly moved by two films. One was *A Man for All Seasons*, starring the great English actor Paul Scofield and based on Robert Bolt's magnificent play about St. Thomas More. The other film was *The Pawnbroker*, starring Rod Steiger.

I think being raised on television, as opposed to books, had much to do with my love and appreciation of film. As a boy I was fascinated by World War II documentaries; it was watching these documentaries that gave me my initial awareness of the horrors of the Holocaust. *The Pawnbroker*, directed by Sidney Lumet, was one of the first films to examine the murder of Europe's Jews from the perspective of a survivor. Even now I still consider Rod Steiger's performance the best acting I've seen in any film. The emotional power he brought to his role overwhelmed me—I can still remember my walk back to the dorm after seeing the movie. I felt empty. My campus surroundings seemed irrelevant.

The good films I was seeing began to draw out of me feelings I'd locked up inside. Both *One Potato, Two Potato* and *The Pawnbroker* made me feel the wrong of racism and the pain of loss. I was just beginning to grow up emotionally. I had a long way to go, but I was starting to recognize my feelings and connect them to what I was learning, not only in school but also in life: what I was hearing, what I was seeing. The most difficult part for me would be sharing my feelings with others. That's something I continue to work on, and struggle with, to this day.

Another powerful evening for me took place at the Student Union, in the large main lounge. Twelve hundred people from the university community had gathered to hear the poet and critic John Ciardi speak. I happened to be studying or playing pool in the Union at that time; I wandered into the lounge, curious to learn what had drawn so many people there. It took only a moment to figure it out. Today I can't remember what Ciardi talked about, but I do vividly remember his wit and brilliance and the way the members of the audience hung on every word. That adulation from the audience was infectious, making this event a new and exciting experience for me. As with Bishop Sheen, I was more taken by the man's bearing and voice and inflection than by what he said. For me this was an evening to appreciate "performance" in the world of ideas and thought. Ciardi blended insight, humor, and the forcefulness of his mind to hold the audience rapt, to engage his listeners both intellectually and viscerally. Afterward I began to discover that what I was learning at college could be not just interesting but truly stimulating.

Up to this point I'd gotten by academically, but barely—I was given many Cs. But now my studies began to have new meaning for me. Professor Peter Snow, in the political science department, piqued my interest in Latin America; my concern for the region would continue throughout my congressional career and beyond. I'd been introduced to Latin America by my grade-school teachers, the nuns from the Order of St. Joseph. They educated us in the rudimentary facts of Mexico, Central America, and the Caribbean, always setting the instruction in the context of "liberation" from criminal leaders like Somoza in Nicaragua and Duvalier in Haiti. Professor Snow made clear for me the United States' colonial and wretched past in the region, and sparked in me a fascination with the populist leadership of Perón in Argentina, Vargas in Brazil, and Cárdenas in Mexico. The issues and personalities were captivating and romantic; I was drawn to them. It would be years before I began to read Octavio Paz, Carlos Fuentes, Mario Vargas Llosa, and the incomparable Gabriel Garcia Marquez: violence and love all mixed in a stew of magic realism. It's delicious for my mind.

In general, I was learning how a college education and a college campus could enrich my life. I came to like being in that type of environment. I liked being near the Iowa Writers' Workshop. During my time on campus, the Writers' Workshop was producing extraordinary writers, such as Mark Strand, who grew into one of the country's most important poets, becoming the US poet laureate. Kurt Vonnegut, teaching at the workshop, was writing *Slaughterhouse-Five*. I didn't know about those two giants at the time. I would read their work later in my life.

THOMAS, JOHN, FRANCIS: RELIGION AGAIN

Roger LaMont and John Ficeli were, like me, Catholic, so from time to time we would meet on Sunday morning and walk the mile along the Iowa River to attend Mass at St. Thomas More Chapel, located just down the riverwalk from the university art buildings. We were products of a Catholic culture and education. We felt connected to our faith.

In college I went through the process of sorting out all the simple and wrong lessons about my faith that I'd learned in grade school and ignored in high school. In Professor Sherwood B. Tuttle's geology class I learned that the earth was billions of years old and not created in six days, as Genesis has it. The progressive and populist pope, John XXIII, had convened the Second Vatican Council, beginning the process of opening the Church and its followers to other religions. It was no longer a sin to visit a temple, mosque, or Protestant church; you no longer needed to be a Catholic to love God and enter heaven. The work of Vatican II was turning the Church and its teachings in a more realistic and charitable direction.

A Quonset hut, St. Thomas More Chapel reminded you of World War II whenever you saw it. (In fact, Quonset huts were not uncommon on campus; our rhetoric classes were held in them.) The significance of the name of the church was not apparent to me until I saw *A Man for All Seasons*. The film details the struggle of Thomas More, chancellor in Henry VIII's England, to keep true to his Catholic faith in the face of the king's divorce of Queen Catherine, marriage to Anne Boleyn, and sundering of the Christian faith in England.

There are two quotes from that film that I've tried to incorporate into my life and, in particular, into my career as a legislator. I knew when I heard them many decades ago in the dark of an Iowa City movie house that they were filled with truth and wisdom. The first concerns conscience: "When statesmen forsake their own private conscience for the sake of their public duties, they lead their country by a short route to chaos."

The second quote speaks of the law and, I think, applies as I write in 2013 to the Tea Party Republicans who have shut down the government of the United States of America. Thomas More is speaking to Roper, his son-in-law: "And when the last law was down, and the Devil turned round on you—where would you hide, Roper, the laws all being flat? This country's planted thick with laws coast to coast—man's laws, not God's—and if you cut them down—and you're just the man to do it—d'you really think you could stand upright in the winds that would blow then? Yes, I'd give the Devil benefit of the law, for my own safety's sake."[2]

Also in 2013, a new, populist pope was chosen. Francis, the first Jesuit to lead the Church, officiated over the canonization of his open-hearted predecessor John XXIII. As did John, Francis possesses a common touch, as well as the wisdom and tolerance to reach out to those outside the Church's orbit. His humility, humanity, and practical approach to life's challenges have prompted many who have fallen away from the Church to give it another look, another chance.

---

2 Quoted from the original play: Robert Bolt, *A Man for All Seasons: A Drama in Two Acts* (New York: Samuel French), 56.

What Francis is doing today, and what John did half a century ago, is to once again open the doors of the Church. He is offering liberation to his flock. It was that idea of liberation many decades ago that kept me connected to the Church: the idea that, through the teachings of Jesus, the Church would work to free the poor and near poor from poverty; the idea that all work has dignity; and that those performing work need to be justly compensated.

The Dominican theologian Gustavo Gutierrez, a native of Peru, is considered by many to be the founder of Liberation Theology. Gutierrez recently met with Francis. The hope of the impoverished may rest with the new pope's desire to speak for them and to open the gates of opportunity for the dispossessed. To use an old military metaphor from the days of Lyndon Johnson, a "war on poverty" is imperative. The table is set with progressive political leadership in power in much of Latin America. When I think of the possibilities, I recall a line in Isabel Allende's novel *The House of the Spirits*: "My son, the Holy Church is on the right, but Jesus Christ was always on the left."[3]

LOVE'S MAGIC:
SYBIL

Outside of Joann Ulrich in the seventh grade, I never, from my awakening to the existence of girls through my first two years in college, had a steady girlfriend. In fact, I did not date at all during my freshman and sophomore years at Iowa. That inactivity came about not from lack of interest but rather because I was shy, withholding, awkward, and ill at ease around members of the opposite sex. Had my mother been around, she might have been able to clue me in on understanding and being with women. But she wasn't, and I did not have the kind of relationship with my father that would have enabled me to share his wisdom on this

---

3 Isabel Allende, translated from the Spanish by Magda Bogin, *The House of the Spirits* (New York: Knopf, 1985), 154.

subject. Neither one of us would have been comfortable engaging in such conversations, so we avoided them.

Missing this aspect of life saddened me. Eventually I decided that membership in a fraternity might help solve my dating woes; during junior year I joined SAE. The improvement in my circumstances was negligible: Going into my last semester at Iowa I still was pretty much without female companionship. Then one day it all changed. My fraternity brother Joe Burns asked me if I was interested in meeting Sybil Rader. I did not hesitate. She did not know who I was, but I certainly knew who she was. She was tall—five feet ten—with long brown hair.

Joe, the other Burns in my life, arranged for four of us—he, his date, Sybil, and me—to meet for coffee and hot chocolate in the cafeteria of the Student Union. It was a cold February evening; if I remember correctly, Sybil, a skilled swimmer, was returning from the Field House pool. When I saw her in the Union, she was wearing a white wool hat that framed her smiling face. Once we got our drinks and began to converse, I found her friendly and easy to be with. She was smart as well as beautiful, and was studying to be a special ed teacher. I liked her outlook on life: She seemed able to observe life's absurdities and laugh at them. But what came across to me above all, that day and as I got to know her, was how well she treated other people, no matter their station in life.

I summoned up my courage and called her for a second date. I was terrified of rejection, but, *mirabile dictu*, rejection did not come, and we quickly became a couple. In no time I was falling in love, and for the next three and a half months, until graduation, we would study together, go for walks, attend a party or two, take in movies. When we were apart I could not wait to see her again, or at least to hear her voice on the telephone. Being in love was magical. Life seemed so much better.

Both of us struggled as we approached the finish line of our undergraduate educations. Sybil was a much better student than I was, but she was not comfortable with her student teaching assignment at Pine School, a public elementary school on campus, and was starting to

Sybil Rader, fall of 1966

doubt her ability to be a good teacher. I tried to buck her up, even though I had a big problem of my own. I was straining to pass my required course in Latin. I had failed to keep up in class—I just hadn't done the work. Only as finals approached did I appreciate the stakes: If I failed Latin, I would not graduate.

I was on pins and needles right up to the posting of grades. If I made it, I'd be the first in my family to graduate from college. My father, sister, and brother were coming all the way from Michigan for the ceremony. They were even bringing our neighbors and good friends Helen and Roy Livingston. Sybil's mother was traveling from Chicago; our families were to meet for the first time. I needed that passing grade.

I got it—barely. I did not deserve to pass, but my professor took pity on me and I fell over the goal line. Whew!

Late in the spring, before graduation, I asked Sybil to marry me and she accepted. I did not perform this task as I should have. I did not get down on my knee, I did not buy her an engagement ring. But, looking back, what I regret most was not asking Sybil's mother for permission. Sybil's father was deceased. Approaching her mother before the engagement would have shown my respect for the woman; it would have been the proper and kind thing to do. And she might have opened my mind, before I took the plunge, to all that goes into making a marriage work.

But I did none of those things.

I didn't realize my mistake at the time. I couldn't have been more pleased that beautiful spring day as Sybil and I, in our caps and gowns, walked hand in hand among our fellow graduates into Kinnick Stadium, where four years earlier I'd been inspired by the thought of thousands cheering for me. Out of the thirty-five in our class who ended up with a football scholarship, only John Ficeli and I graduated in four years. I didn't have an academic record to brag about, but I was learning and maturing and moving my life forward.

And now I would have a smart, beautiful partner at my side in the journey.

CHAPTER 7

On Our Own

The Air Force, Julie, and a Faraway War

Too Much, Too Fast: Jobs, A Riot, A War, A Wedding

The summer after graduation, 1967, I went back to East Detroit and secured a job as a probation officer for "delinquent" boys with the Macomb County Probate Court. A decade later, when I was in Congress, I would joke with my constituents that "I used to work with delinquent boys, but now I work with delinquent men."

I started my job as a probation officer with the same amount of preparation I'd had for my summer job at the Youth Home: none. On-the-job training was all I had to rely on.

Taking the position meant joining my third union, the American Federation of State, County, and Municipal Employees (AFSCME). For all the protection the union provided, it didn't protect probation officers at the probate court from a burden that crippled them as they tried to serve their clients and the public: an excessive caseload. Mine was eighty boys, all under the age of eighteen, whose offenses spanned the spectrum from school truancy, incorrigibility at home, and petty theft to more serious crimes like breaking and entering and even violence resulting in harm to others.

It was virtually impossible to work with that many boys, most of whom were burdened with significant personal and family problems. Years later, when I ran for the legislature, I campaigned for increased funding to reduce these caseloads. Eventually they were cut in half, to about forty.

Sybil's father had died in 1965, and her brother, Doug, was away pursuing a career in major league baseball, so Sybil and her mother were the only occupants of their home in Northbrook, Illinois, that summer. I liked Evie. Small in stature, she was smart, with a gift for art—painting was her specialty. She worked in retail sales at Carson Pirie Scott department stores in the Chicago area. Together she and Sybil worked on plans for a November wedding.

Both Sybil and Doug had been adopted after living in an orphanage and in foster homes. A year older than Sybil, Doug was the first to arrive on Butternut Lane in Northbrook. Sybil soon followed at the age of two. Her birth mother had named her Karen Joyce, but the staff at the Chicago Children's Home and Aid Society called her Angel. The Raders gave her the name Sybil.

In addition to preparing for the wedding, Sybil looked for a job. Certified for both regular elementary school and special education, she was highly employable; before we had gotten engaged, she'd accepted an offer to teach in the Madison, Wisconsin, school system. But now she looked for a job that would keep us together, and she got one: Starting in the fall, she'd be teaching third grade at Beechwood Elementary in East Detroit. She struggled over the choice but eventually decided to pass up the opportunity in Wisconsin in favor of teaching in my hometown.

Until she arrived in East Detroit to begin her job, I drove back and forth to Northbrook on weekends. It was a five-hour drive on I-94, but the anticipation of seeing her made the trip worthwhile. I usually spent the drive listening to baseball on the radio—the Tigers were red hot that summer, locked in a pennant race that went down to the last day of the season, when the Red Sox finally clinched first place. The games were carried on WJR, a 50,000-watt station that gave me a clear signal all the way. I would leave after work on Friday to arrive in Northbrook at

On Butternut Lane, near Sybil's home in Northbrook, Illinois

around 9:00 p.m. We'd spend the weekend talking about the wedding, going for walks, seeing a little of Chicago, and playing a lot of Yahtzee, a Milton Bradley dice game, with Evie. I was getting to know Evie, the Raders' neighborhood friends, and members of the extended family. Uncle Eddie and Aunt Marge would come over, and Eddie would regale us with stories about the fire and police departments. Northbrook was a middle- to upper-middle-class community, with fabulous schools, services, and recreational facilities. It was a nice place to be.

On Saturday, July 24, 1967, Sybil and I awoke to the news that Detroit was on fire. In the early morning hours on 12th Street, the Detroit

Rebellion—or the Detroit Riot, depending on your point of view—
had exploded. Outside of the Draft Riots in New York City during the
Civil War, the 1967 eruption in Detroit was the biggest, most destruc-
tive civil disturbance in American history. Fueled by racism, poverty,
hoodlumism, and police insensitivity and brutality, the rebellion/riot
exacted a devastating toll on the city. Detroit has never really recovered.

In five days of unrest, 43 people were killed and 1,189 wounded.
Two thousand buildings were destroyed, and 7,200 people were
arrested. Governor George Romney called out the Michigan National
Guard, but it was incapable of restoring order, so President Lyndon
Baines Johnson sent in the 82nd Airborne Division of the regular U.S.
Army. Driving on I-94 through the heart of the city when I returned
to the area that Monday morning, I saw soldiers stationed on the tops
of buildings. In battle fatigues and laden with gear, they held their M1
rifles at the ready. It was eerie and unsettling.

Only days earlier, Newark, New Jersey, had been beset by similar
deadly disturbances. Not only were half a million troops stationed in
Vietnam just as we were about to get married but now our cities were
becoming unhinged, as well. The future looked bleak.

Neither the Vietnam War nor the disturbance in Detroit was the premier problem dogging us as we prepared to tie the knot. The issue we
dealt with was religion: Sybil was Protestant, I was Catholic.

Still engaged with my Catholicism, I argued that we should marry
in the Catholic Church. Sybil reluctantly agreed, so we scheduled a date
for the nuptials to be held in St. Norbert's Catholic Church in Northbrook. However, the pastor at St. Norbert's insisted that Sybil take the
Pre-Cana counseling course—so named because Jesus turned water into
wine at a wedding feast in Cana—at the parish rectory. After several
sessions, Sybil was distinctly uncomfortable with elements of what she
was being told. "I don't believe in some of this," she said to me.

I was wrong to push the Catholic framework, and she was right to
resist it. Both of us were opposed to the Church's teachings on birth

control, and both of us objected to the pastor's insistence that the children of our union be raised Catholic. I tried to see Sybil's side in this clash of cultures but thought we could just skate through the issue and then be done with it. I was wrong in that assessment and wrong in pushing her along this route. She wanted to please me, so she completed the counseling.

At the end of the summer we got an apartment in East Detroit on 9 Mile Road, about a mile from my boyhood home on Ego. The location was favorable: It was within walking distance of Sybil's school and only a twenty-minute drive to the court building where I worked. Financially, we were doing well. Each of our jobs paid between five and six thousand dollars annually, a comfortable salary back then. But while the commute and the wages were fine, our future was still in doubt because of the war. I thought my work as a probation officer might be the kind of social work to exempt me from military service. My goal at that point was to engage in more community service, then run for political office in a city where the name Bonior was known and respected.

For Sybil, our new setup posed more of a challenge. She was moving into a community where she had no friends other than my family members, whom she hardly knew. She was entering a brand-new profession with worries based on her unfortunate experience at the Pine School in Iowa. She was planning a wedding (no stress there!). So all of this—new partner, new home, new job, the wedding, new religious questions, soon a new marriage—pressed upon her. I was blind to the stress I had placed on her. It was all too much, too fast. I regret that I did not see matters more from her perspective.

We walked down the aisle at St. Norbert's on a Saturday in November, she a gorgeous bride, I a nervous groom. Evie had done a superb job with the arrangements: The flowers were lovely, the food was delicious. Sybil had three bridesmaids: two college friends, Vivian Fabro and Barb Pitts, as well as my sister, Nancy. I chose John Carlin to be my best man. My pals David Deigel, Bill Beals, and Dante Rotondo also made the trip from Detroit to join the celebration. After the morning ceremony, we adjourned to the formal banquet room of a nearby hotel for a luncheon reception. About a hundred guests attended—thirty to forty of my family and friends who'd traveled from Detroit, the rest on Sybil's side. We spent our wedding night at the Holiday Inn in Chicago, on Michigan Avenue, overlooking the lake.

Honeymoon? Didn't happen. On Monday both of us had to be at work.

We did get away a few months later. In February, I saw a newspaper ad announcing a twenty-five-dollar round-trip air fare to Boston. While a weekend in the cold of a Boston winter would not exactly make up for our missing honeymoon, we nonetheless decided to take advantage of the low rate and see this historic city, which neither of us had ever visited.

Off we went. After checking into a midpriced hotel downtown, we set off to explore the city. The temperature must have hovered in the single digits—readings not ideal for romance. But because it was so cold, few tourists were taking in the sights, so the city seemed to be all ours as we visited Old North Church, Boston Commons, Paul Revere's home, and, mercifully, a museum that got us out of the weather. Even in the cold I was inspired by the roots of our country's history. Back then the "Tea Party" was a historical event only.

Whatever cozy feeling we had, however, was soon upended. On Saturday evening we decided to splurge on dinner at the famous—and famously touristy—Union Oyster House. Big mistake. We both wound up with food poisoning and a trip to Massachusetts General Hospital.

Somehow we limped back to our hotel and then to the airport for our return to Michigan.

A Zigzagging Line:
My Path to Military Service

In addition to all the new private stress we faced in our young lives, there was the ever-looming public question of the war in Vietnam. As did millions across the country, we wondered what impact the war would have on our future. My student deferment had expired upon graduation; I was now classified I-A, "Available for combat service." I appealed that status, making the case that as a "social worker," I was performing a service important to the community. My draft board didn't buy it; the three-person panel voted 2–1 to refuse the appeal. I would later learn that my draft board, Selective Service Board 300, in Roseville, Michigan, presided over one of the nation's highest percentages of draft-eligible men serving in the military. One reason for the high rate was the low number of young men from Macomb County who went to college. Another was the pride Macomb County families took in their tradition of military service. Many fathers, uncles, and grandfathers had served in World War II and Korea; their service to their country in the past steered many from the working and middle classes into the military of the present. And finally, the county draft board was simply a tough bunch, not about to let eligible men escape service.

The war was heating up, and the armed forces demanded a constant supply of manpower—not only because casualties were high but also because troops were sent to Vietnam for tours of only one year. With public discord over the war threatening to boil over, a presidential primary was staring LBJ in the face. On March 12, Senator Eugene McCarthy, an antiwar Democrat from Minnesota, stunned the nation by garnering 42 percent of the vote in the New Hampshire balloting. The most wrenching year in decades, 1968, was upon us. All hell was breaking loose.

On March 31, I was watching television in our apartment after dinner as I pondered my options regarding military service. Only days before, the mail had contained a notice from my draft board calling me to report for a physical examination.

I was alone that night—I think Sybil was at her school attending a parent conference—as I waited for President Johnson to come on TV to address the nation about the war. Near the end of his remarks, Johnson shocked not only "mah fella Americans" (as he always opened such speeches) but also the international community by withdrawing from the presidential campaign. "I shall not seek," he said, "and I will not accept, the nomination of my party for another term as your president." Even most of Johnson's aides were caught by surprise. Of course, I was, too. McCarthy, New Hampshire, and the Tet Offensive had altered the course of American history. In the midst of the war and all the attendant domestic turmoil, the country would see a wide-open race for the White House.

I reported for my induction physical at historic Fort Wayne, just across the Detroit River from Canada in the Delray section of Detroit. Constructed in 1849 on Native American burial grounds that date back nine hundred years, the star-shaped fort was designed by the famous Civil War architect Montgomery Meigs, the quartermaster general of the Union Army. During the Second World War, the army used Fort Wayne as a supply depot; during the Korean and Vietnam Wars, it became an induction center. Looming over the fort, to its immediate south, is the mammoth Ford Rouge complex. The Rouge was at one time the largest manufacturing facility in the world, employing 100,000 workers.

The day I arrived for my examination in April 1968, the fort was packed with young men following a thick yellow line on the floor that zigzagged along, taking us from station to station as each element of our physical condition was judged and documented: eyes, ears, heart, lungs, feet, weight, reflexes, and mind. Some inductees were too heavy to serve, while others sought disqualification by conniving to boost their blood pressure past acceptable levels. But in the end, most "passed" their physicals, retaining their I-A classification.

At the end of the examinations, a sergeant ordered us outside, onto the fort's grounds, then lined us up in a straight line and instructed us to count off by threes. A comedy of errors, not an exercise in military precision, ensued, as many of the inductees—there must have been fifty to seventy-five of us—could not figure out whether they were "one," "two," or "three." The exasperated sergeant finally walked along the line and assigned a number to each person. The humor stopped when he told all the threes to take one step forward. After they did, he made an announcement that must have blown the minds of many of the nervous young men standing before him. (It certainly blew mine.) "Congratulations," he said in a loud, proud voice. "All you threes have been inducted into the United States Marine Corps." To this point in the Vietnam War, all draftees had been assigned to the army; the elite fighting force known as the Marines had accepted only men who chose the Corps of their own free will. But that arrangement was not meeting the needs of the Marines who were bearing the brunt of the fighting in the northernmost area of South Vietnam—I Corps—which abutted the Demilitarized Zone dividing the South from Communist North Vietnam. The Department of Defense, therefore, had just issued an order calling for thousands of Marines to be inducted. I knew that day at Fort Wayne that there was only one place Marines were going, and it was not Europe. I was a two. Whew!

After passing my physical, all that remained was for me to await my induction notice in the mail. When I got it—ordering me to appear shortly for the beginning of my army training—I immediately began a search for an alternative. All the reserve and National Guard units nearby were filled. Because I had a college degree, I thought that army officer candidate school might be a possibility. Wrong: The only officer slots available were in engineering and medicine or dentistry; there were none relating to my college background in political science and sociology. I was left with enlistment in the navy or air force, both of which were accepting volunteers (if you can call someone who enlists to avoid the draft a "volunteer").

My decision as to which branch of service I should choose centered on (1) being stationed on land so that Sybil could join me—that eliminated the navy—and (2) my desire to establish military credentials for a future political career. While I admired conscientious objectors, and those who went to jail or left the country rather than serve in a war they despised, a future in politics was weighing heavily on my mind. And so, even though I was opposed to the war, and even though our policy in Vietnam was becoming more and more unpopular, I felt that I needed to serve in some capacity. I was right in that judgment—having a military background paid off later when I ran for office in Macomb County, with its working-class population that took great pride in military service.

There was a catch, however: Enlistment in the air force or navy meant a four-year commitment, whereas an obligation to the army or Marine Corps was only half as long. While I certainly preferred a two-year hitch, I judged the longer option to be measurably safer. I was married, I wanted a family, and I did not believe in this war. So I chose a four-year enlistment in the air force.

I could still end up in Vietnam, but I saw this course as my best chance not to.

DEATH OF A PROPHET:
MEMPHIS, APRIL 4, 1968

On February 1, 1968, in the city of Memphis, Tennessee, a malfunctioning compressor in the back of a garbage truck crushed sanitation workers Echol Cole and Robert Walker to death. The two men were in the back of the truck because the day was rainy, and city rules forbade them from taking shelter anywhere else. The conditions for Memphis sanitation workers—nearly all of whom were African American—were deplorable: no union, no benefits, poverty wages, and unsafe working conditions. On February 12, they went out on strike. Garbage piled up. After the city hired scabs, scuffles ensued.

My union at that time, AFSCME, was at the center of this struggle. The national leadership sent Bill Lucy, who would rise to the union's number-two position, to negotiate with the city. After I got to Congress, Bill, who also founded the Coalition of Black Trade Unionists, became a good friend of mine. In 2002, he walked door-to-door on my behalf during my campaign for governor of Michigan.

To Bill Lucy, as well as to prominent civil rights leaders like Bayard Rustin, Roy Wilkins, and the Reverend Jim Lawson, it was becoming clear that the Memphis sanitation workers strike was no ordinary labor dispute but rather an important event in the civil rights movement. The issues were so clear and the cause so righteous that the situation screamed for justice.

The nation's most prominent civil rights leader, Martin Luther King Jr., took notice; on March 18 he addressed an audience of thousands at the Mason Temple in Memphis. The strike was still in force when he returned to town ten days later to lead a march to city hall. After violence broke out, the procession did not reach its destination, but King, refusing to be deterred, vowed to return. Workers' rights were human rights to King, who understood the plight of the working poor and recognized that with the legal structure of Jim Crow torn down, the civil rights movement needed to shift toward the struggle for economic justice. On April 3 he returned to Memphis and the Mason Temple, where he told his audience that threats to his life didn't "matter with me now, because I've been to the mountaintop." Whatever his personal fate, this modern-day Moses wanted his listeners to "know tonight, that we, as a people, will get to the promised land!" As he often did when he visited Memphis, King stayed at the Lorraine Motel. At 6:00 p.m. on April 4, he was standing on the second-floor balcony outside his room when James Earl Ray, a fugitive from the Missouri State Penitentiary, shot him dead.

For millions in the country and around the world, King's murder was a dagger plunged deep into their hearts. Martin Luther King Jr. was more than just hope. He was action. His magnetism and spirituality, bolstered by his political and physical courage, pushed the nonviolence movement forward even when others were rejecting it. Certainly, many in America were glad to see King dead. But the large majority of the nation saw his decency and his bravery. And deep down they understood that what King was doing for the Memphis sanitation workers was about as noble and right as it gets. The sadness, grief, and anger over his death were profound.

Unfortunately, if understandably, the sorrow over King's death manifested itself in a form this apostle of nonviolence would not have condoned. Beginning the night of the murder, violent rebellion broke out across America. When I left work at the probate court in Mount Clemens the next day, I saw fire a mile away, in and around the city's downtown. Burning and destruction likewise visited Detroit, Pontiac, Flint, and Benton Harbor.

Four days after the shooting, the slain leader's widow, Coretta Scott King, led a silent march through the streets of Memphis on behalf of the striking workers. A week later, the men went back to work after the city recognized their union and granted them a pay increase.

Fast-forward thirty-five years to Wayne State University, where I work at the Walter Reuther Library and Archives. We honor the sacrifices of all involved in Dr. King's last campaign, which adopted as its slogan the words "I Am a Man" to signify the basic human dignity of the striking workers. Several of the now-retired sanitation workers attended our symposium on the strike. James Lawson and other key figures spoke.

Today the Service Employees International Union (SEIU) runs a Justice for Janitors (JFJ) campaign that serves as one of the modern models in the fight to obtain justice for low-wage workers. The JFJ efforts in Los Angeles during the 1980s and in Houston and Miami during the 2000s helped tens of thousands of janitors, cleaners, and caretakers join a union and receive the decent compensation in wages and benefits that flowed from their exercise of collective strength. In April 2006 I took part in the campaign at the University of Miami. I walked a picket line, supported a hunger strike, and took on, through American Rights at Work and in the press, an insensitive university president who ignored the needs of her low-wage workers. Some of these employees had loyally and competently served the institution for a decade or more yet still received only the federal minimum wage, causing them enormous hardship as they tried to support themselves and their families.

Sadly, this university president was Donna Shalala, the former secretary of health and human services under President Bill Clinton.

AIRMAN BONIOR:
I JOIN THE AIR FORCE

The clock on my civilian life had run out.

I arrived at Lackland Air Force Base, in San Antonio, Texas, on May 6, ready to get all of the hair removed from my head. At twenty-two, I was the old man in my squadron, which was made up almost entirely of eighteen- and nineteen-year-olds fresh out of high school. For me, basic training was a mixture of intensity and boredom. No hair? So what? It felt good. Bounce a quarter off my tightly made bed? No problem. I had been making my bed with hospital corners since I was eleven years old. Spit shine my boots and shoes so I could see my reflection in them? Easy. I had been polishing the shoes in my family since I was ten. Drill sergeant screaming at me? Big deal. Coaches from the "old school" had been yelling in my face since I was in sixth grade. Ironically, the name of my drill sergeant was Sergeant Love. No kidding! And he was a lovely guy, with a big smile and a well-developed sense of humor. He tried to be a hard-ass but couldn't get there. He was always giving guys a break.

While the training was relatively easy for me, being away from Sybil was not. I missed her terribly. After her school year finished in early June, she headed back to Northbrook, where she got a job as an usher in a movie theater. More than the drills and the discipline, it was the isolation that made my two months of training nerve-wracking: We were allowed no contact with the world outside our barracks except for the letters we might receive at mail call, the most anticipated event of each day. Sybil's frequent letters sustained me. After a month on the base, we were allowed a phone call. I called Sybil, and on June 7, the day after my twenty-third birthday, I learned that Robert F. Kennedy had been assassinated in Los Angeles the night of June 4, after he'd won the California Democratic presidential primary. It was the first real piece of news I'd heard since arriving at Lackland.

I was devastated. Only two months had gone by since Martin Luther King Jr. had been murdered. It seemed that the country was falling apart.

As basic training drew to a close, I needed my next duty assignment. I received a form asking where I wanted to be stationed; I was stunned that the air force cared one bit what I wanted. After conferring with Sybil, I filled out the form: For my domestic choices, I topped my list of installations with Norton Air Force Base in California and my list of geographic sectors with Region 5, which included the western United States. Next in order of preference were Selfridge AFB, in Macomb County, and the Midwest. I was sure I hadn't a prayer of getting these picks. Even more unlikely were my choices for postings overseas: Italy, then Spain. *Fat chance*, I thought.

But before the air force could send me someplace, it needed to train me for something, and the something it had in mind was being a radio intercept operator. To fill that job, I'd need to learn Vietnamese and Chinese. According to various aptitude tests we'd all been given, I had the ability to learn these languages.

They hadn't talked to my Latin professor.

Toward the end of our two months of basic, I was interviewed by a young lieutenant who told me that the air force wanted to send me to language school in Monterey, California. The Monterey part sounded fantastic; later, it would turn out to be one of my favorite places on the planet. However, I was not buying the idea of Vietnamese and Chinese.

With as much respect and humility as I could muster, I told the lieutenant that I probably would not do well if they sent me there. He stared at me for what seemed like a long minute and then got rid of me with, "That will be all, airman. You are dismissed." I stood up, saluted, and returned to my barracks wondering what in the world the air force would have in mind for me.

Two weeks after my act of mild insubordination, basic training ended. I was not the only graduate without a new assignment: There were around twenty of us being held over an extra month as the air force figured out what to do with us. Because I was older and, presumably, had shown some leadership ability, I was designated to be in charge of my barracks and the twenty fellow airmen who shared my uncertain future. We were in limbo. We had nothing to do except wait and stay out of trouble. The good news was that we could perform those demanding tasks away from Lackland: We were now free to leave the base and visit San Antonio.

My first day in town I visited the Alamo, in front of which I saw Nelson Rockefeller giving a speech. The moderate Republican governor of New York was campaigning for his party's presidential nomination. I don't recall what he said; what I do recall is that I was astonished by how short he was. Later that day, perhaps inspired by the exploits of the Alamo's defenders (or attackers), I took a horseback ride through Brackenridge Park. Big mistake. I had neither skill at riding nor chemistry with horses, and my mount obviously could tell. (I doubt he constantly tried to nibble the shins of riders who knew what they were doing.) Before my ride ended he played a joke on me that scared me half to death.

There was a tourist train that ran around the park. The horse and I came to a crossing and got halfway through it, when, right over the tracks, he decided to stop. I pleaded with him, I kicked him. I sweet-talked him, I cursed at him. I pulled the reins right, I pulled the reins left. I rocked back and forth, I rocked up and down. Still, he would not budge. I thought, *This animal is stupid! Do I want to be on top of him with a train roaring toward us?* And then I saw the train. Coming toward us. It wasn't a big train, it wasn't pulled by a magnificent, huge locomotive, but it *was* a train, and I knew that the answer to my question was, Hell, no! When the train was about a hundred yards away—with thoughts of the headlines my death would generate: "Airman on Horse Run Over by Train"; "Train Runs Over Horse; Airman Also a Victim"— I gave up trying to convince the horse to move and decided that if the horse wanted to be run over, that was his business; I needed to get to safety. Off I jumped. But, fine horseman that I was, one foot stuck in the stirrup. I finally wiggled free and stepped well away from the track. Meanwhile, the train was barreling toward the horse. Then, with only moments to spare, the horse walked off the track at a leisurely pace. He had the whole thing under control. No doubt the beast had pulled this gag on tenderfoot riders before.

After the train went by, the horse looked at me with an expression that said, *Hey, cowboy. What's keeping you? Let's get out of here.* We were late; of course, it was my fault.

By this time a small crowd had gathered to witness the pathetic spectacle. As I got back on my evil horse, I decided that I'd had enough of Texas. I was ready to leave.

While in limbo I volunteered for some medical experiments at Brooks AFB, also in San Antonio. I was told that the tests, which occupied the better part of a day, had something to do with astronaut training; I don't remember exactly what I did, but I know that I survived with my faculties intact. On another day I went to see Claude Lelouch's film *A Man and a Woman,* starring Anouk Aimée and Jean-Louis Trintignant. The scenery, musical score, and chemistry between the leads made for an intense romantic film that put me over the edge. I had to see my wife. I could stand to be away from her no longer.

As it happened, it was only hours later, when my orders arrived the next day, that I learned my separation from my bride was almost over. I was being sent to the army quartermaster school at Fort Lee, Virginia, where I would learn to be a cook. At that time the two lowest rungs on the military career ladder were occupied by military police and cooks. I figured that this assignment was the air force's way of punishing me for refusing language training. I would be a cook. Translation: I would be doing kitchen police (KP) duty—pots, pans, and floors—for the next several years. Fortunately there would be some actual cooking, as well.

I took a deep breath and accepted my fate, feeling I'd made the right decision in turning down the previous assignment—a more likely ticket to a combat unit—even if I was in for years of scrubbing away burned-on sauce and caked grease, peeling gigantic pots of potatoes and carrots, and mopping up floors covered with grime, soot, and spilled foodstuffs.

But my future in food mattered little to me. What did matter was that my new location was set, and Sybil would be permitted to join me there. I was going to be reunited with her after three long months of separation.

The summer of 1968 was the hottest of my life. Moving from the dry Texas heat (regularly a hundred degrees Fahrenheit, although it felt like Celsius) to the wet Virginia heat (high nineties), it seemed as though all I did that summer was sweat. I received permission to live with Sybil, who had given up her teaching job in Michigan, outside the confines of Fort Lee. We found a tiny log cabin with an attic bedroom in Hopewell, Virginia, about seven miles from the fort. The whole place added up to no more than an efficiency apartment, with five hundred square feet of space at the most. The bedroom was particularly cramped—you couldn't stand up in it without hitting your head on the slanted ceiling. The cabin was owned by a Presbyterian minister, whose short stature explained the dimensions of the place. Next to the cabin was his church.

We had no air-conditioning, so the whole cabin was hot. But our bedroom was the worst: The heat rose to the attic and stayed there, creating what must have been three-digit temperatures as we tried to sleep. Thankfully, we both were used to living without air-conditioning—we hadn't had it in any of our homes.

Since my airman's pay was only $110 a month plus another $100 for food and lodging, it was good that Sybil got a job stuffing envelopes for our landlord's church, even if she was paid minimum wage. (Or was it even that high?) We would be here only seven weeks; once my training ended, I would most likely be sent elsewhere. It helped to know that she would not be doing this work for a long time.

Twenty-four airmen, all recently released from basic training, made up my cooking class. Tom Drum, a young banker with a business degree, was, like me, married and living outside the fort. Our air force careers paralleled each other, from Texas to Virginia to our next assignment.

My course work at quartermaster school included (1) introduction to cooking; (2) small quantity cooking; (3) cake and pastry baking; (4) meat cutting; (5) field mess operations; and (6) garrison mess operations. This last course—learning how to work in a large indoor "mess hall" (or "chow hall")—occupied most of our time. I found the coursework interesting for the most part and picked up some skills that have remained useful ever since. I learned how to bone a ham, cut up a chicken, and assemble and clean a meat-slicing machine. In meat-cutting class we wore metal-mesh gloves so that we could start our culinary careers with five digits on each hand. We did the cutting in a refrigerated cooler, so we were constantly moving from the Virginia heat into the chill of the meat locker, and back out again. This repeated change in temperature made me nauseated.

Nausea also afflicted me during extended periods working in the bakery. As inviting as a kitchen stocked full of fresh doughnuts, cakes, brownies, and pies could smell, my repeated exposure to this wonderland of sugar turned my stomach. This is coming from someone who to this day is ruled by a vicious sweet tooth.

The most practical lesson I learned in cook school was "Clean as You Go." This slogan was hammered into us from the day we arrived, and it's a maxim I still rely on forty-five years later whenever I am in the kitchen. The idea is that it is a lot more efficient and healthy to work in a clean, safe kitchen. So while waiting for water to boil or the oven to heat up, you should use the time to clean up around you and organize yourself for the next step in your project.

Sybil and I took advantage of our location by touring historic Virginia. We also didn't mind spending time in our air-conditioned '65 Olds Cutlass. Gas was cheap at thirty cents a gallon, so on weekends we explored colonial Williamsburg, William and Mary College, the Civil War battlefield at Petersburg, Thomas Jefferson's grand estate at Monticello, the University of Virginia, and the Appomattox Court House, where Robert E. Lee surrendered to Ulysses S. Grant to end the Civil War.

But even though I found the history fascinating, all of this touring felt strange and frivolous, adding to the guilt I felt knowing that 500,000 fellow servicemen were fighting a war half a world away. I expected there was a fifty-fifty chance that I might join them when cook school was finished.

I didn't. My orders were to report to the 479th Tactical Fighter Wing at George AFB near the town of Victorville in the high desert of California. I graduated cook school on September 13, 1968, just as the Detroit Tigers were getting ready to wrap up the American League pennant. I had until October 6—over three weeks—to arrive at George, so I could see the sights on my way out.

The air force cut me a check for $153 that was supposed to cover nine days of travel. Sybil and I were thrilled to be on our way to California.

ROAD TRIP:
MAKING OUR WAY WEST

The idea of California was enchanting to me: the Pacific Ocean, Big Sur, Yosemite, Los Angeles, San Francisco, San Diego, Santa Barbara, the mountains, the Mojave Desert, Mexico just over the border. There would be so much to see and do, even with our thin wallets. I had no idea how long I would be stationed in California, but we were determined to make the best of our opportunity while it lasted.

But first we had to get there, and we intended to see as much of America as we could before we hit the West Coast. I'd long been fascinated by the idea of driving cross-country—I'd listened to "Get Your Kicks on Route 66," the popular song, first recorded in 1946 by the great Nat King Cole, that summed up what has often been called "the romance of the American highway." No highway had more romance attached to it than Route 66, the road taken to the West by countless travelers in the days before the building of the interstate highway system. The song lyrics include a list of towns along the historic route—Joplin, Missouri; Oklahoma City; Gallup, New Mexico; San Bernardino, California, among others. Now was our chance to see them all.

We left Hopewell, Virginia, with our belongings packed into the Cutlass and drove into Washington, D.C., where we were to stay with my father at the Shoreham Hotel. Dad was in the capital on business for his job with the Office of Economic Opportunity. We made the mistake of parking our car on the street, a block away from the hotel, and leaving inside it most of the cargo. I didn't think to drag the stuff to the hotel with us; we'd just have to repack it when it was time to leave.

Error, Bonior. When I went to get the car in the morning, I found that much of what we'd brought with us was gone. I cursed my stupidity as we pulled out of Washington, driving a car noticeably lighter than before. At least our gas mileage must have been better as we drove to East Detroit—we did all 530 miles in one day.

We stayed only two days in Michigan, just long enough for us to say our good-byes to family and friends and load up the car and a small U-Haul trailer with household items and barely used wedding gifts. Because I was just an airman, at the lowest enlisted grade, I didn't rate having the air force ship our goods to California. We packed the trailer as full as we could.

Our next stop was Northbrook, and we'd be going with a passenger: my brother, Jeff, twelve years old and growing. Sybil and I asked him to ride with us on this leg of our trip. We made room for him in the backseat among the boxes packed with cookware and linens. I was aware that my posting to California might mean that I would miss his high school years. This trip would give us a little time together before we separated.

When we arrived in Northbrook, we made plans to watch Sybil's brother play baseball. At that time a rookie starting at third base for the Houston Astros, Doug Rader would build a substantial and impressive career in the major leagues as a player, coach, and manager. The Astros were in town for a series with the Cubs at historic Wrigley Field. It was exciting to see him play. At six feet two and 210 pounds, with bright red hair, Doug was flamboyant on the field and off. Around the league he was known as the Red Rooster.

It was especially good to spend some time with Evie. Over my weekend visits the previous summer I had started to form a warm relationship with her. The time Sybil and I spent with friends and family, in Michigan and Illinois, was important to us. On my two-hundred-dollar-a-month salary I did not think we would soon be able to get back to the Midwest. As it turned out, I was right: We did not return for three and a half years.

After Sybil and I put Jeff on a bus back to Detroit, it was time for us to head west. The trip from Chicago to San Bernardino, where Sybil and I would live while I worked at the base, was two thousand miles. As we set off toward southern Illinois, the ride felt like a familiar drive through rural Iowa: plenty of broad fields of corn, some harvested, some not. We passed through Springfield; I've never been back, but reading *Team of Rivals,* by Doris Kearns Goodwin, has given me the desire to return and experience the place where Abraham Lincoln lived and worked.

Our trip through St. Louis might have provided an opportunity to visit JaJa and Busia's old neighborhood and parish, St. Stanislaus Koska, the center of Polish life in the city, but I was not then aware of my grandparents' roots in that town. Continuing west through Missouri, we drove through Joplin, where I thought of Robert Cummings. On *The Bob Cummings Show,* his television sitcom known in reruns as *Love That Bob,* the actor frequently referred to his roots in Joplin. Sadly, when I now hear of Joplin, I think of the terrible tornado in 2011 that destroyed so much of the town and killed 162 people.

After about eleven hours on the road we pulled into Tulsa, Oklahoma, where we got a room for the night. Driving through Oklahoma had the feel of oil, just as Iowa had the feel of corn and Michigan the feel of cars. The next morning, as we drove through Oklahoma City and out to Amarillo, Texas, we passed one oil derrick after another, all surrounded by dry, barren fields. The desolate landscape reminded us of John Steinbeck and the migration west from Oklahoma and other states of the Great Plains afflicted by the Dust Bowl of the 1930s. Unanchored soil had turned into "black blizzards" that blew so hard, a man might see only a yard in front of him. Tens of thousands of "Okies" lost their farms and homes and made their way to California, as Steinbeck so poignantly described in *The Grapes of Wrath,* still one of my favorite novels. This mass upheaval had taken place just three decades prior to our passing through the region.

The long days on the road gave us a chance to talk about our future. I have struggled my whole life to extricate myself from the habit of living in either the past or the future. The ride west gave me a chance to experience the present, as indeed I did, soaking up all the new and fascinating sights on our journey across the country. Sybil and I spoke about what we were seeing. But the trip was too long, and the temptation too great, not to map out what was ahead for us. I was always presenting Sybil with a blueprint; it's the way I was then and still am today, always coming up with plans. To me it felt like we were driving not just west but into the unwritten chapters of our lives. A line from Proverbs went through my head: "Where there is no vision, the people will perish." We planned and dreamed and tried to envision how everything would turn out.

We decided we wanted to not live in poverty on my air force pay of two hundred dollars a month and we wanted to start a family. It made sense to build some cash reserves, but it would not be easy. I was locked into my meager salary cooking. At George AFB I would work two days on, two days off. On my days off I would do some substitute teaching, but the assignments were hit or miss. Sybil, with her credentials in elementary and special education, plus her experience teaching in East Detroit, would no doubt be able to bring in additional income. As to having a child, we decided to put it off.

We spent the next night in Albuquerque. I'll never forget driving into a stunning sunset as we approached the city. The expansive sky was evolving into a brilliant red color against the silhouettes of the buttes and mountains. The lights of the city tried to compete with the painted skyline but fell short. The sky and the lights together evoked for me a spirituality I will always remember. I was transfixed, I was in the moment. I knew then why New Mexico is called the "Land of Enchantment." To this day, when I hear the word *Albuquerque*, I think and feel red sky.

Our long, earnest discussions in the car took place against the backdrop of the car radio. The musical offerings tended toward country and western, with a smattering of Motown, and almost no classical. In the evenings we'd find major league baseball, almost always either the Astros, Doug's team; the Atlanta Braves, at the time the only other Southern team; or the St. Louis Cardinals. Millions of fans throughout the Midwest, South, and West had developed allegiance to the Cards before teams began to populate the western and southern halves of the country. And they were able to follow the Cards thanks to the immense power of the KMOX transmitter. Unfortunately, my beloved Detroit Tigers, coming to the end of a spectacular season, were nowhere to be found in the radio land of the rural plains and Southwest. But I would be able to catch some of the games played a short time later, when the Tigers came back from a 3–1 deficit to beat Bob Gibson and the Cardinals in the World Series.

Hungry for information in this pre-Internet age, we also listened to talk radio. The civil rights movement, the war, and the presidential election were the topics discussed. This was the supercharged year of 1968; both parties had recently concluded their national party conventions. A politically wounded Hubert H. Humphrey was trying to catch a resurrected Richard M. Nixon, whose promises to end the war—though he wouldn't say how—and restore "law and order" had given him the lead in the race.

If we needed a break from the hashing and rehashing of the issues of the day, we could tune in to matters of a less temporal nature: Reverend Ike, out of New York, and Oral Roberts, in Oklahoma, both expressed distinctive religious points of view as powerful as their pitches to get into our wallets. And defying classification was Larry Glick. Because he broadcast on 50,000-watt WBZ out of Boston, we could pick him up loud and clear well into Texas, before he got a little scratchy as we neared New Mexico. Sybil liked to listen to Glick. Interesting and funny, he hosted a regular set of callers who made you feel as though you were sitting around the pickle barrel in the country store swapping stories. He came on at midnight, eastern time, and didn't leave the air until 6:00 a.m. He was the companion of many third-shift folks, long-distance truck drivers, and insomniacs. Years later, when we came back East, Sybil would listen to his show.

From Albuquerque we headed for Las Vegas. The scenery on the way was stunning, with red rocks and buttes that reminded me of all those old black-and-white cowboy films I'd seen as a kid. Now it was in front of us, and in living color: soft blue skies, crimson rocks, taupe desert, and those orange-scarlet mesas and buttes that gave the landscape its dimension.

The landscape changed as we climbed up to seven thousand feet and Flagstaff, Arizona, where we saw huge mountain pines. Soon snow would create a white blanket that would last until spring.

From Flagstaff we continued west to Kingman, Arizona, and then we left Route 66 and took Route 93 north to Boulder City, Nevada, and the Hoover Dam. We just had to stop and explore this man-made wonder. Later, while in Congress, I would challenge the building of these mega-dam projects. But in 1968, even though the structure resembled a giant scar on the desert's surface, I was still impressed and overwhelmed by the engineering that went into the dam's construction.

It was dark when we came over a rise and saw the bright lights of Las Vegas. My gambling fever had been cured by losing all my summer earnings at the racetrack a few years earlier. Nevertheless, the glamour of this place drew me in, making me eager to see what "Vegas" was all about. I had yet to learn what great environmentalists like David Brower, Wallace Stegner, and Wendell Berry were saying in the eternal debate surrounding the American West: preservation or development. But on this evening, the city, bejeweled with light, looked magical.

I don't recall where we stayed once we got to town, or what we did that evening. I imagine we ate dinner in a café or diner, then took a walk along the strip. We might have stopped for a drink, Sybil perhaps ordering a glass of Lancers wine and me a bottle of beer—Stroh's, Detroit's own, if they had it. She and I might have talked about how the car was riding low and bumpy, on rear shock absorbers that were shot after the long journey. We expected an uncomfortable ride the rest of the way.

Thinking about it now, Did we even have auto insurance?

In the morning we started down Route 15, which we took all the way into San Bernardino. We stopped in Victorville to check out the high desert town, set at an elevation of three thousand feet. Victorville, with its ten thousand permanent residents, was home to George AFB, where I would work. The mission at the base was to train F-4 fighter pilots; the dry desert air and the site's isolation from substantial population centers made it perfect for that task. The 479th Tactical Fighter Wing trained not only American pilots at the time but also some Iranians who were learning to fly the jets for America's ally, the shah. My job was to help feed the pilots and the support personnel—about five hundred people altogether.

After a brief look at Victorville and George AFB, we headed for the Cajon Pass. We took it through the San Gabriel Mountains and drove down to San Bernardino, the biggest city close to the base.

A THOUSAND EGGS: COOKING FOR THE AIR FORCE

We found a second-floor, one-bedroom apartment at 2927 Harrington, on the far eastern side of San Bernardino, near the foothills of the mountains. The buildings of the complex were two stories high, arranged in a rectangle around a courtyard that featured a swimming pool. Our home was next to Interstate 15, which would take me the forty miles back up through Cajon Pass to the air base.

Our first task was to furnish our apartment, and do it cheaply; luxury was definitely not in order. We purchased mostly used furniture: for the bedroom, a bed, a dresser, two end tables, and a couple of lamps; for the kitchen, a small table and two chairs; for the living room, an old sofa. We'd brought a TV with us from East Detroit but nothing to put it on. So we bought some red bricks and four pine boards that we stained red; with these materials we built a bookcase. The television found a home on the top shelf. Once Sybil got her teaching job, we could afford to join the Book-of-the-Month Club. With that membership, plus some old paperbacks and textbooks we picked up, we began to fill the shelves.

We put the radio in the kitchen so we could listen to music as we did the nightly dishes. To decorate the walls we depended on the San Bernardino public library. The library allowed card holders to borrow, for one month, framed reproductions of great paintings. We usually checked out French impressionists, so the work of Monet, Degas, and Cezanne, as well as the post-impressionist Van Gogh hung from our walls. Later, when our financial situation improved, we went over to Highland Avenue and bought a basic stereo unit at a discount retailer called Two Guys.

All these were simple, inexpensive joys. But they were *our* joys.

We lived simply in our food and drink, too. We drank inexpensive Portuguese wine—either Mateus or Lancers—that came in distinctive bottles suitable for use as vases or candle holders once the wine had been consumed. We were so inexperienced that we were oblivious to all the great low-cost California wines that filled the shelves across from the bottles of Mateus. But we were also supporting the California migrant workers' strike and grape boycott led by the legendary labor leader Cesar Chavez.

When we wanted fresh oranges the size of softballs, we drove a short distance to a Catholic convent located on Redlands Boulevard between the cities of San Bernardino and Redlands. Payment for the fruit was strictly on the honor system: The nuns set large, brown paper grocery bags filled with oranges on the front porch of the convent with a sign instructing buyers to leave their money in a small wicker basket placed near the bags. San Bernardino was surrounded by huge orange groves. The aroma was heavenly. And so were the oranges.

Sybil shopped at the commissary at Norton AFB, in San Bernardino, where prices were low. We'd buy six frozen slabs of beef liver for less than two dollars. Sybil did most of the cooking—not only were we traditional in that way but I also had enough of food and stoves and ovens during my fourteen-hour days at the mess hall. She knew her way around a kitchen, producing lasagna that was out of this world. If we ate out, it was usually on Friday night, when a nearby eatery had a special: six tacos for seventy-five cents. Let me be clear: That's seventy-five cents for all six! The first McDonald's was located near our apartment, on E Street, so sometimes we'd forgo the tacos and eat at McDonald's instead. Hamburgers were fifteen cents apiece.

Liver, McDonald's, tacos—what I didn't know about nutrition could fill a book.

In California, as in Michigan, teachers were in demand. With her experience in East Detroit, Sybil was able to land a job, starting midyear, at Muscoy Elementary School. Muscoy, a semirural community located a quick five-minute drive across I-15 from San Bernardino, was populated by working-class and poorer families, many of them Hispanic. One thing that sticks in my mind about Muscoy was the presence of unleashed dogs—some apparently with a home, some feral—that ran around the neighborhood near the school. Every day, one German shepherd would hide behind a tree, then dart out to chase our car as we drove to and from the school. We were always afraid we'd run over the nasty, snarling canine as it ran alongside our front wheels, out of our vision.

The school itself was so basic that it didn't have a real school building—just a series of cheap, freestanding prefab classrooms; you had to go outside to walk from one room to another. The school grounds contained neither a gymnasium nor a cafeteria. In good weather the kids ate their lunch outside; if it rained, they ate in their classrooms. Both locations were accessible to roaming dogs. Sybil recalls a large one wandering into her third-grade classroom and making itself at home on the cool floor in the back. The poor mutt was just trying to get out of the heat.

Sybil was pleased to work with dedicated teachers, to instruct a diverse student body, and to team with those parents who showed an interest in their children's education. Still relatively new to teaching at the time, she now recalls two major lessons she learned at Muscoy. First, you cannot outshout a class of third graders. Eventually, she figured out that when she stood silently at the front of the class for a few moments, the kids would start to catch on to the fact that she wanted their attention. And when she spoke quietly, the kids had to listen more attentively than they did when she spoke loudly.

The second lesson was that not all teaching had to be about cursive writing and multiplication. Upon hearing that some of the pupils were teasing a boy who had come to school wearing his sister's coat, Sybil stopped drawing on the chalkboard and started to talk about how it feels to be cold, how teasing hurts, and how to be a better friend. Some weeks later she decided that at least some part of her homily had gotten through to the kids when a boy came up to her and said, "My friend doesn't have shoes to wear to school, so I let him use mine."

After the summer break, Sybil was back at Muscoy Elementary teaching a new class of third graders. We had decided over the summer that the time had come to start our family, and in the fall she became pregnant. We were elated. Although suffering from morning sickness, Sybil kept teaching. But then she stopped—not because she was physically unable to keep working but because Muscoy had a rule prohibiting pregnant women from teaching past their fourth month.

Fortunately, times have changed.

On October 6, soon after we arrived in California, I reported to the base to begin my career as a cook. My friend Airman Tom Drum and I, on the same path from Lackland to Lee to George, were assigned to the same shift in the mess hall. Tom and his wife, Trisha, lived five minutes away from us in San Bernardino, so Tom and I would take turns driving to work. The forty-mile trip through the pass took us an hour in good weather, so to arrive at our starting time of 4:30 a.m., we needed to leave at 3:30. Leaving after our shift ended at 7:00 p.m., we arrived home no earlier than 8:00. If we'd just finished the first day on, in our two-day-on, two-day-off routine, we had just a few hours to rest before rising the next morning at 3:00 to do it all over again.

When we arrived in the chow hall at 4:30 a.m., the bakers were just finishing up baking the night away, leaving the sickly sweet smell of pies, cakes, brownies, and doughnuts pervading the mess hall and kitchen. As low men on the totem pole, Tom and I got all the worst jobs: mopping the floors, scrubbing pots and pans, cleaning the vats and deep-fat fryers, and whatever other KP was needed. Since we were both older than most of the other airmen and had college degrees, the tech and master sergeants who ran the mess—air force lifers—were resentful of us. As a consequence, they cut us no slack, making sure to keep us in our place. Whenever a top-ranking officer was scheduled to visit the mess hall, all hell would come down on us in anticipation of his visit. "Clean this," the sergeants would bark. "Clean that." "Scrub over here." "Make this shine." I often ended up spending an hour or more cleaning the grill with a grill block, a brick-shaped block of stone you rubbed on the grill's surface. I worked it back and forth until the grill gleamed.

Under normal, more sane circumstances in the kitchen, my first job in the morning was to walk into the large cooler, take out a thousand eggs, and crack them into cereal bowls, ten to a bowl. The first order of business was to determine if any of the eggs were bad with blood; if so, all ten in the tainted bowl would be discarded. The eggs that passed inspection would then be taken to the line for "breakfast to order." When the troops came in, starting around 5:30 a.m., they could order virtually anything they wanted. They could have eggs cooked any way they liked them, with a choice of four meats: ham, bacon, sausage, or hash. The bacon was Tom's department—while I'd be cracking eggs, Tom would be pulling large rashers of bacon out of the oven. We also served sausage in white gravy poured over freshly baked biscuits—SOS, as it was known, for "shit on a shingle"; it was my personal favorite, although probably the least healthy of our breakfast selections. Potatoes, grits, oatmeal, and cold cereals were standard fare, as well as pancakes and French toast. We were constantly replenishing the chow line's supply of doughnuts, bread, and regular toast, as well as its assortment of hot and cold drinks. Outside of the navy, the air force was reputed to serve the best food in the military. Perhaps the coast guard would dispute that assessment, but there could be no disputing the likelihood of gaining weight if one did not control oneself in the George AFB mess hall.

The floors of the hall were covered with hard, unforgiving tile, making my legs ache after fourteen hours on my feet. Finished with our shift, Tom and I would pile into our car and head for the pass. The high desert at dawn and at dusk was spectacular. In winter, the mountains would be snowcapped, and the reds and golden yellows of the sinking or rising sun over the desert would cast a magnificent hue that ran along the horizon as far as the eye could see. No matter how tired I was, I never failed to be awed by the grandeur of the opening and closing of the day. I was humbled by my lowly position in the world of cooks; I was even more humbled by this extraordinary display of nature.

Our ride up or down Cajon Pass seemed like a crap shoot, a roll of the dice as to whether we'd come out alive, for the weather was unpredictable and dangerous. As high as four thousand feet above sea level, the road was susceptible to wind, fog, and sometimes snow as it snaked around hills. The fog was the worst—there were a number of trips when we had to turn back or pull off the road, in both cases hoping no one would crash into us. It was terrifying; we could not see ten feet in front of us. At other times the Santa Ana winds would come roaring off the desert and through the pass, buffeting the car left and right. When the winds got to gale force, sixty to eighty miles per hour, the California Highway Patrol would close the road and we'd have to get to a phone to notify the mess hall of the problem. "I remember the dreaded winds along the Cajon Pass," says Sybil. "Sometimes the troopers would order the semitrailer trucks off the road to Victorville. Otherwise, the large flat sides of the trailers would act as sails, and the wind would blow them right off their wheels." How we ever survived those three-plus years on that road I will never know. We were lucky, certainly. But as treacherous as the ride was, it was nothing like being on patrol in a rice paddy or in a firefight on Hamburger Hill.

Tom and I kept reminding ourselves how fortunate we were.

SNOWY MOUNTAINS, SANDY BEACHES:
TOURING THE GOLDEN STATE

People around the world would give just about anything for a chance to see California—and we were living there. We made it a point to experience the best of that beautiful and bountiful state whenever we could get away, but to properly explore California required both a little time and a little money. To fulfill those preconditions, I needed to get out of the mess hall, where I'd been working an exhausting schedule for a year and a half. After looking around the base for a different assignment, I decided to switch to education counseling. I had a college degree, and that background seemed likely to appeal to whoever made the personnel assignments. The education office on base was in an old barracks. I talked to the three sergeants who worked there and found out that two of them were close to the end of their air force service. Tom applied to transfer out of cooking the same time I did, and we were both successful: I got the education office, and Tom got what he wanted—the finance office. We both changed to regular work hours: nine to five, Monday through Friday.

This change took place around January of 1970, when Sybil was leaving her teaching job in Muscoy and getting ready to have our baby. We would lose her solid salary, the kids would lose an exceptional teacher. But I was moving up, in both rank and pay. Now that I was a sergeant, my monthly check shot up to almost three hundred dollars; add in my lodging allowance and subsistence pay, and I was pulling down around five hundred dollars a month. This number was close to what Sybil had been making as a teacher.

With my new work schedule, my weekends were free, and so, with my bulging wallet in my pocket, we spent our Saturdays and Sundays touring the Golden State. We could take longer trips, too, because I now got thirty vacation days a year.

For a short getaway we might travel about fifteen miles north, into the San Bernardino Mountains and Forest, to visit the mountain communities of Crestline, Lake Arrowhead, and Big Bear Lake. Driving from San Bernardino up to Crestline took a good forty-five minutes of negotiating one switchback after another on a two-lane road. Once up near Crestline, we would look down on a thick layer of smog, present day in and day out, covering San Bernardino and the valley below like a blanket. It was a real eye-opener to see the filthy air we were breathing daily. But the air was clear and crisp in these small mountain hamlets built among the tall pines and mountain lakes. Swiss chalets and log cabins formed the majority of the structures in the villages, as well as at the nearby roadsides and lakesides. The snow at Big Bear Lake, at about seven thousand feet, remained on the ground into the spring. That snow and the tall pines made me homesick for northern Michigan.

We also loved the beach. A favorite spot was Laguna Beach, an hour's drive from San Bernardino by way of Riverside. Laguna had a small but growing art community, as well as a bunch of quaint, funky bars and restaurants right on the beach. Walking the beach usually entailed hopping over enormous strands of ocean kelp, with their attached horns—parts of the kelp that looked like you could actually blow into to produce a sound—that would wash up on the beach and give off a briny scent. Unlike many Southern California beach communities, Laguna was small and isolated; its remoteness allowed us to feel that it was "our place." I liked that.

Another notable beach visit occurred soon after we had purchased a new car. Before describing the trip, however, a personal confession is in order from this Detroiter. All the cars I have owned over my life have been union made. So far, so good. *However*, two of them were manufactured in Europe. One was the Austin American, made in England (despite its name), which we bought in 1970. (The other was a Volkswagen camper with a pop-up roof.) A compact, economical four-seater, the American was designed to compete with the popular Volkswagen Beetle. It proved to be an uninspired choice: With its puny engine, it was hardly suited to the often demanding California terrain.

On this particular weekend we decided to go camping on the beach at Point Mugu State Park, near the town of Ventura. At no cost to us, I checked out from the base a variety of equipment—tent, sleeping bags, cooking gear, and some other odds and ends—and stuffed it into our little car. We left after work on Friday and arrived, following a two-hour drive, in the early evening. For the most part we enjoyed our weekend on the beach, swimming, walking, reading, and generally relaxing. However, I had not counted on how loud the ocean sounded when you slept right next to it—it was soothing and threatening at the same time. The upshot was that the ocean kept me up at night. Sybil recalls other nocturnal problems: "We had to pitch a tent in the dark, with no instructions, apparently unaware that the support poles went *outside* the canvas. At some point, therefore, our shelter partially collapsed. Also, a dog barked all night. It was no wonder we didn't get any sleep. Still, we did find the whole scene humorous." On Sunday, exhausted but happy, we packed up and headed for home. The ride was fine—until we came to a steep pass. Slowly we chugged up the hill, with all the pluck and determination of The Little Engine That Could. But before we got to the top, a rod went right through the engine block of our new car. That's what I got for not buying American. I don't recall how we traveled home, but that hill ruined not only our car but our weekend, as well.

With my vacation time and our new car—a used Dodge Dart with a Slant Six engine—we took a week's trip up the coast to San Francisco. The scenery was gorgeous. We saw Big Sur and toured Steinbeck country: Carmel, Monterey, Salinas. We motored along 17-Mile Drive, with its magnificent views and ubiquitous deer that made the road and people's front lawns their home. When we got to San Francisco, we were drawn, like many young people, to the Haight-Ashbury district to see the hippie scene and the drug culture; unfortunately, the area attracted a sizeable homeless community, which included many teen runaways. But we were excited to play tourist as we saw the more positive sights of San Francisco, like the Golden Gate Bridge, the streetcars, and Chinatown. We visited hilly neighborhoods and huffed and puffed as we walked up and down the inclines.

On more than one occasion we drove down to San Diego, traveling through Redlands, Palm Springs, Indio, and the Coachella Valley to see Doug's Astros play the San Diego Padres. The Red Rooster always left us good seats. While we were in town we would visit the world-famous zoo and then the beach at La Jolla. On the way down or back we would stop in Indio to buy dates. I grew up eating date-filled oatmeal cookies and still have a passion for dates.

As Sybil's due date got closer, we moved to a two-bedroom apartment on the first floor of our building. Our new home was about fifteen feet from the apartment of our landlady, Mrs. H. While Sybil was at home waiting to give birth, she noticed that when African Americans would come to rent an apartment, Mrs. H. would not answer her door. Seeing this persistent pattern, Sybil finally called the air force office that dealt with equal housing opportunities and discrimination. An investigation ensued, and the authorities put an end to the landlady's odious practice. Soon our complex was integrated. Sybil was a real heroine.

Among the friends we made at the apartment complex was a sweet couple, Ann and John Reed. Sybil found Ann easy to confide in. John liked to come over to our place to play me in an Asian strategic board game called Go; I was not much competition for him, but we enjoyed each other's company. Once he and I rented an air force recreational cabin (at maybe five dollars a night) close to the mountains outside Bishop, California. Bishop sits at an altitude of more than four thousand feet, but nearby White Mountain Peak and Mount Humphreys both rise much higher, to more than 14,000 and 12,500 feet, respectively. We spent three days there, just the two of us, drinking a few beers, playing Go, and soaking in the wonders of mountain stream fishing. The stream was fast, bordered by steep banks lined with an assortment of pine trees. I still have that picture in my mind. The scene was gorgeous, and the roaring sound of water mentally transported me to a state of relaxation. Years later, when I wanted to leave the stress of my work, I would think of this peaceful memory.

Playing Airplane:
Julie Arrives

As Sybil's pregnancy progressed, we began to get the baby's room ready. Because we didn't know the sex of the child—prenatal identification of a baby's gender hadn't yet become routine—we couldn't decorate completely, but we bought the essentials, including a crib. The BX (for "base exchange," the retail military store) sold such items at cost. Sybil and I constructed shelves in Julie's room. I borrowed a drill from John Reed, reamed out some holes, bolted a couple of ladders perpendicular to the wall a few feet apart, and attached boards to the steps. We got an old rocking chair and a small dresser from the secondhand store. We slapped red, white, and blue paint on everything. "We made quite a nice little room for our baby," Sybil recalls.

With the date approaching, we considered names. If the baby was a girl, she would be called Natalie or Julie. If a boy—well, I can't remember what names we liked.

Sybil was to have the baby at Loma Linda Hospital, a Seventh-day Adventist facility not far from San Bernardino. Because the health facility at George AFB had no obstetricians on its payroll, we had to find a local doctor to handle the prenatal care and delivery. (The air force covered the cost.) Sybil found Dr. Herbert Henken, who was associated with Loma Linda Hospital, which happened to be a teaching facility. We did not know it at the time, but he was a preeminent authority on delivering breech babies. His expertise came in handy when he discovered our baby to be in the breech position. He tried to "turn" our baby, but without success. Nevertheless, Julie was luckily delivered, in a room full of medical students, by a doctor who was teaching a dying art. In the years since, virtually all babies in the breech position have come to be delivered by C-section.

On May 18, 1970, Julie Marie Bonior was born, weighing six pounds, five ounces, and measuring 19¾ inches. While Sybil was doing the hard work, I paced the floor in the waiting room. I felt relieved when I was told that mother and child were fine. Sybil liked Loma Linda, a vegetarian facility that emphasized healthy, natural living, and she liked her doctor. Mother and daughter stayed at the hospital for four or five days after the birth—the norm back then, but not now. And then they came home.

Julie was wonderful to have but a handful to make comfortable—she was colicky those first three months, with much crying and screaming. We rocked and burped her constantly. Eventually, we figured out that white noise sometimes calmed her, so we would run the vacuum cleaner to get her to sleep. But it was mostly Sybil's loving touches and cuddles, and her soothing lullabies and voice, that calmed our daughter.

Once Julie started eating solid food, I enjoyed feeding her baby rice and other pureed delights out of a Gerber's jar. We might play "airplane" with a spoonful. Or I might sing out, "Over the teeth and through the gums, look out, stomach, here it comes!" When she'd eaten enough, I would gently try to wipe away the carrot mash all over her face and bib; she'd move her head side to side and up and down to avoid my hand and the towel. Not long after feeding, one of us, most often Sybil, would change Julie's cloth diaper. We kept our home well supplied with Vaseline and baby powder to soothe Julie's soft baby skin. At some point we joined the modern era and switched to paper diapers.

We looked forward to each new skill our daughter learned. In those first weeks we marveled at how she reacted to light, and then at her intense focus on our faces. Her first smiles and laughs made up for all her stomach discomfort, even though that upset sometimes would last through the night. Back then it was customary for a child to have a playpen; that's where she spent a lot of time when not in our arms or in the stroller for a walk. When she learned to roll over—all by herself!—our excitement was so great you would have thought she had just graduated from Yale. She learned to crawl. She learned to lift herself up holding onto the side of her crib and playpen. I think her first word was *duck*.

"Julie was a cautious, late walker," says Sybil. "She always preferred toddling around, grasping someone's hand or finger for support." Some of Julie's first steps occurred on the lawn in front of our apartment. We have pictures and memories of her early walking, clasping both out-stretched hands together in front of her, as if pointing at something, and then waddling forward, step by slow step. After that adventure, she would plop onto her seat on the soft grass, her face full of pleasure at her achievement.

When Julie was only a couple of months old, we would take her into our courtyard swimming pool and let her swim. Really! We read somewhere that if you put infants underwater, they naturally hold their

Julie, me, and a bag of oranges from the convent,
San Bernardino, February 1971

breath. So with great trepidation, when Julie was maybe six or eight weeks old, we took her to the pool. Sybil and I stood about one foot from each other, submerged Julie, and pushed her back and forth. Then we pulled her out of the water to see if she was okay—she was! We repeated the exercise, and each time she was fine. Little by little, in subsequent visits to the pool, we increased the distance to three or four feet. Because of this early exposure to water, Julie got comfortable in the pool and grew up to be a fine swimmer. Let me caution, however, that today this practice is not recommended for babies under six months old.

Soon it was time for Julie's first Christmas. "We were so poor," recalls Sybil, "that we had a five-dollar limit on gifts for ourselves. But with the help of family and friends, Julie did better. One night, just after we'd finished decorating the tree, we turned off all the lights, carried Julie into the room, and suddenly lit up the tree. I couldn't take my eyes off her face. It was full of pure wonder and joy, wrapped up for an exquisite moment."

In 1970 and 1971, a number of earthquakes hit Southern California. San Bernardino sits right on the San Andreas Fault. Whenever we felt tremors, Sybil and I would run into Julie's room, just a few steps from ours, snatch her from her crib, and hold her tight as the building shook. During one quake, I grabbed Julie and ran to stand beneath the front doorjamb, supposedly a relatively safe place to be. As I held her, I watched the water in our pool sloshing back and forth, with some of it spilling over the sides. This might have been the Sylmar earthquake, which hit 6.5 on the Richter scale.

Cindy and Mike Reusswig, from Newton, Iowa, were our neighbors a few doors away. Mike, an air traffic controller, was also stationed at George AFB. They were a great couple with a daughter, Amy, about Julie's age. We often tried to get these toddlers to play together, but "together" is not a concept easily grasped by one-year-olds.

Evie and my father, both thrilled to be first-time grandparents, visited after Julie's birth. Although many miles separated them from their new granddaughter, they had hopes that the distance would soon lessen.

Sybil and I considered making California our home once I got out of the air force, but the tug of family and opportunities back east was too strong. As stunning as California scenery was to look at, we were appalled by the dirty air in and around Los Angeles. Breathing in the pollution was a problem for me, affecting my lungs and eyes. The two of us agreed that Southern California was not a healthy place to live.

The day of Julie's birth was one of the happiest days of my life. Of course, my role in her birth was nothing compared to the role her mother played, but it was wondrous to know that I had played a part in creating this beautiful infant. I felt a completeness in fulfilling my biological imperative to procreate. I'd had no prior hint—no thought or emotion or inclination—that I would feel this way upon becoming a father. But I did. And now it was time for the real work: loving and protecting Julie, giving her the best possible chance to grow up healthy, providing her with opportunities that would offer a path to a good life.

When Julie was just a couple of months old, we took her to Los Angeles to see the Astros play the Dodgers. She slept through most of her first baseball game despite all the cheering that surrounded her. Her uncharacteristic calm made me think about finding a recording of cheering crowds to help soothe her during those nights when she would not go to sleep. However, I never got such a record, so we stuck with the vacuum cleaner.

Starting at second base for the Dodgers was Ted Sizemore. I'd played high school basketball against Sizemore in Detroit, where he'd starred for Pershing High School along with future basketball Hall of Famer Mel Daniels. We'd practiced against Pershing often during the season, and I'd always ended up guarding Sizemore, who was about my size. So it was a multiple thrill for me to take Julie to her first game, where I saw on the field both Doug and a guy I'd spent hours competing against in high school.

A Second Chance:
A New Job and Grad School

I knew back at Iowa that my mediocre grades would block me from admission to graduate school. Nor did my standardized test scores help: In my senior year, I took the Law School Admission Test (LSAT) and the foreign service exam and did poorly on both. Subpar grades and test scores were giant obstacles for me, because I knew how important a master's or law degree would be in my pursuit of public office.

What was I to do?

In the fall of 1967, three months after my graduation from Iowa, I enrolled in two night classes at the University of Detroit. The idea was to begin to establish a better academic record. One course, in English literature, centered on the writings of Dr. Samuel Johnson and his biographer, James Boswell. The reading left me infatuated with Johnson's and Boswell's grand tour of Europe; I would act on that passion four years later by taking my family on a European tour during my last year in the air force.

I was even happier with the second course, a film appreciation survey that featured eight classic films, including Ingmar Bergman's *The Seventh Seal*, Akira Kurosawa's *Rashomon*, Orson Welles's *Citizen Kane*, Federico Fellini's *La Strada*, and Elia Kazan's *On the Waterfront*. We were required to write reviews of three of the eight, plus an additional film of the student's choosing. I selected a recent release, *The Graduate*, by Mike Nichols. Little did I know back then that this stylish examination of a generation's angst would, with the passage of time, be considered a classic on the level of those other great films. I did well in these two classes. I was building confidence in my ability to climb the academic ladder.

But once I got to California, my onerous cooking schedule made it impossible to continue my classroom education. By this time I was becoming more and more interested in history, and in pursuing a master's in the subject. To accommodate my schedule and feed my interest,

I enrolled in two correspondence courses in US history given by the University of South Carolina. Taking the two courses entailed hours of laborious work, including weekly typing—at the snail's pace my rudimentary keyboard proficiency permitted—of answers to questions that were meant to test not only my reading comprehension but also my analytical skills.

The grueling work convinced me that a different tack was in order. So here was another reason to get out of the chow hall and into a regular schedule: I wanted to continue my education in a real classroom setting.

Before I could pursue a master's in history I needed to find a school and a program that would work with me. As an education counselor, I was familiar with all the programs at George AFB and at the colleges and universities nearby. Chapman College, in Orange, California, offered a number of classes right on the base, so I decided to investigate. Visiting the main campus, an hour's drive from our apartment in San Bernardino, I found that the school maintained a graduate program in history. It was on this campus, in early 1970, that I met a man who would play an important role in my life.

Bob Ramsay, the dean of the liberal arts school, was a retired navy admiral in his seventies. Having arranged an appointment in advance, I walked into his office to introduce myself and found a portly man with snow white hair, a white mustache that sloped down his face, and an easy, patient way about him that made him seem grandfatherly. After noting his venerable image, I introduced myself as Sergeant David Bonior, United States Air Force. After some small talk, I laid out my marginal academic record and asked for his advice on what it would take for me to gain admission to the history program.

He asked some basic questions, probably to gauge how hungry I was to get into the program. He was not a big talker, but what he did say made it clear that he was thoughtful and engaged in our conversation. The upshot of the meeting was that, to my delight, he was willing to work with me.

The plan we worked out was that I would take the Graduate Record Exam, in effect an SAT for admission to graduate programs in the humanities, and enroll in four courses, each one counting three hours toward a degree. The courses would center on nineteenth- and twentieth-century European history, with a particular focus on Russia and Germany. Once I had completed the four courses, Dean Ramsay would evaluate whether I should be admitted to the program itself.

I was elated. He was providing no guarantee, but the door was open. He was giving me a second chance at academic success.

I became absorbed in my studies. The topics were fascinating, the classes small—seven or eight students—and the four professors excellent, especially Kurt Bergel and Robert Gueswel.

I took two courses per semester, driving to campus after work at the base, usually on Tuesdays and Thursdays, when my classes met from 7:00 to 9:45 p.m. The three-destination round trip on school days— home to base, base to campus, campus to home—added up to 160 miles. I would drive those miles for two years, in the spring, summer, and fall terms of 1970–71.

My marks in the first four courses reflected my newfound dedication to the life of the mind: three As and a B (if I remember correctly). The GRE did not go as well, yielding a score below what I needed for admission. But Dean Ramsay didn't give up, suggesting that I take it again but prepare for it this time. The idea of studying for this type of exam had never occurred to me. I went to a bookstore and purchased a thick volume designed for that purpose. It contained questions, answers, and exercises to improve my skills in math and reading comprehension. I studied this book religiously for four months, and on my second try my GRE score zoomed up 150 points, enough for admission to the program once I completed another four courses. I was on a roll: In my second batch of courses, I earned grades similar to those from the first go-round.

Dean Ramsay looked at the twenty-four hours of course work I had completed, as well as my improved GRE score, and admitted me into the program. He also credited eighteen of the twenty-four hours toward my degree. To get my master's in history would require a total of thirty hours' worth of course work, plus a thesis and an oral exam. So I needed only four more courses, at three hours each, to finish the classroom component. I was elated to get the news that I was on track to graduate. Like Jerry Burns, Dean Ramsay was a pivotal person in my life. He gave me a break—a big break—when I needed one.

Back at George AFB my job as a counselor was to educate and advise military personnel on their educational opportunities. I shared my responsibilities with Sergeant Merle Patterson, from Emporia, Kansas. Rock-solid folks from the plains, Merle and his wife, Susie, became friends with Sybil and me. Merle kept preaching to me about this up-and-coming political figure in Kansas, a guy named Bob Dole. Merle thought he would be president someday. While Senator Dole did not quite make it to the White House, he got pretty far and served his country well. His self-deprecating sense of humor helped his career and made him a likeable fellow. And Bob Dole knew how to cut a deal.

Merle and I worked with people of nearly all ranks, from airmen to colonels, offering information and guidance on goals that ranged from acquiring a GED—the equivalent of a high school diploma—to attending law school, and everything in between. We also discussed career education programs in the military, such as the War College in Washington, D.C.

Merle and I worked well together advising our young clients on how to pursue a college degree. After all, one of the main advantages of military service was that Uncle Sam would pick up the cost of your education, giving you a golden opportunity to advance yourself. Two of the most active programs on our military bases were those run by the University of Maryland and by Chapman College. Maryland's programs were world renowned, since they were offered on almost every American military base, both in the US and around the world. Chapman's reach was not as extensive, but its programs were prominent on military

Sergeant Bonior, education counselor, 1970

installations in California. What really put Chapman on the map in higher education, however, was its innovative and popular Semester at Sea. Students would take classes on board a ship as it traveled the world.

Another important part of our work was advising people who hadn't finished high school about how to improve their reading skills and earn their GEDs. Previously, the air force and navy had generally required a high school diploma for enlistment. But during the Vietnam War, with a pressing need for more and more manpower, the Department of Defense changed the rules. Under the new program, called Project 100,000 for the number of service members to be added, the air force and navy accepted recruits without a high school diploma or its equivalent and with substandard academic skills.

There were often gaps in my workday, allowing me to crack a book and read, study, or write. I was fortunate that I could get much of my studying and homework done during working hours. With a wife and baby at home, and with so many hours spent in the car, I needed every advantage I could find to get my work done.

My course work included the requisite number of hours in American history, but Russia and Germany were the focus of most of my classes. The idea of the German national character was a theme that constantly seemed to surface as I studied Europe during the nineteenth and twentieth centuries. My master's thesis centered on the complicity of German industrialists with Hitler and the Nazis. Krupp and I. G. Farben were my case studies. Krupp used slave labor in its factories, producing armaments for the Nazi war machine. Farben produced Zyklon B, the pesticide used to kill Jews en masse in the gas chambers at Auschwitz. I was overwhelmed by the enormity of the Germans' crimes against humanity. Hitler and his thugs were the epitome of evil; I wanted to understand who was complicit with them.

When I finished my two summer courses in July 1971, all that remained for me to graduate were two courses plus my thesis and oral exam. So I decided that before the fall semester began, I would act on that notion of a Dr. Johnson-style European Grand Tour that had entered my mind four years earlier. Sybil and I had been talking about it for a long time. I had accumulated thirty days of leave, and we had saved enough money. The armed forces of the United States would subsidize the journey by allowing us to fly at the low military rate and to sleep in American military installations in Germany. I know I was asking a lot of Sybil to take this trip with a fourteen-month-old child, but the odds were that Sybil and I might never find that much simultaneous time off to travel for as long as we did at such a bargain price. I saw a once-in-a-lifetime chance to see the world.

With reasoned concern and well-founded trepidation, my wife agreed to go.

THE BELLE OF BRUSSELS:
OUR GRAND TOUR OF EUROPE

Looking back, I wish I'd understood how stressful it would be to take such a young child on a monthlong trip to Europe. We had no help on this adventure: no family, no nanny, and almost no money. What I had was a belief that it would all work out. Sometimes I get an idea in my head, then fall in love with it. Then I massage the idea and tweak it so that I can preserve the core of the original concept while rendering the plan practical enough to work. Regrettably, however, I sometimes ignore common sense, neglecting the need to pull back on the brainstorm, especially if the idea is "big."

Well, for us this idea was "big": It represented perhaps our only chance—ever—to see Europe. My belief in the feasibility of the plan came in part from *Europe on Five Dollars a Day*, a popular book first published in 1957 by Arthur Frommer, who had come up with the idea of inexpensive travel in Europe when he was a US army corporal serving in Germany. By 1971, his plan for seeing Europe cheaply had under-gone years of refinement. I was one of many who bought the book and dived into the excitement of making a dream come true.

Frommer's guidebook wasn't the only travel innovation that would make our trip easier and more fun. Around this time, a backpack baby carrier was introduced to American consumers. We purchased one, and when we got to Europe, we noticed the effect produced by this equip-ment—still a novelty east of the Atlantic—and its passenger. Passersby were all smiles seeing the adorable toddler, with her shocks of blond hair and gorgeous hazel eyes, riding around on our backs. Julie was a big hit and so were we, happy to accept the delight of perfect strangers. The owners of bakery shops would give her treats. Even leathery-faced Alpine mountain climbers used to toting tents and pickaxes—not babies—on their backs couldn't help but wave and smile. These positive interactions helped sustain us through the more challenging moments in our trip.

We began our journey by flying to New York, where we changed planes for our flight to Frankfurt, Germany. During this transcontinental, trans-Atlantic marathon—thirteen hours in the air, plus another four hours taken up by ground transportation and waiting in airports—we took turns trying to occupy the attention of our daughter. For much of the flight time I stood in the rear of the plane bouncing up and down and swaying left and right, trying to create a rhythm for the little girl strapped into the contraption on my back.

We were relieved when we arrived.

Julie and my glasses

At the airport in Frankfurt we rented a station wagon, then traveled the twenty miles to our practically free lodging at a military facility in Wiesbaden. With all three of us exhausted, and Julie, especially, off her normal schedule, we spent a couple of days resting, allowing our bodies to become adjusted to the time change, before we ventured out to Frankfurt. I regret that the only memory I have of that city is taking the streetcar, which reminded us of our visit to San Francisco.

Our next destination was Amsterdam, a five-hour drive away. We broke up the trip by stopping in Cologne, where we visited the great cathedral that is now a UNESCO World Heritage site. Work started on the cathedral in 1248, was stopped in 1473, then resumed again in the nineteenth century until the structure was completed in 1880. Massive and grand, it commands the landscape in its location just off the Rhine River. A monument to German Catholicism, the cathedral is today one of Germany's most visited landmarks, hosting over six million people per year.

I remember that we stopped in a large department store near the cathedral to buy something essential, but I don't remember what the product was. Diapers? A blanket for our ill-fated night of camping later in Belgium? Whatever it was, I can safely say that with our meager finances, we did not purchase caviar, diamonds, or any other luxury item.

From Cologne we continued up along the Rhine toward the Dutch capital. Our ideas about Amsterdam—canals, dikes, windmills, little Dutch boys like the mascot for Dutch Boy paint, Anne Frank's house, tulips, Van Gogh, and nightlife (not that we were in any condition to participate in it)—filled us with anticipation. We stayed in a small blue cottage just outside the city, with waterfowl on the adjacent canal. Is this where Julie fell in love with the word *duck*? I know that we left that pastoral, peaceful setting to tour the city. Did we visit Anne Frank's house or any museums? Again, I don't remember.

After two or three days we were off to Brussels, Belgium, a short 125 miles away via Antwerp. I did not know in the summer of 1971 that Antwerp was the port at which my grandfather John Gavreluk boarded the SS *Lapland* in 1912 bound for the United States and Canada. Had I been aware of that crucial event in our family history, I would have prevailed upon Sybil to visit his point of embarkation.

Brussels was a pleasant surprise to me, looking and feeling like what I'd imagined an old European city might be. I remember round domed buildings and broad boulevards lined with stately plane and beech trees. By some wonderful chance I had booked a room in a charming hotel in the center of town. Thank you, Arthur Frommer! For now, at least, we were living the high life: no hostel, no fleabag hotel, no camping. And our daughter was the belle of Brussels. Everywhere we visited—patisseries, hotel lobbies, or the sidewalks of Rue Neuve and Avenue Louise—strangers were enchanted with the lovely girl on our backs. She brought out the best in people.

The next city on our itinerary was Paris. However, for some reason, I'd come up with the cockamamie idea of not going directly to the city but first camping overnight in a wooded area, in Belgium near the French border, that had seen heavy fighting in the two world wars. This was one of my big ideas that should have been overruled by common sense, but I pressed forward with the plan. It was a lot to ask my wife and daughter to adjust to a new continent, a time change, and a month in motion. Now, once they were starting to settle into a pattern, I introduced the fun of spending a night in our station wagon in the woods in the middle of nowhere.

In my defense, I was trying to save money. Still, it was a bad idea. If I'd wanted to cut costs, maybe I should have scaled back our accommodations in Brussels. But here we were, in the woods, with no camping equipment other than a twelve-inch collapsible stove and a small can of Sterno for fire. I had bought a few cans of soup and a loaf of French bread for dinner. We folded down the backseat of the station wagon, and after the soup we piled in the back end of the vehicle and tried to sleep on a chilly August night. Mother and daughter were reduced to tears. I don't recall, but I hope I took the blame and apologized.

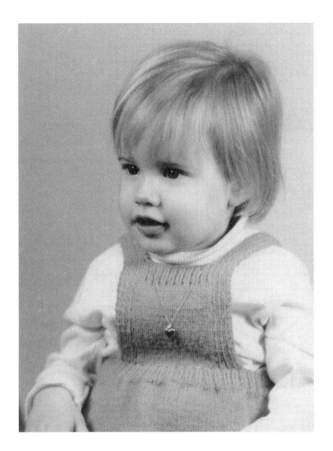

The belle of Brussels

On to the City of Light.

I booked a room at the Hotel St. Vincent DePaul, near the church named for the same saint, a Catholic priest who devoted his life to serving the poor. The designation seemed apt for this inn, a fleabag walk-up near the Gare du Nord railroad station. Our gaudy but threadbare room on the fourth floor featured the most sagging bed I have ever slept in. Lying in it, we felt as though we were at the bottom of the hull of a great ship, with steep sides engulfing us. We were nervous bringing Julie to bed with us, fearing she might get lost belowdecks and suffocate.

Sybil rigged up a separate sleeping area for Julie. We stayed in these digs for three backache-inducing nights.

In the daytime we stretched our spines by walking the streets of Paris for hours on end, seeing all the famous sights: the banks of the Seine, Notre Dame Cathedral, Luxembourg Gardens, the Eiffel Tower. And of course we took breaks in our sightseeing to let Julie run and play in the city's parks. It was wonderful watching not only mother and child play but also Parisians enjoying our small family's interactions.

Driving away after our last night in Paris, we got on the Peripherique, a circular beltway around the city. Right after we exited that road to head south toward Lyon, I was driving at about fifty-five miles per hour when something hit our front windshield, causing a thousand tiny cracks to appear all over it. Sybil immediately commanded me to stop the car before the glass could explode onto us. Barely able to see through all the cracks, I pulled the car over to the far right lane of the freeway, braking as I glided onto the shoulder. Just as I was about to stop, the windshield burst apart, with all the tiny pieces of glass falling into the car, mostly on the dashboard and into our laps. Had I not stopped when I had, the glass would have flown at us at high speed, no doubt seriously injuring all three of us. Sybil's fast thinking and a little luck had saved us from catastrophe.

After Sybil and I breathed a collective sigh of relief, I noticed an emergency phone on the grassy bank just ahead of us. I had taken two years of French in high school; I thought to myself, *This is where it will pay off.* After making sure Sybil and Julie were okay, I walked the fifty yards to the phone and picked up the receiver. Someone at the other end came on the line and asked me a question in French that I did not understand. *Je ne comprends pas* should have been my response, but I froze after the word *Je.* We were at a standstill.

But just then a large tow truck pulled up behind us on the shoulder. As vehicles continued to whiz by us, the truck's driver, a large French mechanic wearing a beret, got out of his cab and assessed the situation. I wasn't about to try to speak French again; fortunately, he understood what we were saying and spoke back to us in broken English that was ever so much better than my frozen French. After he attached our car to his towline, all four of us got into the front seat of his cab. When he learned that I was American and in the military, he reacted coldly, announcing that he was a member of the French Communist Party and then talking about the war in Vietnam. Perhaps he was surprised when we found common ground, agreeing that both the French and the American efforts in Indochina were disastrous. As we continued to converse and he learned more of our politics, he warmed to us. As we wove through the narrow Parisian streets, he assured us that his garage could fix our car.

What a relief!

The good news was that we were rescued. The bad news was that it would take the shop all day to locate and install the proper replacement windshield. Sybil and I took from our car what we would need that day for Julie—toys, clothing, diapers, feeding and drinking utensils—and set off. Luckily it was a beautiful day, making our lives a bit easier as we played with her on the historic paths of the Avenue des Champs-Élysées near the Arc de Triomphe. Our car was ready late in the day. We got in and drove four hours to Lyon.

After a night in Lyon, we drove to Geneva, Switzerland, where we spent two days before crossing the Alps into Italy via the seven-mile Mont Blanc Tunnel. The scenery at four thousand feet was breathtaking, especially the massive, sheer side of Mont Blanc, which rose to fifteen thousand feet. It was August, but it felt like December as we looked at the snow covering parts of the mountain.

Within hours we pulled into Milan. From there we drove through northern Italy and then up and across Austria on our way back to Germany, where we would stop at the Bavarian mountain resort of Garmisch-Partenkirchen. Originally two separate towns, Garmisch and Partenkirchen were joined by Hitler to facilitate hosting the 1936 winter Olympics. In May 1945, the American 10th Army captured Garmisch and established a POW camp there, as well as a resort for American fighting men. My father was in Germany during 1945. I know he spent time in Bavaria; thinking back now, I wonder if he visited this spot for R&R. In the years following the war, the army continued to operate the rest camp, turning it into a popular holiday and vacation spot for US military personnel. The cost to us of staying in this beautiful mountain resort was negligible. It also featured an impressive medical facility that we visited because Julie came down with a low-grade fever. The excellent care she received, and her quick recovery, underscored my faith in the "socialist" medicine offered by the US military.

For the next three days, we unwound in our suite, which included a full kitchen and ample living space. The scenery outside the apartment was spectacular, with lush green pines up the mountainsides and fog that danced in and out. With creature comforts and the comfort of English spoken by all present, this place was the perfect stop before we headed to Munich for our flight home. We took excursions away from the camp; one I have cherished involved taking a train from Garmisch to the upper reaches of the Zugspitze, at ten thousand feet the highest point in Germany. Near the very top of the peak you could pick up a foot trail, above which was strung a cable you could hang onto as you made your way up and around the summit. I took the trail, carefully, without Julie on my back. It was exhilarating and fun.

Thirty days and nights on the road in foreign lands had taxed our patience and stamina, but for the most part the adventure was memorable and exciting. It opened us up to a new and broader world. It brought context to our lives.

But now it was time to return to California and close out our lives there.

DECISIONS:
LIFE AFTER THE AIR FORCE

The country was war weary in the fall of 1971. Peace talks to end the fighting in Southeast Asia continued in Paris, while US troop levels had dropped to a fraction of what they had been just a couple of years earlier. Somehow I had escaped a tour of duty in Vietnam.

The air force had initiated its Early Out program, which allowed personnel to apply for early release from their military obligation if they attended school upon discharge. In my case, I could shave three months off my service, moving my date of discharge from May to February, a change meaningful to me because candidates for statewide office in Michigan needed to file their intentions by the first Friday in May. Without Early Out I might have missed the opportunity to run for the office I had in mind to launch my political career: a seat in the Michigan House of Representatives.

My Chapman degree program finished in February, so I needed another educational destination in order to qualify for Early Out. I applied to a school of auto mechanics located at Gratiot and 7 Mile in Detroit. Fearing that the authorities who would read my Early Out application might wonder why the holder of a master's degree wanted to learn how to fix cars, I rationalized my choice as follows: I was return-ing to Michigan to reclaim my old job as a probation officer for juvenile boys. Many of these boys had mechanical interests. An education in auto mechanics would help me relate to my clients and thus do a better job for them and for the community. With troop levels plummeting in Vietnam, the air force was in such a hurry to shrink its active-duty force that the authorities bought my argument. I sent fifty dollars to the school as a nonrefundable down payment. I had no intention of enrolling once I got back to Michigan and knew I'd have to forfeit the money, but it bought me three months of civilian life and a shot at the legislature. Best fifty bucks I ever spent.

With perfect timing, I graduated with my master's in history in

February of 1972. Over the two years of my studies at Chapman, I had filled up our handmade bookcase: William Manchester's *The Arms of Krupp*, Will and Ariel Durant, Nietzsche, Marx, Mikhail Bakunin. I'd learned a lot from all that reading, and I took immense pride in the new academic record I'd established. Not since my sophomore year at Notre Dame, when I made the honor roll each marking period, had I felt this sense of achievement. Earning my degree had been hard, but I'd learned to find the work enjoyable and to understand how significant a building block it was in my character. I had always felt capable of performing demanding physical endeavors in sports and at jobs, but until now I'd never been quite sure that I was up to the intellectual rigors of academia and, eventually, lawmaking. Chapman and my master's degree changed that for me. A newfound confidence and a strong base of historical knowledge helped me go forward with my career.

Another piece of good timing came when the California State Highway Department surprised us with the news that our apartment building was being "taken" for a road project and we would be forced to move. The State of California would compensate us for the trouble of relocating—which we were about to do anyway—to the tune of fifteen hundred dollars (if I remember correctly). This windfall covered our rent for a few months in Michigan, as well as some of our expenses traveling back east.

Although we had not accumulated much in the way of possessions in our three and a half years in California, it was still a bonus that we did not have to haul our things across the country—this time, since I had attained the rank of staff sergeant, the air force shipped our belongings back to Michigan. In addition, the highway department cut us an additional check specifically for moving expenses. The upshot of all this good fortune was that we had a little nest egg with which to reestablish our lives back East.

But before we could invest that money in our future, we needed to figure where and what type of work the future held for us.

One of the options I was pondering was teaching at a community college in Florida or Michigan. I figured that with a master's degree, plus my background in helping military personnel with their higher education needs, I'd be a perfect candidate to perform veteran outreach aimed at boosting a community college's enrollment numbers. Florida was an option because Sybil's mother and brother now lived there. The idea of living in that sunny climate, with its spectacular beaches and clean air, appealed to us. I researched numerous Florida colleges to gauge my chances of employment; I was particularly interested in Indian River Community College, near Stuart, Florida, where the Raders had their home.

But in the final analysis, the most compelling factor in the place we would settle and the work I would aspire to do was that mental picture I'd carried since my visit to the Michigan legislature when I was twelve years old. I could not shake from my mind that image of the lawmakers in session and the idea that I might someday take part in such work. On the question of "where," Florida offered a unique opportunity. Living in the South did not appeal to me, but South Florida wasn't the South—not demographically, that is. It was full of Northerners who had come looking for good retirement weather, as well as countless immigrants from the Caribbean and Latin America who had come looking for opportunity.

In addition, the Florida legislature had a multi-representational system, featuring two or three seats from each district. I thought this arrangement might prove an advantage for a new person like me, who could outwork a field of candidates, come in second or third, and still grab a seat. On the negative side, statewide politics were more conservative in Florida than in Michigan, and I knew nobody there except for a few family members. So while the idea of a career in Florida had its attractions, the reality of running as a complete unknown and, if I won, serving in a largely conservative legislature was too daunting.

In Michigan my choices were clearer. First, I had a job waiting for me at the probate court. And unlike in Florida, I would not be starting my political career from scratch. I had friends and family in East

Detroit, where the Bonior name was well known and well liked. More-over, the district's incumbent, a Democrat, was retiring. But a nagging feeling, almost an instinct, told me to run elsewhere. I was proud of my father's record of success, I was proud of the name and reputation he had worked so hard to build. But it was *his* success, it was *his* reputation. I had helped him in all his campaigns, but now I wanted to achieve my own success, separate from his.

These were the thoughts racing through my mind as I plotted my future in the fall and winter of 1971–72.

CHAPTER 8

A Thousand Votes

Finding Success, and Making Mistakes,
as a Legislator and a Father

A MAP ON THE BACK PAGE:
CHOOSING A LEGISLATIVE DISTRICT

W e made the trip from San Bernardino to Stuart, Florida, in our Dodge Dart. I would end up buying three of these cheap and simple cars. This one was blue, used, and not much to look at, but boy, was it durable and reliable. In 1972 there were no seat-belt laws, and child-restraint seats had barely been invented. We should have been frightened flying across I–10 with a child, not yet two years old, sitting untethered in the backseat or on her mother's lap in front. Detroit and the auto industry were absolutely irresponsible, indeed, morally bankrupt, as they fought such safety measures tooth and nail. I shudder when I think back to how lucky our family was to escape serious injury and death in a car.

Sybil, Julie, and I made our way across the Southwest in the middle of February, glad to be below all that icy weather up north. We had now escaped four northern winters, and we were spoiled. I don't recall much about that trip except that it felt like an eternity getting across Texas, particularly west Texas. We were in a hurry to see Evie and to hit the Florida beaches. The industrial look of Beaumont, Texas, vaguely sticks in my memory, as do the Gulf Coast resort areas of Biloxi, Mobile, and Pensacola. Passing by a number of military installations, I realized how significant the armed forces were to these cities and to the South generally. I found it ironic that Dixie, which had committed treason against the Union a hundred years earlier, was now the beneficiary of so much federal military spending. And I felt uneasy traveling through the land of racial terror that had enslaved millions of families for centuries and, up until only eight years earlier, had enforced the rigid system of Jim Crow segregation. I had the same feeling as I'd had traveling through Germany: I was glad to have seen it but also glad that I did not live there. Southern hospitality? Not for me, thank you.

After a week with the Rader family in sunny Stuart, about a hundred miles north of Miami, I left Sybil and Julie and flew up to Detroit to set up the next phase of our lives. Staying at our home on Ego in East Detroit, I could see that my father was busy and apparently happy with his growing programs at the Office of Economic Opportunity. Jeff, now a strapping sixteen-year-old, had established living quarters in the finished basement, using the rattan furniture stored down there to fashion a comfortable nest. A lover of music, Jeff had a guitar he'd taught himself to play. My grandfather, now seventy-eight, still looked physically fit, although mentally he was showing subtle signs of depression and confusion.

The first morning after my arrival it was bitterly cold—so much for avoiding another winter. I snatched the *Detroit Free Press* off the front stoop and brought it into the house to read over coffee. On the back page of the front section was a full-page layout featuring maps of Michigan's legislative and congressional districts, newly redrawn for the 1972 elections in accord with the 1970 census. My eyes quickly went to the state house map. The East Detroit district had changed little: It was pretty much the same safe Democratic district that had been held by longtime Democratic incumbent Harold Clark, whose only claim to fame as far as I could remember was the candy—Clark Bars—he passed out during his campaigns. There would be no bonanza for candy lovers this year: Harold was not seeking reelection.

But there was another seat I was attracted to. Republican David Serotkin, a smart young lawyer who had graduated from Princeton

University, represented a district centered in Mount Clemens, in Macomb County. Unbeknownst to me at this time, Serotkin was seriously eyeing a step up, perhaps in response to the change in his district under the reapportionment: It had been made more Democratic by the addition of some areas in largely Democratic Clinton Township and some Democratic precincts in Sterling Heights. He was thinking of taking on Congressman James G. O'Hara, the veteran Democrat whose district also included Mount Clemens. Serotkin was considered a thoughtful legislator and enjoyed a good reputation in the community, making him an attractive candidate and a dangerous opponent, both for me in a legislative contest and for O'Hara in a race for Congress. In his midthirties, Serotkin was ambitious and on the prowl for his next opportunity.

The fit for me in the East Detroit seat was almost perfect. I'd been raised in this heavily Catholic, Democratic, and pro-labor community. And after two decades of my father's political activism, our family was well connected. Yes, there was my father's defeat for reelection for mayor, but I could sense from friends and neighbors that the city had begun to realize its mistake. Election would have been easy for me in East Detroit, but the temptation to strike out on my own, in a new community, was strong. What's more, I was never one to shy from a fight. I figured that with the added Democratic precincts, I could win in greater Mount Clemens.

I discussed my idea with my father, who was supportive, and I ran it by a few friends. Then I called Sybil. We had already made up our minds to choose Michigan over South Florida; I told her about my inclination to run for the Mount Clemens seat. I also told her what I'd found out about my job at the court: My old one was not available, but the court had offered to hire me as an adoption caseworker, a position that interested me. I also shared with her another offer that came out of the courthouse: Judge George Denewith of the circuit court suggested we rent a home he owned in Clinton Township, which is adjacent to Mount Clemens. Clinton Township was the largest and, at fifty thousand residents, most populous municipality in the newly redrawn legislative district. All in all, in just a week back in Michigan I'd made good progress in finding work, a potential home, and a starting point for a career in politics. Sybil agreed to give all of it—including the race in Mount Clemens—a try. I flew back down to balmy Florida for a little more rest before driving with my family back to the cold North.

But it was March. Spring was just around the corner.

Our new house was set in a semirural area, on Elizabeth Road near Michigan Route 59, better known as Hall Road. I worked for many years in Congress to get funding to upgrade M-59 to the premier road it is today. With six lanes divided by a boulevard, this thoroughfare is where the commercial, educational, and cultural communities thrive in Macomb County. It's home to Macomb's best and largest theater venue, to Macomb Community College and its library, to satellite campuses of Wayne State University, Oakland University, and several other colleges and universities, to the county library, and to two upscale shopping malls. The road also divides the county politically, with, for the most part, Republicans living in Macomb's more affluent north side and Democrats toward the southern end.

But back in 1972, M-59 was a two-lane highway with farms on either side. Our house on Elizabeth sat about a hundred feet back from the road on a five-acre plot of land. Across M-59 from us was Judge Deneweth's 150-acre farm. Directly across from us on Elizabeth was an 1850 farmhouse being lovingly restored by its owner. Running behind that house, and behind all the houses on that side of Elizabeth, was the North Branch of the Clinton River.

Our house was a blond-brick ranch built in about 1940, with two bedrooms and an unfinished basement that contained a vital piece of equipment: a sump pump, which automatically kept our basement dry even though we lived so near the river. Our home was not the most beautiful place in the world but it was solidly built, with thick walls made of sturdy, old-fashioned plaster, and it offered pastoral views out the windows. The living-room picture window in the front framed a nice view of the old farmhouse across the road. The kitchen window in the back overlooked an expansive yard with a large oak tree. I rigged a swing over one of the tree's sturdier limbs. To round out the recreational possibilities, Sybil and I constructed an elaborate aluminum swing set, with a slide and glider attached; we placed the set under that beautiful, shady, big old tree. The side bedroom windows faced four acres of cultivated land that contained a few rows of grapevines, an old pumpkin patch, and some rows of flowers. On the other side of the house was a detached garage located near a wooded area. We would construct my campaign signs in that garage.

Julie and her swing set, fall of 1972

The setting was bucolic enough that deer, raccoon, rabbits, fox, coyote, and an assortment of birds became our frequent visitors. At night we could hear the fast-moving traffic on Hall Road, but we also reveled in the sounds of crickets, frogs, and cicadas. In early summer, fireflies lit up our backyard, which was located next to the small forested area that separated us from Hall Road. And oh yes, there were plenty of mosquitoes.

The people restoring the farmhouse across the road had young children. I was gone most of the time, either working or campaigning, so this friendly family would provide some company for Sybil and Julie. By and large, however, we were too isolated in this spot. So, when our lease ran out after the election, we moved to a more populated neighborhood.

My new job as an adoption caseworker was based in the same probate court building where I'd worked as a boys' probation officer before my military service. That location gave me two advantages: Commuting time by car from our new home was two minutes, and I already knew Judge Castellucci and his staff. Some of his top people were also political operatives in Clinton Township. When I mounted my campaign, I was able to recruit some of these seasoned veterans, like Frank Marella, as well as some newer court workers, like Stan Kemp.

As a caseworker I visited homes, interviewing both the birth mother and the family in line to receive the child or newborn. Then I prepared a report for the judge, who would preside at a hearing on the adoption. I worked closely with agencies like Catholic Social Services, Lutheran Social Services, and Child and Family Services. These adoptions were delicate, sensitive matters, in which my primary responsibility was always to protect the children. In retrospect, I did my job well, but I wish I'd been better trained. Today the job would require an MSW (Master of Social Work) degree.

"My Name is David Bonior": The Primary

Serotkin made it definite: He was giving up the Mount Clemens state seat to run for Congress.[1] I called Dad and some friends to tell them I was moving ahead with my race for the seat. Then it was time to begin my campaign.

Like most neophyte campaigns, mine began with close friends and family. High school pals and army veterans Dave Deigel and John Carlin had preceded me in returning from military service and were now established in jobs with Macomb County. Dave, a wizard with numbers and budgets, was working in the county controller's office. His long career with the county government would culminate with his promotion to controller, making him Macomb's top financial officer.

John, who held my old job as a juvenile probation officer, had returned home from Vietnam after heavy combat duty with the army's First Cavalry Division, which suffered a higher rate of casualties than any other unit during the war. Years later, when I started the Vietnam Veterans Caucus in Congress and worked on legislation affecting the veterans who had come home to indifference and even scorn, I often thought of John, his time in combat, and his service to our country. I wish I had been more generous in expressing my gratitude to him when he got back after a year at war.

Both John and Dave did amazing amounts of campaign work, as did my father. Dad's years as chair of the County Board of Supervisors had helped him develop an extensive network of friends and political and business acquaintances in and around Mount Clemens and throughout the county; he reached out to them now to ask them to support me.

---

1 David Serotkin may have regretted that decision, for he lost the race to O'Hara. But he put himself in a good position to run for Congress again four years later—against me.

Our friend Cheryl Krysiak, a history teacher at Mount Clemens High School, was tireless in her efforts, as were Shirley and Joe Druin, active members of the St. Theclas Catholic community in Clinton Township. These people, together with my siblings, aunts, uncles, and Sybil, made up the core of the campaign's volunteers. Eventually, some people I met by knocking on their doors—a few teachers and some others—joined our team, too.

I ended up with two opponents in the Democratic primary. Twenty-one-year-old Ed Bruley, a former Catholic seminarian active in the Catholic social justice movement, had a reputation as a savvy community organizer. Ed and I would later form an alliance and close working relationship that still thrives after four decades. But in 1972 he lacked the experience and financial resources to make a credible run for the legislative seat.

My other primary opponent was former state representative Victor Steeh, who had held the Mount Clemens seat in the 1960s. Victor came from a highly respected, progressive Lebanese American family. His brother George had served in the state senate and then as a distinguished circuit court judge. George's son, also named George Steeh, is today a federal district judge in Detroit. The Steeh family was, and still is, beloved in the African American community. But the rap on Victor's candidacy in 1972 was that his time had passed, that he needed to give way to someone new.

So I ended up in the middle of my two opponents: one considered too young, the other past his prime. It was a good position to be in. And, politically speaking, my résumé sparkled. It contained all the pieces that said, *He's one of us.* I was: A Polish-Ukrainian Catholic former seminarian born in Hamtramck and raised in Macomb County. A graduate of Notre Dame High School, the University of Iowa, and Chapman College. A military veteran. Married, with a young daughter. An adoption caseworker. And, last but certainly not least, a union man. All of these characteristics and life experiences connected me to the county's voters, often establishing common ground with individuals via more than one category.

My job now was to get this information to the eighty thousand residents who lived in the district.

In a football game, I knew that the best way into the action was to just go out and hit somebody; in this case, I would hit some doors. There is no better way to campaign than to meet neighbors on their home turf. I had gone door-to-door many times as a kid campaigning for my father or his friends, so I felt no shyness, no reluctance to forge ahead.

In April, as I got ready to begin knocking, I decided that what I lacked in experience I would make up for with effort. "I'm simply going to outwork my opponents," I told myself. I could not wait to get going. My first street was Marvindale, in a heavily Catholic and Democratic precinct in Clinton near St. Theclas. I was charged up, feeling great to finally be out there in the public arena. However, I was carrying about as unprofessional a piece of campaign literature as you could imagine: I had typed up the highlights of my background, plus my views on half a dozen issues, and run off copies on an office Xerox machine. No professional printing—and it showed. I pledged to myself that I would do two hours of door-to-door each weekday and four hours each day on the weekend. But as John Carlin made sure I understood, I badly needed a professional piece of literature. So, quickly, I got it.

Because of my father's connection to the printing trade, we were able to stretch our campaign dollars. He was a distribution agent for a silk-screening company; they gave us a discount to produce our signs and literature. We were innovative in the material we handed and mailed out, soon opting for paper cut into a semi-round shape that would stand out in contrast to all the standard rectangular mail pieces, sent by other candidates, that would flood people's mailboxes. We wanted voters to say, "Hmm, this looks interesting" when they picked it up. Although this format added to the cost of the pieces, the expense would pay off if recipients actually read what we were sending. Knowing

My first printed campaign piece was *rectangular.*

the tricks of the printing trade, Dad helped guide us in our decisions. John Carlin helped design our most popular piece, which was a three-quarter circle that folded open to reveal a family portrait, my résumé, and statements on a few issues.

Door-to-door is pretty simple. Knock on the front door (or ring the doorbell—but often it doesn't work). When someone answers, introduce yourself. "Hi. I'm sorry to trouble you. My name is David Bonior and I'm a candidate for state representative. When you have a minute, I would appreciate it if you looked at my campaign literature." You then hand them the piece, shake their hand, and thank them for their time. Most will be polite, take the literature, and then terminate the contact. Some will peruse the handout while you're still there. They'll look for a connection. "Oh, I see you went to Notre Dame. My brother went there." From that common thread a conversation might flow. Some will say that they either don't vote or are not interested. Some will tell you they're Republican. A small number, maybe one or two a day, will express interest in working for your campaign.

If nobody answers the door, which happens about 40 percent of the time, you leave them the literature on which you've handwritten, "Sorry I missed you at home. David Bonior." To keep the flow of your knocking efficient, before you begin your day you should write out your

"Sorry I missed you" message on fifty pieces, which you will carry along with the "clean" pieces as you make your rounds. You stick the signed piece in a place where the resident will notice it: in the screen door, maybe, or wedged aside the door handle.

Oh yes, one other crucial technique must be kept in mind. When your hand goes up to knock on the door, use your right foot to brace the screen door shut until it is clear that no dog (or dogs) is about to come flying out at you. The one time I did not follow my own advice, a German shepherd shot through the doorway and started gnawing on my shin.

The filing deadline was during the first week in May, and I needed petitions signed to get my name on the ballot. I got some of the signatures as I went door-to-door; volunteers got the rest. We turned in more than enough signatures to qualify. The next step was to make a formal declaration of my candidacy, because even though I'd been actively campaigning in neighborhoods every day for a month, I needed to make my quest official and, most importantly, attract press attention. So early in May I got up to talk to some thirty friends and family members, plus a few educators and labor leaders, who had gathered at the Mount Clemens Holiday Inn. I regret to say that my announcement speech was less than compelling. I was not a polished or aggressive speaker, although I was sincere. I spoke about jobs, education, the environment, and issues affecting senior citizens. When I got to the part about the elderly, I read the lyrics of Paul Simon and Art Garfunkel's song "Old Friends"; that is, I read *all* the lyrics of the song. I read about the elderly people sitting on a park bench "like bookends," and about how it's "terribly strange" to be seventy years old.

It so happens that I am barely short of seventy at this writing. Simon's words seem as moving and real to me now as they did forty-two years ago. Even then I understood that time moves quickly and that before you know it you may find yourself on a park bench, with most of your life behind you. These days, many of my contemporaries among my friends can't believe they have reached senior age. "How did this happen?" they ask with a shrug of their shoulders and an impish smile on their faces. But seventy, and seventy-plus, were always there, staring us in the face through our grandparents, coworkers, and about 12 percent of the US population. And so, even then, I parted with Paul Simon's lyrics on that point: For me, aging was not strange. My thoughts from 1972 were what they are today: Make the most of your time. Do good works. Take on worthwhile fights. Struggle for justice.

Nevertheless, that poem that day was a downer. Reading it was a melancholy way to end a speech that was supposed to project a positive, can-do spirit. My choice probably had people raising their eyebrows, as if to say, *This guy needs a lot of work.* They were right; my speaking and presentation skills had room for improvement, to put it mildly. But because I felt so strongly about social justice, I believe people thought I wasn't a lost cause. I was painfully cognizant of my shortcomings and worked hard over my career to overcome them. Over the course of my thirty years as a legislator, I grew to be an accomplished public speaker, sought after to speak at rallies, conventions, and dinners. But back in 1972 it was all new to me, and a bit overwhelming. Over time I discovered different techniques that worked, like short poems, jokes, and parables mixed into the text. I learned to vary the pitch of my voice and to offer people hope in my concluding remarks.

Each evening, after the door-knocking had ended, John, Dave, and I would meet in my garage to construct campaign posters and signs. The work entailed lots of glue, wood, nails, and staples, and lasted for a couple of hours. A six-pack of beer was another integral feature of each evening, as was fighting off the army of mosquitoes that regularly found its way into the lighted space. The signs ranged in size from the four-feet-by-eight-feet model we placed along large roads and highways, to the more manageable lawn signs that were easy to mass assemble. As we went door-to-door, if a voter seemed interested in my candidacy, we'd ask if he or she would take a lawn sign. Many did agree to have us stick a Bonior for State Representative sign on their front lawn.

I believed in my candidacy so strongly that I borrowed three thousand dollars from the First State Bank of Fraser to infuse the campaign with start-up funds. It took me years to pay the bank back, but taking out the loan proved to be a wise investment. If you do not believe in yourself, it's awfully hard to get others to believe in you. The three grand bought signs and literature, with enough left over to invest in several fund-raising events, the proceeds of which we used for mailings and for purchasing ads in newspapers and on the radio.

Neither of my two primary opponents had much visibility, nor did they knock on any doors that I was aware of. Soon I became the favorite in the race and began to garner endorsements from individuals and organizations.

On primary night, the first Tuesday in August, we celebrated my first electoral victory: Bruley, 1000 votes; Steeh, 2,200; Bonior, 3,700. As pleased as I was over winning the nomination, I had no illusions about the mood of the electorate: It was not friendly toward Democrats.

The fall race would be harder.

NIXON, McGOVERN, WALLACE, BONIOR: THE FALL CAMPAIGN

The Republican candidate, who had won his primary unopposed, was a conservative radio talk show host named Ed DeWitt. A fixture at WBRB, a station that billed itself as "The Voice of Macomb County," he was smart, smooth, and articulate. He lived with his wife and two children in Harrison Township, the more Republican part of the district. The biggest asset he had going for himself was that 1972 was shaping up to be a landslide year for the GOP. A red-meat Republican issue, cross-district busing to achieve racial balance in public schools would dominate that year's campaigns in Michigan, especially in the Detroit suburbs. Busing had been ordered by the courts and was thought to be on the way. Nor did it help to have South Dakota Senator George McGovern at the top of the Democratic ticket. McGovern, a wonderful man and fine public servant, who had fought courageously in World War II, had led the anti-Vietnam War movement in Congress. Everyone could see that he would be crushed by President Richard Nixon, who was seeking reelection.

All these factors spelled trouble for us.

By the time I won the nomination in August, busing had been a hot issue in the state for months. Michigan's presidential primary had been held in May. In addition to McGovern, the frontline Democratic candidates were Hubert Humphrey and George Wallace. Senator and former vice president Humphrey was a Minnesota liberal and longtime progressive warhorse on social justice issues, particularly African American civil rights. The combative Alabama governor George Wallace, on the other hand, had been a leading segregationist during the early '60s. By 1972 he had shifted from explicit to coded racism, presenting himself as an angry populist critic of all things Washington. Although Wallace's appeal outside the South had been limited—he'd carried five states of the Confederacy running as a third-party presidential candidate in 1968—in 1972 his campaign struck a chord in this state on the nation's northern border. Anti-liberal and anti-Washington fervor was running through Michigan, set off by the cross-district busing expected to soon begin.[2] It was the hottest political issue I encountered in my thirty years of elective politics. Wallace capitalized on the busing issue brilliantly, lambasting the federal government, which had imposed this burden on ordinary citizens. With a curl of his lip, he mocked Washington's "pointy-headed bureaucrats" toting fancy government briefcases that, he said, contained nothing more than a peanut-butter-and-jelly sandwich.

On May 15, the day before the balloting in Michigan, a gunman tried to assassinate Wallace at a campaign rally in Laurel, Maryland.

2 As it turned out, the U.S. Supreme Court struck down the plan for cross-district busing in the Detroit area, and no such busing ever took place. Supreme Court rulings relevant to the busing issue include *Brown v Board of Education*, *Swann v Charlotte-Mechlenburg Board of Education*, and *Milliken v Bradley*.

Wallace survived the attack, but his grievous wounds confined him to a wheelchair for the rest of his life. Although the shooting would ultimately end the Alabaman's presidential aspirations, it did not hurt him in the following day's voting. He placed a comfortable first in Maryland and ran away with Michigan, taking 51 percent of the tally, compared to 27 percent for McGovern and 16 percent for Humphrey. His share of the ballots in Macomb County was stunning: 66 percent. Detroit and its suburbs made up one of the most segregated metropolitan areas in the country. Greater Boston and greater Chicago were much the same.

There was not an issue I disliked more in my career than cross-district busing, which exacerbated racial tensions and divided communities. Yet it was the overriding issue we all faced in our campaigns during those years. I thought a better approach to this real educational and racial challenge was passage and enforcement of a much stronger fair-housing law. This was not the answer many of my constituents wanted to hear, but living in mixed neighborhoods seemed to me preferable to busing children far away from their homes.[3] Although people asked me about cross-district busing as I knocked on doors, not many folks bothered to find out my position on the issue, oddly enough. Rather, they just told me how they felt—and did so with much fervor. My Republican opponent, in his speeches and literature, charged that I supported "forced busing." Among voters, the general view was that Republicans opposed busing and Democrats supported it. I was opening myself up to that charge by advocating integrated neighborhoods: The stereotype was that because Democrats favored integration, they also supported cross-district busing.

---

3 A few years later, when our son Andy was in second grade in Alexandria, Virginia, he attended Jefferson-Houston School, a predominantly African American Alexandria school across town from our home. His commute by bus took thirty minutes each way, some twenty-five minutes more than he would have needed to walk to our neighborhood school. Andy liked the predominantly black school and, when he got home, would entertain his mother with stories of life on the bus. Sybil liked Andy's teachers, and we all adjusted to Andy's new school and bus ride

But I wasn't about to abandon my solution, for I felt strongly about it. I had seen it work in California when Sybil helped integrate our apartment complex, and I believed in 1972, as I do today, that we all are enriched by a diverse community. One of my first acts as a member of the legislature was to join with State Representative James Bradley of Detroit in authoring a fair-housing resolution that would have put teeth into the enforcement of state housing laws. With the storm of George Wallace just past, and the specter of court-ordered busing on the horizon, the Judiciary Committee, where my housing resolution was sent, did not give it the time of day.

In Miami in July, in yet another fractious Democratic National Convention, McGovern was crowned the party's standard-bearer for the fall election. In 1968 the Vietnam War had been far and away the central issue that disrupted the party's quadrennial gathering. In 1972 the war still lingered as a point of bitter contention, but the issue had been blunted by Nixon's program of "Vietnamization," under which the number of American troops in-country had been greatly decreased. More than the war, this year it was the cultural wedge issues, often centered on race, that tore up the Democratic coalition. In the fall, the AFL-CIO, headed by George Meany, would fail to endorse the Democratic nominee for the first time in decades.[4] The convention was a mess. The disorder and discord caused the nominee to deliver his acceptance speech at three in the morning, when virtually nobody was watching. And the South Dakotan's hasty pick as his running mate, Thomas Eagleton, turned disastrous just weeks after the convention, when revelations that the Missouri senator had undergone electroshock treatment for depression forced McGovern to drop him from the ticket. After numerous prominent Democrats turned down McGovern's request to take Eagleton's spot on the ticket, McGovern settled for Kennedy in-law, and founding director of the Peace Corps, Sargent Shriver.

---

4 McGovern would get his revenge thirty-five years later when he publicly campaigned against the Employee Free Choice Act, which would have made it easier for workers to join a union.

McGovern was a good man, but his flawed candidacy harmed thousands of down-ballot Democrats all across the country. His campaign ended with one of the most lopsided results in American history. The president carried forty-nine states; his challenger took Massachusetts and the District of Columbia.

I saw this electoral storm brewing by early spring. In the larger scheme of things, my race was a sideshow; the top of the ticket would dictate the closeness of my race. My best weapon was my door-to-door work, and I kept at it, campaigning as the underdog fighting a heavy Republican tide. I believed that if my race was close, I would prevail— as long as I met enough people. So from the kickoff of my campaign in April, until Election Day in November, I knocked on the door of virtually every voter's home in the district. My opponent, Ed DeWitt, and the local Republican Party did everything they could to tie me to the national Democratic ticket. I did not run away from that ticket, as did many members of my party. I proudly included the word *Democrat* on my literature and signs.

As the returns started to come in on election night, it was quickly apparent that Democratic candidates around the country, and in Macomb County, were going down. Somehow we hung on, winning 52–48 percent, which translated to a margin of a mere one thousand votes. Door-to-door had made the difference. I was exhausted, but flush with hope and idealism.

RIGHT CAUSE, WRONG TIME: WORK, FAMILY, AND A BAD DECISION

After the election, I was pumped. I was eager to add my voice to changing Michigan and the world. I got my chance to speak up right away.

With Nixon's national security advisor, Henry Kissinger, in and out of peace talks with the North Vietnamese, it looked and felt as though the nightmare of Vietnam might finally be coming to an end. In late

October, the two sides reached a deal, prompting Kissinger to announce, "We believe that peace is at hand." But then the deal fell apart. In December, Nixon and Kissinger responded with a massive air attack on North Vietnam, particularly on the country's capital, Hanoi, and its main port, Haiphong. The B-52s and fighter jets executing Operation Linebacker II, known more widely as the Christmas Bombing, produced casualties in the thousands. The Nixon administration argued that the strikes were made necessary by Hanoi's lack of "seriousness" at the negotiating table. In fact, it was America's ally, South Vietnamese president Nguyen Van Thieu, who had balked at signing, insisting on a long list of changes that caused the North Vietnamese to withdraw consent. The public rationale for the bombing was a lie: The attacks were meant to bring not Hanoi but Thieu back to the bargaining table, by demonstrating to him that the US stood ready to use force against the North if it violated the terms of the agreement. Once the show of force was completed, Nixon gave Thieu an ultimatum: Accept the terms of the negotiated agreement or lose America as an ally. Thieu buckled, and by the end of January, America's war in Vietnam was over.

December's sudden escalation of the war was greeted in the US with dismay, skepticism, and anger. Support for US involvement in the war had plunged, with 60 percent of the nation telling Gallup in January that sending American troops to Vietnam had been a mistake. It was in this atmosphere that 100,000 people gathered in DC around January 20—the date President Nixon would be sworn in to serve his second term—to protest the war at a "counter inaugural."

I wanted to be part of that protest against a war I considered to have been wrong from the beginning. It was now fourteen years since the first US soldier had been killed in Vietnam. Fifty-eight thousand had followed, along with as many as two million Vietnamese. The war had divided our country as no other conflict had since the Civil War. It had drained precious resources that could have been used for health, education, housing, infrastructure, and the fight against poverty. What's more, whereas during and after World War II the US had accumulated enormous international goodwill, much of world opinion now considered America to be the globe's number-one "bad guy." In short, the war had been, and continued to be, a disaster.

As an elected leader, I felt I had both an opportunity and a duty to lead my community in speaking out on this central issue in our nation's life. But as a husband and father, I had a different obligation: to be with my family, for my wife was about to give birth to our second child. Clearly, in retrospect, my family responsibilities in Michigan should have trumped my desire to protest in Washington. But I organized a busload of about forty Macomb County citizens to travel to our nation's capital for the demonstration, and off I went with them.

Our second child might appear any day, and Julie was only two and a half years old. Moreover, while my constituents had narrowly elected me, they had voted overwhelmingly to grant President Nixon a second term. So a good case could be made that by protesting at the start of that second term, I was putting my desires ahead of not only my family's needs but also the will of the citizens I'd only weeks before been chosen to represent.

It was one of the biggest mistakes of my life.

My place should have been with my family, especially considering that Julie had been born in breech position. Andy, fortunately, was not turned the wrong way. Nevertheless, a red light should have gone off in my head telling me to stay home and let others carry the day in DC. Now, every four years, when a president is inaugurated on January 20, I celebrate my son's birth. But the occasion is also always a reminder that I made the wrong choice in being far away the day he was born at St. Joseph Hospital in Mount Clemens.

Our bus trip was purposeful, our colleagues proud and happy to be going. We sang songs and told stories on the more than five hundred miles of highway: south to Ohio, through the Buckeye State, slicing through western Pennsylvania, dropping down to western Maryland, and then pulling into DC. We visited our senators and stopped by the office of every Michigan member of the House, reading to each chief of staff a well-thought-out document, which we'd composed during the trip, laying out the case against the war. On Inauguration Day, we roamed the Mall between the Capitol and the Washington Monument. Many protesters had slept on the Mall the night before, although we'd bedded down in a cheap hotel in Northern Virginia.

As our activities progressed, I periodically checked in with Sybil and Evie, who'd come to stay with her. I was hoping that our child would arrive late, permitting me to be back in time for the birth. But on the morning of the twentieth, when I called Evie from a pay phone at a restaurant off Route 1 near Fort Hunt Road in Alexandria, she told me that Sybil had given birth to a big boy weighing seven pounds, seven ounces. Mother and child were doing fine, Evie said. Sybil and I had already decided on names; if the baby was a boy, his name would be Andrew David. And so it was.

When I got back to our bus, I relayed the news to my traveling companions, who let out a cheer. I was happy, but the feeling was bittersweet. I was thrilled over my son's birth but wished I were home with my family.

Once again I was trying to do too much in too short a time. A baby, a new job, and an upcoming move into a new neighborhood were generating a lot of stress for this young family.

Essentially the job of a Michigan state legislator is located in the state capital, Lansing, a two-hour drive from Mount Clemens. When I first arrived in town, I met with House Speaker Bill Ryan to try to convince him that I should move my family to Lansing. I'd been away so much, taking evening classes when I was in the air force, that I was already feeling guilty at the prospect of being away from my family for much of each week. The Speaker, as well as Majority Leader Bobby Crim, were both adamant that bringing the family to Lansing would be a monumental political mistake. They argued that because I'd won with only 52 percent of the vote, I would inevitably be targeted by the Republicans in the next election. Living with my family out of district would open me to GOP charges that I was out of touch with my constituents. I immediately saw that they were right and agreed to keep my wife and children back in Macomb County.

In 1972 Michigan was one of a handful of states with a full-time legislature. The annual salary, eleven thousand dollars, almost doubled what I'd been making. Plus, the health and pension benefits were generous, and I qualified for a travel allowance and a per diem for each day away from home.

The legislative calendar kept me busy. Our first session of the week would take place on Monday evening, giving members a chance to travel to the capital earlier that day. Occasionally, sessions would go through Friday, but most often the week would end on Thursday, allowing me to hit the road back to Mount Clemens late that afternoon. I'd set a light work schedule on Fridays, taking the day to stay close to my family.

The legislative calendar pretty much followed that of the school systems: We had generous time off during holidays, including two to three weeks around Christmas and New Year's and another two weeks around Easter, plus we recessed for a month in the summer. Those breaks gave me time with my wife and children, but for a substantial part of the year I was not home most of Monday through Thursday. Those long stretches of separation were not good for the family. We missed each other.

We became homeowners for the first time with our purchase at 301 Riverside, one block outside Mount Clemens in Clinton Township. Built in 1929, the modest—it cost us roughly twenty-six thousand dollars—two-story brick featured a detached garage in the backyard and interior space measuring sixteen hundred feet. The front door opened into the living room, which included a fireplace and a large picture window that looked onto a wooded area across the street. Adjacent to the living room was a small dining area, next to which was the kitchen. We took our meals there, at a table that overlooked the yard, and we used the unfinished basement for laundry and storage. A staircase from the living room led up to the second-floor bedrooms. Andy and Julie shared a room that overlooked the backyard; the room was small, but large enough for a three-year-old and a newborn. The bedroom Sybil and I shared overlooked the front of the house, the woods across the street, and the Clinton River beyond. There was also a tiny third room upstairs that the previous owners might have used as a sewing room but could serve as another bedroom.

Andy and Julie, 1974

The house sat in a lovely old neighborhood. Large oak trees shaded winding roads that followed the curve of the Clinton River. In a wooded area across the street from us was a walking trail that took you a short hundred yards to the river's edge and a view of the tall buildings in downtown Mount Clemens, a mere fifteen-minute walk away.

Several blocks away from our house was the Clinton River Spillway, a man-made appendix to the Clinton River. Running from Mount Clemens two and a half miles straight to Lake St. Clair, the spillway was constructed to alleviate flooding along the banks of the natural river as it passes through Clinton Township, Mount Clemens, and Harrison Township before draining into Lake St. Clair. There was a wild beauty to the spillway—more so, ironically, than to the natural river, whose banks were built up with homes in all three communities. The spillway, on the other hand, was bordered on each side by about a hundred yards of open space and/or woodlands. Bird life was abundant, with a plenitude of red-winged blackbirds. In high school and during breaks in my first years in college I would come to the spillway with friends to drink beer. If you were lucky enough to have a date, it became a place to do what we then called "necking."

Decades later, when I was in Congress, I led the successful effort to build a bike and walking trail along the entire length of the spillway, right up to its terminus in Lake St. Clair. Soon, master gardeners led by Patrice and Brent Avery were planting gardens of all kinds along the route, including butterfly gardens. Our neighbors, Ed Bruley and circuit court judge John Bruff, both avid and accomplished gardeners, also pitched in. All these passionate and creative people gave their time in order to serve the common good and the beauty of the community. Soon Detroit Edison joined the bandwagon and planted new trees.

The houses on our block and neighborhood varied in style and size, with colonials, ranches, bungalows, American craftsman, and modernes mingled together. Our street was quintessentially middle class. The Suklock and Burns families lived on either side of us; farther down the block were Fire Chief Walker and County Controller Sherwood Bennett, as

Entertaining Sybil and the children with a hand puppet

well as the Papkes, Taylors, and Fosters. John Foster became a personal and political friend who, decades later, would serve on the county circuit court, becoming its chief judge. Julie and Andy befriended many children from these families. It was a nice place to live.

Even though we lived in Clinton Township (a wise political move considering it was the largest community in my district), it felt as though we lived in Mount Clemens proper, which began at the far end of our block. We would walk to downtown Mount Clemens to buy ice cream, shop in Priehs Department Store, or get a marvelous corned beef on rye at Litwak's kosher delicatessen. Sybil and I would take the kids to the pool at the YMCA downtown, where Julie learned to swim and Andy frolicked as his dad launched him high into the air and caught him right before he hit the water.

Established in 1818, Mount Clemens still carries the charm of an old county seat. The size of the population in 1973 was about what it is today—it's held steady over the years at sixteen to twenty thousand. When we lived there, its pleasant neighborhoods were home to middle- and working-class families. Ethnically, the town was mixed, with African Americans, many of whom had a connection to the military via nearby Selfridge AFB, making up about a quarter of the population. Blacks held responsible positions, as teachers and administrators, in the town's school system. A small but active Jewish community, large enough to support one synagogue, also resided in Mount Clemens. Leaders of that community were successful in business and medicine.

Mount Clemens's notoriety came from the discovery in the 1870s of "curative mineral water" emanating from underground springs. People came from all parts of the US to partake, and majestic hotels, all featuring bathhouses, sprang up. This tourist trade and the phenomenon of the water played out with the Great Depression, but the hotels remained, both downtown and on the city's edges. In 1973, the Arethusa, Medea, St. Joseph, Murphy, and Colonial hotels still adorned the city.

Downtown Mount Clemens, located along the Clinton River, featured an attractive green area on the riverbank sloping down toward the water. Thousands of people would gather there on summer evenings to hear concerts, mostly of rock music. Shadyside Park, at the junction of the river and the spillway, was another popular destination. The downtown also had two movie houses, the Jewel and the Macomb. When I was a kid growing up in Hamtramck and East Detroit, the Jewel in Mount Clemens and the Fox in Detroit were the two area theaters for big-time movie premieres. In the late 1970s, the Jewel became a porno house. The Macomb fared better, turning into a nightclub and a venue for stage productions and concerts.

As the county seat, Mount Clemens had many governmental buildings, including the thirteen-story county building, the cornerstone of which was laid in 1931. From the exterior of the top floor, a set of large gargoyles glared ominously upon those passing by at street level.

Regrettably, the old Victorian-looking courthouse, built in 1881, was razed in 1930. But because the county had grown so dramatically after World War II, in the 1960s many called for construction of a new court building. A passionate battle was waged within the board of supervisors—the county's governing authority—over the location of the new building: either along the river and next to the thirteen-story county building or at a satellite county campus away from the heart of the city. My father, who chaired the seventy-member board, argued vigorously for the downtown location. He was joined by the mayor of Mount Clemens, Abe Levine; together they argued that building the structure away from the city center would doom the area to urban decay. Their reasoning convinced the supervisors, the building was put up downtown, and Dad and Abe were credited with saving the city. My father took great pride in that battle and his leadership of it.

In front of the Macomb County courthouse, which my dad built

Andy grew into a strong, independent, healthy toddler who slept soundly and ate like a champ. One of my fondest memories of him in his pre-walking days was seeing him buckled into his Jolly Jumper, a seat suspended by elastic straps attached above the kitchen doorjamb. The elastic cords would allow Andy to use his ample legs to propel himself into the air—a good six inches above the ground. Playing in this contraption brought pure joy to Andy; watching him brought pure joy to his mother and me. When he was not in his jumper, he and his sister would often be playing piggyback; the back in question was mine, on which they would sit as I crawled across the living room floor on all fours. Then, abruptly, I'd flip over, catching them as they dismounted. Lying on my back, I might then instigate a game of "tickle" and watch them squirm and squeal to our mutual delight, or maybe I'd choose "airplane," in which I'd hoist one of the kids into the air with my two feet on their chest then propel them into the air with my legs and catch them with my hands before they crashed down on me. Nowadays when I see Andy engaging in similar acrobatics with his three children, I get lost in these memories.

Andy was active and adventurous, as we found out during one nerve-wracking episode when he was only eighteen months old. All four of us had gone to Metro Beach Park on Lake St. Clair to let the kids play in an elaborate toddler play area, called Tot Lot, near the beach and lake. Sybil and I were enjoying watching them play when, for no more than a minute, our attention turned exclusively to Julie. When we looked back to where Andy had been, he was gone. We scanned the entire playground; he was nowhere to be found. Panic set in; within seconds, every parent's nightmare flooded our minds. One of those nightmares told us to immediately check the water's edge. We grabbed Julie and ran toward the beach, where we found Andy, calm as could be, pointing to the lake. "I go water," he said. Immense relief engulfed us. We would have to keep a close eye on this kid.

Andy was a free spirit. When he was three he found some coins at home and wandered down the block to Frank's Drug Store to buy

Andy and me

candy, something he had seen his older sister do with Sybil or me. He never complained when Sybil enrolled him in ballet class with a roomful of girls at Grace Episcopal Church. "Julie was not enjoying her ballet lessons," Sybil recalls, "and as I had already paid for the remainder of her lessons, I asked Andy if he would like to take her place. He wanted to, so I stuffed him into her pink leotard tights and he joined the fun. He finished the classes and proudly showed me how to do a 'gwan pee aaa'—that is, a grand plié."

Like his father, he loved balls and was always up for throwing, catching, batting, shooting, or kicking them. Julie was the same way. It was clear early on that both children not only liked sports but had natural athletic ability.

A full-time mom, Sybil made it her business to help our children explore their creative side, often working with them on simple crafts projects. I tried to do my part. We both would read to them, and I would take them exploring the wooded area across the street from our house. The trail to the river was about a hundred yards long, but to the children I imagine it felt endless as they tramped through this dark, wooded enclave. I'm not sure how much sank into their two- and four-year-old minds, but on these little walks I would talk about trees and their leaves, the bugs we found, and the birds we could hear "if we're very quiet." Today Julie lives in Colorado, where she and her husband, Brian, often take to the mountains and the trails with their three children. Andy and his wife take their kids hiking, too, sometimes along the Billy Goat Trail that runs along the Potomac River just outside DC or up Old Rag Mountain in Shenandoah National Park. So perhaps our walks in the woods, and our short excursions in our camper, helped spur in both Julie and Andy an interest in the outdoors.

One day my sister called Sybil and told her of a conversation with our family friend Helen Livingston. Helen had relayed to Nancy news about a fifteen-year-old girl, then living at the Macomb County Youth Home, who needed a foster home. Sybil and I talked about this girl and soon got to thinking about taking her into our family. We had the space—there was the small room upstairs that could be turned into a bedroom. Sybil discussed the matter with Julie and Andy, and the vote was unanimous: We would share our family and home with Debbie Talent. Debbie became like a big sister to Julie and Andy. Because I was away a good part of most weeks, Sybil spent more time with Debbie than I did. Debbie was both company to Sybil and, being a teenager, a challenge. But overall, she was a wonderful girl who needed a family. She had been attending L'Anse Creuse High School—L'Anse Creuse was the name of our local public school district—so her education suffered no disruption when she moved in with us. Three years later, she would graduate from L'Anse Creuse. When I was elected to Congress in 1976 and we moved to DC, she chose to stay on in Mount Clemens to be close to her boyfriend.

Carving a jack-o'-lantern with our foster daughter, Debbie, 1976

ALLIES, COLLEAGUES, MENTORS:
FINDING MY WAY AS A NEW LEGISLATOR

As bad as my decision to attend the counter inaugural had been for my family, it did bring me positive political outcomes. First, it set a pattern to which I would adhere throughout my thirty years as a legislator: I would follow my conscience on important and controversial issues. I remembered Edmund Burke's words on public service: "Your representative owes you, not his industry only, but his judgment; and he betrays, instead of serving you, if he sacrifices it to your opinion." I'd made a tough call, one out of step with the majority opinion in my district, at the absolute beginning of my legislative career. Perhaps I had not acted in my self-interest, if my self-interest was ensuring a long tenure in office. But I knew who I was and what I stood for, and that inner core helped me push forward on issues of human rights and economic justice even if my words and deeds sometimes rubbed against the prevailing thought in my district.

Second, the bus trip expanded my reach into the ranks of Michigan McGovern activists like Ed Bruley, Chris Koch, Elsie and John Shore, Carol and Fritz Eberhardt, and Ron and Brenda Oakley. These progressives and I decided to build politically at the local level and formed a group we called Locofoco. We borrowed the name from a faction of the Democratic Party active during the 1830s and '40s. Also known as the Equal Rights Party, the Locofocos opposed entrenched machine power, generally approaching politics from a Jacksonian populist point of view.

Our small group of activists met weekly, usually at either the Koch or Eberhardt home, committing ourselves to take our values to the ballot box by running candidates for school board, city commission, and county commission. "After McGovern lost so horribly," recalls Chris Koch, "a whole group of us that had gotten to be friends on his campaign started this little group just to run local candidates. We'd failed so miserably at the national level; that's why we decided to start working locally. My husband, Allan, was our first candidate. He ran for school board. He lost but came very close."

Ed Bruley recalls that our Locofocos originated during that trip in January 1973: "There was the Christmas bombing, and David organized a bus. A lot of people on that bus were from Mount Clemens. We formed a little group in Mount Clemens and Clinton to run people for school boards and city councils. And we started to put together a nucleus of how we were going to organize things." Ed had organized his own bus to go to DC that week, and one of the passengers was Kathy Gille. The two buses traveled from Michigan in convoy, and our two busloads of activists hung out together in DC, forging friendships and political bonds. From those early connections resulted a political and personal connection with Ed, Chris, and Kathy that has lasted these past forty years. All three would hold leadership positions in my

First Locofoco members (l. to r.): Brenda Oakley,
Ed Bruley, unidentified, Ron Oakley

congressional operation. Chris and Ed ran my Michigan office for the whole twenty-six years I served in Congress, while Kathy spent twenty years as my top legislative confidante in Washington. The genesis of our involvement together was the trip to DC; it led to our mutual commitment to build something different and unique in Macomb County politics, a way of operating that would spread to other areas of Michigan. My eventual election to Congress, and all the support systems that came with a congressional office and staff, helped us elect many progressive candidates at the local and state levels. From the modest beginning of our weekly Locofoco gatherings grew a major movement that thrived and grew in Michigan over decades.

The drive from Mount Clemens to Lansing took two hours. The drive was one of the worst parts of the job; I never looked forward to it. Nevertheless, I kept myself occupied in my Dodge Dart listening to public radio, especially when it broadcast the Senate Watergate hearings, which were riveting. The legislative session began at around seven, Monday evenings, allowing me to spend a little extra time at home before I disappeared for three days. I would usually leave for Lansing after lunch and pull into my assigned parking space in the back of the capitol at around 3:00 p.m.

When I first arrived in Lansing, I stayed at the Jack Tar Hotel directly across the street from the capitol. The Jack Tar was the grande dame of Lansing hotels, although it was now less grand than merely old. My colleagues in the legislature frequently referred to it as a firetrap, and that description made me nervous. But it was convenient. Its bar would start to fill up at around five o'clock, after our work sessions had concluded; a lot of legislative business got started or finished over a martini or beer. The restaurant in the hotel was informal, featuring a buffet breakfast table free to any legislator. Lobbyists had arranged with the hotel to pick up the tab.

The thought of being consumed in a conflagration at the Jack Tar was unsettling, so I went looking for other accommodations. My first stop was the downtown YMCA, where bare-bones rooms—with a shared bath—went for six dollars a night. I'd lived in dormitories during college; I was back in one here, tramping down the hall in my bathrobe to the showers. While the price was right, the wine bottles and drug paraphernalia I'd find in the bathroom kept me from considering the Y my home away from home.

Stuck on the six-dollar price of a room, I ventured to a Motel Six, so named because six dollars was, indeed, the price of a room when the company was founded in the early 1960s. My memories of this establishment center on a vibrating machine attached to the bed. For a quarter, you could shake yourself silly for two minutes—a novelty that wore off quickly in what proved to be a grim, depressing place.

It took until my second term, but I finally found better housing. At the urging of Perry Bullard, who sat next to me in the legislature, I rented a room from him in a spacious house three blocks from the capitol. The new digs represented a huge improvement over the previous three locations: I now lived with interesting people in a regular house. Besides Perry, Iner Bolin, the chief administrator of the Michigan Supreme Court, resided there, as did John Cleveland, who turned out to be the great-grandson of President Grover Cleveland. The only drawback was Winston, Perry's cat. Never before having lived in a house with a cat, I only now discovered that I was acutely allergic to the species. My aggravated asthma notwithstanding, I was glad to be spending my Lansing nights in this house.

My room was comfortable, my bed was soft, but for me the main attraction of the location was Perry, who was always filled with energy and passion. Born in Cleveland in 1942, he received a BA from Harvard and then, in 1970, a law degree from the University of Michigan. In 1966–67 he flew combat missions in Vietnam, coming home highly decorated for valor. Soon after his discharge, he joined Vietnam Veterans Against the War and publicly renounced his thirteen awarded medals. Before being elected to the legislature from Ann Arbor, Perry had worked as a law clerk in the Michigan Supreme Court. Aggressive and impatient, he rubbed many older members the wrong way. But he made up for his abrasiveness with his ardor for justice and civil liberties, areas in which he demonstrated resolve and leadership.

I was proud to be his friend.

Young, male, highly educated, and progressive, our 1972 freshman class was motivated by the need for change. Older, established, and generally more conservative veteran legislators, who seemed to think we were a bunch of hotshots and know-it-alls, derisively dubbed us the "Kiddie Caucus," a name the Republicans also embraced as a way of driving a wedge into the Democratic caucus as a whole. The legislation we introduced and the speeches we gave were often received as threats to the existing order.

Which they were. We wanted a more progressive tax structure; more, tougher, and wiser environmental laws; more open government;

more protections for workers; more emphasis on human rights; and more social services for the economically disadvantaged. We were the "more" wing of the Democratic party, while the Republicans were the party of "less." Among my colleagues in the caucus were H. Lynn Jondahl of East Lansing, Howard Wolpe of Kalamazoo, John Otterbacher of Grand Rapids, Bill Broadhead of Detroit, Gary Owen of Ypsilanti, Paul Rosenbaum of Battle Creek, and Charlie Harrison of Pontiac. Not all the veteran legislators scorned us. Seasoned liberals like Dale Kildee, Joe Forbes, James Bradley, Phil Mastin, Earl Nelson, Morris Hood, Ray Hood, and Jackie Vaughn III often worked in coalition with us. Much of our common purpose came from our having opposed the war and supported the civil rights movement.

In retrospect we had an exceptionally talented and committed state house, and I include the Republican caucus in that assessment. GOP members were, for the most part, serious and thoughtful legislators. Both caucuses enjoyed skilled leadership: the Democrats from Speaker Bill Ryan and Majority Leader Bobby Crim, the Republicans from Minority Leader Dennis Cawthorne and Taxation Vice Chair Roy Spencer. The dynamics for a productive and engaging legislative session were there: aggressive and talented new members, capable and respected leaders, plus a governor whom just about everybody liked and admired.

Bill Milliken came from Traverse City, where his family owned and operated Milliken Department Store. The Millikens had a long tradition of public service. Bill's grandfather and father had both served in the state senate; his father had also served as mayor of Traverse City. His mother had served on the Traverse City school board. During World War II, Bill flew fifty combat missions as a waist gunner aboard a B-24 bomber; he was wounded over Austria and decorated for bravery. After the war, he came home to run the family business but soon found himself engaged in politics. After following his grandfather and father into the state senate, he served as lieutenant governor under Governor George Romney, then as governor after Nixon appointed

Romney secretary of housing and urban development.

In office 1969–1983, Bill Milliken still holds the record as Michigan's longest-serving governor. A politically moderate Republican who occasionally crossed over to the left, he possessed both a businessman's economic instincts and a progressive's social values. During my first weeks in Lansing I was the recipient of his generous hospitality and genuine charm.

In an effort to get acquainted with newly elected members of the legislature, the governor invited about a dozen of us to the governor's mansion for cocktail hour one day. We all took seats on the mansion's sun porch, enjoying our drinks and talking. Shaped like a half moon, the sun porch was all windows, with shades that on this day were open, allowing the low winter sun to bathe the room. As we chatted, the governor, in his congenial manner, tried to learn a little about each of our backgrounds. About twenty minutes into the gathering, the sun hit me square on, naturally highlighting me among all the guests in the room. Noticing that the sun was in my eyes, the governor got up, went to the window, and drew the shades. I found it a lovely gesture. However, because he drew the shades only far enough to block the sun for fifteen minutes, light was soon pouring onto my face once again. And again he got up and went through the same drill. "Is that better?" he asked me. I was flabbergasted that the governor of Michigan was so attentive to a lowly, twenty-seven-year-old freshman from the other party. "Yes, it is," I replied, and then I thanked him, probably too profusely. "You're welcome," he said with a gentle smile.

Over the years I've wondered if the governor was consciously using the occasion, and my moment in the sun, to show off his graciousness. At the time I thought his gesture toward my comfort was simply considerate of him. Later, however, I realized how politically astute it was for him to bond as he did with twelve brand-new legislators, all of whom must have been thinking, as I was, *What a nice guy. I look forward to working with him.*

I would have my chances.

TOXINS, TRASH, AND TAXES: ISSUES

A cornerstone of both Governor Milliken's career and mine was fighting for a clean environment. During my second term, he and I worked closely on two pieces of legislation that became law. The first was a bill I authored. Sent to the Marine Affairs Committee, which I had chaired since arriving in Lansing, the bill banned the use, sale, manufacturing, and distribution of polychlorinated biphenyls, a dangerous set of chemical compounds more commonly known as PCBs.

The subject of chemical poisoning was prominent in the state and national conversation at this time, in part because in 1971 US Senator Phil Hart, a Michigan Democrat, had held the first congressional hearings on dioxin poisoning from Agent Orange. A defoliant used in Vietnam to clear patches of jungle, Agent Orange theoretically made it easier for US and South Vietnamese forces to pursue their enemy. (I would spend a decade working on the Agent Orange issue while in Congress.) While I was in the legislature, I read that PCBs were carcinogenic to animals and, probably, to humans, as well. I also learned that these toxins were leaking into our environment from a variety of sources, the most prolific of which was containers found in every neighborhood atop telephone and electrical poles. The containers, each the size of a large kitchen trash can, were filled with the stuff in order to cool phone and electrical lines so they would not overheat. I resolved to investigate using my committee.

After many months of hearings and research, we concluded that PCBs were indeed toxic to humans. We further noted that there was a safer alternative. The governor supported my legislation to ban PCBs, as did the environmental community and major editorial boards around the state. The chemical companies, adhering to their dogma that "less government regulation is best," did not like the bill. But since they knew there was a workable, less dangerous substitute, they did not throw all of their resources against us. On March 26, 1976, in the middle of my race for Congress, I stood next to Governor Milliken as he signed my bill. Soon thereafter, other states, and then Congress, introduced PCBs legislation patterned after mine. With passage in Congress, the ban became law across the country. It was a wonderful victory.

The other special success was passage into law of the bottle-deposit bill. I did not write this bill but was an active supporter and cosponsor. And when the bill was, um, bottled up in committee, I was engaged in the statewide campaign to get the measure on the ballot.

I took my direction from the main legislative author of the bill, my Consumer Committee chair, Lynn Jondahl. Bright, articulate, witty, and hardworking, Lynn was one of Lansing's most capable legislators. When the bill came up for consideration in committee, we could muster only four votes, well short of a majority, to move the bill to the floor, for we were up against a concerted campaign waged against the bill by the Michigan Chamber of Commerce and the soft drink industry. After almost three years of this stagnation, as the state's streets and sidewalks and parks and beaches became more and more blighted by littered bottles and cans, a coalition decided to gather enough signatures to get the law on the statewide ballot. Alan Fox, a dynamic young Michigan State student on Lynn's staff, helped craft the statewide petition drive and would coordinate the strategy to convince the voters to approve the ballot proposal. The proposal, which registered 75 percent support in the polls, provided for a five-cent deposit on each pop and beer bottle and ten cents on each can, to be refunded when the container was returned. The nickel deposit was the highest in the country.[5]

Governor Milliken joined the coalition to get it on the ballot and became the first person to sign the petition. Lynn, Alan, and I, along with numerous environmental leaders and activists, hit the streets to garner the 400,000 signatures needed.

We got them. The measure appeared on the ballot in November 1976, when Michigan voters approved it by a 2–1 margin.

5 In 1989 the bottle deposit was lifted to a dime, making it again the highest in the country.

In approving the legislation, Michigan followed the lead of Oregon and its Republican governor, Tom McCall, who had seen a similar law pass in that state in 1971. Michigan and Oregon were both ahead of most other states on environmental issues. Of course, we both had breathtakingly beautiful states to protect.

Many of us remember a time in the 1940s and '50s, when we were youngsters; we'd pick up bottles in parks or on roadsides to redeem for a penny or two at the local corner store. But this practice was catch-as-catch-can, just a means for some bottlers to cut manufacturing costs. There was no law on the books. A friend of mine, Tom Leen, was a locomotive engineer who worked a railroad route between Detroit and Toledo. After the law was approved, Tom told me he had begun to take all his empties with him onto the train in Detroit and throw them off the train as it chugged down to Toledo. The idea was to help the homeless men who lived along the tracks. When he'd return to Detroit the next day, all of the cans would have been picked up.

Today 95 percent of Michigan's pop and beer bottles and cans are returned, and Michigan is a cleaner state for it.

Of all the forty-eight chief executives whose portraits hang in the rotunda in the state capitol, Bill Milliken, in my opinion, ranks at the top. Governor Milliken has always been an underrated and under-appreciated public servant. In all my years as a legislator, I don't think I served with a more decent man. I hold him in the highest esteem.

With Bill Milliken, Bill Ryan as Speaker, and Bobby Crim as majority leader, Michigan was blessed with political leaders whose kind hearts complemented their sharp minds, whose devotion to the public good, paired with their formidable political and legislative skills, brought tangible improvement to the lives of millions. I was most fortunate to have worked with them.

Although I was branded a member of the Kiddie Caucus, I worked at developing relationships outside that circle, seeking out the leaders, committee chairs, and other old pros, like Joe Snyder, Warren Gomaere, and Tom Anderson. I came to respect and admire all of them. Gary Owen, a smart man with a million-dollar smile, was another freshman who tried to branch out beyond his fellow newcomers. He was astute and skilled at making friends with legislators from different backgrounds and caucuses. Gary and I worked together on behalf of mobile park residents who were being ripped off by unscrupulous park owners imposing excessive fees and rules. Gary and I helped overhaul the law governing those establishments. After I left the legislature, Gary went on to be elected Speaker. He served with great distinction.

When I arrived in Lansing, the legislature was completely new to me. Yes, I had seen the lawmakers in session as a kid, and yes, I had worked on campaigns for legislative candidates, and yes, I'd done some reading. But I still had little sense of how the place worked, and freshmen received no orientation to break us in. Like so many of my colleagues, I had no previous experience as an elected official—not on a school board, a city council, or a county board of supervisors. So I did what I did best back then, and that was to listen, learn, and absorb the atmosphere around me. Someone once told me, "Kid, you will never be beaten by the speech you never gave." In other words, shut up and learn something before you run off at the mouth. Some of my colleagues in the Kiddie Caucus were bright, with silver tongues, but they lacked the timing to go with their other political skills. Timing in politics and in legislating is terribly important; it takes patience to learn the right timing in a body like a state legislature. When to speak, when not to speak; when to cut a deal, when to hold out—all were part of the requisite skill set if you wanted to be effective. If you kept quiet and watched closely, you'd soon enough find out who the real pros were. As a member of the Taxation Committee, I figured this rule out early. The knowledge would pay me great dividends.

I knew almost nothing about local and state taxes, yet here I sat, a freshman, on the Taxation Committee. Fortunately for me, the panel's chair was George Montgomery, a sixty-five-year-old former teacher from the city of Detroit. When the general session of the house would end between 5:00 and 6:00 p.m., we would adjourn to the bar at the Jack Tar Hotel. Over the course of my first year, I would drink beer, while Chairman Montgomery, on the next bar stool, downed his Scotch. He was an excellent teacher, and I was a good listener. It was here that I learned the theories behind progressive taxation, as well as the legislative pitfalls in getting progressive taxation passed. The chairman educated me about property taxes and the assessment processes that accompanied them. In other settings, my eyes would glaze over if I were subjected to a discussion of assessment processes. But Representative Montgomery made the subject fun by coloring his lectures with real-life legislative war stories that would have me either laughing or crying. A few Scotches or beers will do that.

In committee or on the house floor, when the issue was taxes, I always voted with the chairman. He appreciated my attitude—my willingness to acknowledge my limitations and to be the master's apprentice—and took me under his wing. After my first year, his concern for me resulted in my receiving a gift I did not deserve but was elated to accept. Not coincidentally, this gift also had the virtue of being a shrewd political stroke.

Chairman Montgomery had come up with a plan, which he named the Circuit Breaker, that linked senior citizens' property taxes to their income. He developed it because many low-income senior homeowners were being threatened with losing their homes due to their inability to pay their property taxes. Under his proposed formula, the property taxes of these seniors could not exceed a certain percentage of their income. The state would cough up the difference between what a senior paid and what was owed, sending the funds to the appropriate local units of government so they could run their cities and their schools. The proposal was wildly popular, especially, of course, among seniors. And because it protected the cities and schools, it neutralized much of the natural opposition to any measure that might disrupt funding of city and county governments—local elected officials, teachers, other

Speaking on the floor of the Michigan house, probably 1975

government employees, and the like. After negotiations and some tweaks, the governor ended up supporting it. When the bill was sent back to the house from the senate for final concurrence before going to the governor for his signature, Montgomery got up on the floor and moved that the bill be called the Bonior/Hasper Tax Relief Act. Hasper was Barney Hasper, another member of our tax committee and a long-time champion of seniors. Bonior was David Bonior, a new guy who always followed his chairman's lead.

I was dumbstruck. I was completely surprised.

The house accepted the chairman's recommendation, and soon Governor Milliken signed the bill with my name on it. I had been given a potent, and completely unmerited, accomplishment to take back to my district as a sign of not only my caring but also my effectiveness. Montgomery and the Speaker were keenly aware that I had won my seat by a mere thousand votes. My name on this bill was their gift to me to help ensure I would return after the next election.

PROUD MOMENTS:
STANDING MY GROUND

I was less reticent in the Marine Affairs Committee. In addition to the PCBs bill, I authored the Marine Safety Act. Michigan bragged on its auto license plates that it was a "Water Wonderland." Contiguous to four of the five Great Lakes, with eleven thousand inland lakes and a coastline second only to Alaska in size, Michigan indeed deserved the title. The state also boasted the nation's largest number of recreational boats—more than even California, Florida, or Minnesota. And my legislative district lay in the heart of Michigan's boat world.

With fun on the water come accidents, and thus the need for safety and rescue programs. As committee chair, I worked with the other members to tailor a bill that leveled a fee on boats in order to fund safety and patrol programs, most of which were run by county sheriff departments. On my first try taking the bill to the house floor, it was sent back to committee for revisions in the fee structure. On the second try we passed a bill that raised the money needed for the programs.

We also had some funds left over, money the fees would bring in beyond what the programs would cost. I convinced Appropriations Chairman Dominic Jacobetti, and his subcommittee chair on capital project funding, Rusty Hellman, that we could use the money to build boating access sites in our respective districts. They were as interested in boating as I was, for both of their districts lay along Lake Superior in the Upper Peninsula. Both Dominic and Rusty were seasoned old pros who were more than willing to introduce me to the world of legislative "pork"—and how I loved that pork! I could now bring the bacon home to my district with two boating and fishing parks on Lake St. Clair. Forty years later, when I see these two parks I still take pride in all the joy they have given families out boating for the day or fishing from the docks or the shore. One of the boating access parks is located at the terminus of the hike/bike trail my efforts got built along the Clinton River Spillway. For years Judy and I would take regular round-trip walks along that trail. About halfway through the five-mile jaunt, at Lake St. Clair, we'd stop to rest and take in the smiles on the faces of the people who had come to boat and fish.

While I'm on the subject, a word about much-maligned "pork." Pork is essential to legislative deal-making. Morsels from the pork barrel—pet projects, earmarks, call it what you will—are the items that get fellow legislators on board to get things done. "Support this bill," a leader or a president can say, "and you'll get your bridge." When Congress cracked down on earmarks, it crippled its productivity. Why should a backbencher support my bill if there's no bridge at stake?

By the way, the vast majority of pork projects are desperately needed. Yes, we can all agree that there has been, and always will be, some egregious abuse. But why throw out the baby with the bathwater?

Over the past few years several friends have told me that while visiting the modest home of Nelson Mandela in Soweto, South Africa, now a museum, they saw hanging on a wall a resolution from the Michigan House of Representatives. My name is on that resolution, which supported Mandela's fight against apartheid, as are those of other members of the Kiddie Caucus. Although I have not seen the resolution in some forty years, I know it must have been produced during my second term in Lansing, because among the signers is Jeff Padden, who was first elected to the legislature in 1974. The document is significant to me because it was one of only two such political proclamations posted on the wall of Mandela's small home in Soweto. It must have meant a great deal to him in his struggle.

The main author of the proclamation was my late colleague Howard Wolpe. Howard, who held a PhD in African studies, had been a professor of political science at Western Michigan University. He went on to serve with me in Congress, becoming chair of the subcommittee of the House International Affairs Committee that had jurisdiction over African issues. He led the fight to override Ronald Reagan's veto of a bill imposing sanctions against the apartheid regime. I'm proud to say

Mandela and me, early '90s, in my whip office, the Capitol,
Washington, D.C.

that I was instrumental in whipping that vote. After his time in Congress, Howard became a diplomat for the State Department. Carrying designation as an ambassador, he shuttled back and forth in Africa trying to bring peace to countries riven by regional conflicts and wars.

Howard sat directly in front of me on the floor of the Michigan house, so we often consulted with one another. Our political friendship became a personal one, as well. We often dined together and would play tennis at Michigan State University. Once we took our families to Beaver Island on Lake Michigan. The vacation was not the most comfortable of my life: Swarms of gnats and mosquitoes chased us daily from our cabin, situated well inland, to the island's windswept beaches, where we found relief from the pests.

Representative Wolpe's passion was racial justice, whether in Michigan or South Africa. Back in 1975, the rules in the House allowed a member to write and distribute a resolution without its actually being passed or even formally introduced. Often, this procedure was undertaken to show your constituents or key interest groups that you cared about an issue even if the resolution's chances of passage were nil. An exhaustive search of records of House proceedings did not turn up the presumed Wolpe Resolution regarding South Africa, so I believe Howard circulated the petition among those of us who cared about ending apartheid and supporting Mandela's political party, the then-controversial African National Congress. Once the document was signed, Howard must have sent it to Mandela, then a prisoner of the racist regime at Robben Island. The world has recently seen the passing of the great South African. When Howard wrote and sent the resolution, support from Western governments for Mandela and for the liberation of South Africa was halfhearted at best. It is gratifying to know, four decades later, that our resolution meant so much to this towering champion of human dignity and freedom.

Busing continued to be a divisive issue in Michigan and in the legislature. My fair-housing resolution was too controversial to attract the support James Bradley and I needed to move it out of committee and onto the house floor. Instead, we were wrapped up in trying to defeat an amendment to the state constitution that would prohibit cross-district busing. Busing remained a potent issue in 1975. Members of the legislature had not forgotten the vote total George Wallace had registered in the state's 1972 presidential primary.

Amending the state constitution required a legislative supermajority: two-thirds in favor. We who opposed the measure were up against a determined majority. Kiddie Caucus and Black Caucus members stood firm against the amendment, as did some other labor Democrats. But we were still short of the necessary one-third plus one to defeat it. As far as I knew, among representatives from Macomb County, only Joe

Snyder and I opposed the amendment. The other five, I believed, supported it. Support was no doubt the safer position; I was sure my vote would doom my reelection. But I was not going to vote to change Michigan's constitution to outlaw this remedy for racial and educational imbalance.

Then another Macomb representative, Warren Gomaere, took the floor to speak. Well-liked and respected by his colleagues, Warren was a bear of a man, six feet five, 260 pounds. The premier conservationist in the house, he was an outdoorsman if there ever was one, but he was not known for progressive views on social or constitutional issues. He was known to oppose cross-district busing, so I had assumed that he would take the side of the majority of delegates from Macomb County. I was mistaken. He gave a brilliant speech explaining why putting this prohibition into the constitution was wrong. His argument was cogent, scholarly, forceful, and passionate. It caught almost everyone in the chamber off guard. We defeated the amendment that day, and it was because of that brave speech. In the world of legislatures and Congress, it is almost unheard of that a floor speech will change the outcome of a vote. But now and then someone's knowledge, passion, and courage will fuse together and people will be swayed. Warren's district was next to mine, so to have his company on this vote meant a lot to me, and I told him so. We laughed about how our service would come to an end after the next election—although, as it turned out, we both won our races in 1976—but it was a proud moment for us. A few years later, a similar resolution would surface in the U.S. House of Representatives, this time to amend the U.S. Constitution.

I stood my ground again.

In 1828, Detroiter Patrick Fitzpatrick was hanged, across the river in Windsor, Ontario, for the rape and murder of an innkeeper's daughter. In 1835, however, Fitzpatrick's former roommate confessed to the crime on his deathbed. The case weighed heavily on the members of the Michigan legislature, which in 1846 voted to make Michigan the first

English-speaking territory in the world to abolish capital punishment. In 1962 a state constitutional convention voted 108–3 to include in Michigan's constitution a prohibition on the death penalty for all crimes. Since 1836, only one prisoner has been executed within state borders: US authorities hanged Anthony Chebatoris, convicted on a federal murder charge, in 1938.

By the time I served in the legislature—not much more than a decade after the constitutional convention's near-unanimous vote to ban state-sponsored execution—attitudes among elected officials and the public had changed radically. Lawmakers in Lansing, reflecting the opinion of between two-thirds and three-quarters of the state's citizens, according to Gallup, mounted a serious effort to amend the constitution to reinstate the state death penalty. Again, amending the constitution required the vote of two-thirds of the sitting members of the house, and again a majority of the house supported the measure. And so again, those of us on the other side needed one-third plus one.

I believe the most important function of government is to protect life. Years later, in 1983, Cardinal Joseph Bernadin, Archbishop of Chicago, advocated what he called the "consistent ethic of life," which in Catholic circles is better known as The Seamless Garment. The doctrine expresses the view I'd held since my youth: that all life is sacred, from the womb to the grave. This outlook determined my view of war and of society's obligations toward the caring and nurturing of children. It caused me to oppose not only the death penalty but abortion, as well.

Even though tough votes inevitably arose around these life issues, I did not shy from them. These questions were important to me because they kept challenging my sense of justice and of what humanity really means. I would struggle internally my whole career over abortion issues; most of that private debate would involve the question of when life begins. My views on abortion would modify over the decades; for one thing, I would come to approve of stem cell research. But I have never wavered on the death penalty. I have never believed that the state should be in the business of taking lives.

After a vigorous and passionate debate, we defeated the amendment. Capital punishment is still outlawed in Michigan.

On December 11, 1971, not far from the town of Port Huron, an explosion ripped through a massive water-intake tunnel under construction beneath Lake Huron. Forty-three men were working that afternoon in the sixteen-foot-diameter tunnel designed to run a length of six miles and 230 feet below the lake bed. Twenty-one men died that day from the blast; one more succumbed to his injuries months later.

One of the worst industrial accidents in our state's history, the tunnel explosion was caused by a buildup of methane gas that had been released from shale by drilling. The gas was then ignited by sparks created when a drill bit fell and landed on the concrete lining the tunnel's floor. However, the explosion would have killed no one except for a catastrophic lack of communication between that day's two teams of workers. The men up on the drilling rig thought no one was in the tunnel; the men below did not know there was drilling. Had the tunnelers been aware of the drilling, their supervisor would have kept them aboveground.

As a member of the House Labor Committee for both my terms, and a steadfast labor supporter, I was taken aback to learn, around the end of my first term, that no legislative investigation of the explosion had been undertaken, no public report issued, and no recommendations made for averting similar tragedies in the future. I'd worked tunnel construction and knew firsthand the dangers involved. Three years should have been enough time to figure out what had happened and take corrective measures. I asked Speaker Crim, who had succeeded Bill Ryan, to appoint a special committee to investigate and report back with recommendations. He agreed, naming a five-member committee, with me as its chair. The panel's title was Special House Committee to Investigate the Port Huron Tunnel Disaster, House Resolution 134.

The full house had granted us power to issue subpoenas and administer oaths. Also at our disposal were the staffs of the Labor Committee and the Speaker's office. In addition, I hired Ted Benca, a talented and aggressive student from Michigan State University, to help.

The reason for the tunnel—bringing much-needed fresh drinking water to an ever-expanding Metropolitan Detroit—was not in dispute, and by the time we convened our committee, the tunnel had been in operation for some time. But our hearings, interviews, and investigation uncovered a shocking list of problems: lack of safety inspections, repeated safety violations by the major contractor, and poor communications and inadequate ventilation at the worksite. All of these shortcomings were serious and costly to fix, but the expense of avoiding the problems should have been included in the bids at the outset. Fixing these issues on future projects, whatever the cost, was vital to protecting workers and their families from death, disabling injury, and financial ruin. I was determined to change the tunneling industry's culture of indifference toward its employees and their safety.

In an ironic and tragic coincidence, on November 14, 1975, just as I was wrapping up questioning a witness before our committee, Ted pulled me aside to tell me of a news report that a methane explosion had just occurred underground at a sewer construction site in Mount Clemens, half a mile from my home. One worker was killed, six injured.

At the hearing's conclusion, I drove from Lansing straight to the site of the accident. It was dark when I pulled up to the curb on the quiet residential street where one of the two shafts that ran from the street to the tunnel was located. There was no one in sight; all the rescue efforts and the press were at the other shaft, located near downtown. I gathered myself after the two-hour drive and breathed a sigh of relief— or was it apprehension?—as I turned off the car's engine. And then, to my utter amazement, I watched as an operating engineer got into the cab of the heavy-duty drill used to bore holes down into the sewer construction and started extracting the drill from the ground.

It was methane gas that had ignited in the Port Huron disaster, set off by drilling. Now I was seeing a bit being lifted from a tunnel that presumably still contained pockets of methane gas, which had caused a deadly explosion only hours before. I immediately thought, *I pray to God there is nobody still in the tunnel.* Fortunately, as it turned out, nobody was. But as it also turned out, no one had been checking for people down below between where we were and where the rescue efforts had taken place. The upshot was that the chairman of the legislature's committee investigating the Port Huron disaster was an eyewitness, in his own hometown, to what appeared to be a safety violation reminiscent of one that had contributed to the earlier tragedy. The coincidence was so rich that it earned the front-page headline of the *Detroit Free Press* the next morning.

Our committee issued a comprehensive report, with recommendations, that was signed by all five members and submitted to the full house in July 1976, one year after our panel's creation. Our recommendations were acted upon—administratively, by the state Department of Labor, and legislatively, by the legislature in its next session.

As a result, I believe we fulfilled our purpose of creating a safer job environment for Michigan workers who toiled underground to improve all our lives. For me it was also an essential lesson I carried with me to Congress: the importance of laws and regulations to protect health and safety in the workplace. Today, according to the Bureau of Labor Statistics, nearly five thousand American workers die annually, and three million are injured, in work-related accidents.

We still have a long way to go.

CHAPTER 9

Looking Back, Looking Ahead

Leaving Lansing, Aiming for Washington

As the end of my first term in the legislature drew near, I was proud of the workmanlike record I had put together in the short time I'd been there. Only twenty-seven when I was sworn in in January 1973, I was a young man with a lot of idealism and energy. But something was bothering me: I was spending too much time away from home. It was what I feared when I told Speaker Ryan that I wanted to bring my family with me to Lansing. I now looked at my situation and saw two small children and a teenager at home. I felt that I needed to be there more, so Sybil and I talked about my leaving the legislature.

I liked being a lawmaker. The work was educational and stimulating, and it provided me the opportunity to make a difference in the lives of many people. My marginal communication skills were improving; I'd gotten pretty good at my job. My record as a freshman stacked up well against those of my peers. Did I really want to give all this up? Was there a way to reconcile my responsibilities as a legislator with my duties as a husband and father? Was there a way to stay on in Lansing yet still spend more time with my wife and children?

After much thought I reached the conclusion that the right thing to do was leave the legislature and quit elective politics.

But then two unexpected events derailed my plans.

The first was that, miracle of miracles, nobody filed to run against me in the next election. This situation was the opposite of what my leaders and my own political sense had led me to expect. I had challenged popular views on busing and the death penalty and had survived.

I was not so full of myself as to believe that my one-term track record was responsible for my good fortune. It was more likely that the ongoing Watergate investigation spelled big trouble for Republicans and their candidates in 1974. Well, trouble for them meant an advantage for me. Without an upcoming election to worry about, I could now spend much more time with my family.

The second event came after my reelection, in 1975, when US Senator Phil Hart announced his retirement and my congressman, James G. O'Hara, decided he would run to replace him. O'Hara's candidacy for the Senate left open a congressional seat that included virtually my entire legislative district, minus only the three or four precincts I had in Sterling Heights. So my options for 1976 changed: Now it came down to either quitting elective politics or running for Congress.

I had never seriously considered a congressional run. Yes, I might have fantasized about it once or twice, but election to Congress was not something I thought possible. Nor was it something I hungered for. To this point I truly believed that the state legislature was as far as I would go, and I was happy with that ceiling. But when O'Hara's seat came open, I started to work myself up for a run. My competitive juices ran deep.

I rationalized—accurately, as it turned out—that home life would be better for my family and me were I in Congress. About two-thirds of the members of the U.S. House brought their families to live in and around Washington. This was long ago, another time entirely in the conduct of our nation's elected officials. Members returned home only once or twice a month, on weekends. I knew about that schedule, because Jim O'Hara had kept to it. And when school was out, members might take their families back home with them for a good part of the summer. Today, two-thirds of the members keep their families back home, putting constant pressure on the leadership to limit the weekdays spent in session in DC. Many members fly in on Tuesday and home on Thursday. And little gets done in our nation's capital.

In addition to my being able to see the kids for breakfast and dinner,

Sybil and I were attracted to the high-quality school systems in the Washington suburbs. L'Anse Creuse schools were wonderful, but the school districts in Maryland and Northern Virginia were among the best in the country. Washington also offered rich cultural opportunities with its ethnic diversity and its world-class museums. What's more, as a congressman I'd be paid more than double what I was making in Lansing. And I'd have much milder winters in which to enjoy that windfall.

From a personal perspective, the whole package was indeed appealing.

Of course, I was looking forward to much more than museums and a paycheck. In Congress I would have a voice in the essential issues facing the government and the nation. Here now was my chance to make a difference on questions of war and peace: No more Vietnams, I vowed. Here was my chance to be part of the national debate on civil rights at home and human rights abroad. Here was my chance to make a difference on workers' rights and opportunities. Here was my chance to promote laws that would protect our Great Lakes and preserve our national heritage lands. In the morning, I could walk out the door enraged at something I'd heard on the news or read in the *New York Times* and then, that very day, go to the floor of the House of Representatives to express my opinion and call for action. I'd be able to satisfy my desire to enter the fray on the international stage, to play a part in bringing justice to developing countries, whether by ending apartheid in South Africa or lessening repression in Latin America. I could fight for national health insurance, like that enjoyed by citizens of Germany, Canada, and every other developed nation. I was intoxicated with the possibility of being a player, of bending the arc of the moral universe toward justice, to paraphrase the words the abolitionist Theodore Parker spoke before the Civil War.

I would have the chance to speak out and even lead. After four years of training and learning in Lansing, I was ready to unleash my working-class and religious values, to apply them to matters of national and global importance.

With O'Hara sending strong signals that he would try for the Senate, I knew that I needed to make a firm decision about whether to run. Local heavyweights in both parties were eyeing the seat; the race would be long and difficult. There was no time to waste.

Sybil and I talked, and I decided to go for it. I thought she was fine with the decision, but in retrospect she must have had at least some

*Andy and me; we used this photo in my
first congressional campaign.*

desire to slow down our lives. However, there was no slowing down when the prize was so big. If I was to make this commitment, I needed to pour my heart and soul into the campaign.

From the days my grandparents decided to leave Europe and seek a better life in America, through my years in the Michigan legislature, I felt that maybe, just maybe, a plan had been developing that had me destined for public service. The values my family and neighborhood had instilled in me, together with my deep religious faith, propelled me forward. The athletic talent I had inherited from my father had set me on a course of discipline, confidence, and leadership that would transcend the games I played and prepare me for a life of participation at the highest levels of public service. I might not have been the smartest young man, or the most articulate, but I had vision and dreams. And that vision and those dreams were centered on a community that operated in an environment of peace and justice. I now would have the opportunity to expand my reach onto the national stage.

I felt ready. I was eager to take on the challenge. I was determined to win.

ACKNOWLEDGMENTS

A special thank-you to my editor and friend Michael Takiff, executive director of Gravitas History. His guidance, suggestions, corrections, wit, and understanding of history made this writing journey a pleasure. We found each other while Michael was conducting interviews for his acclaimed book *A Complicated Man: The Life of Bill Clinton as Told by Those Who Know Him* (Yale University Press, 2010). I am a Detroit Tigers and Washington Nationals fan, Michael a passionate fan of the Nats' divisional rivals, the New York Mets. We often tease each other by signing off our email correspondence or phone conversations with "And I hope your team loses."

Sincere thanks also to:

My sister, Nancy, whose personal goodness and vivid recollections helped identify many of the holes in my own memory. Her interview and picture archive helped immeasurably.

My brother, Jeff, for his research on the book, as well as his interview and photo archives. His stories of conversations with our father aided in creating the picture of Dad's wartime service in Europe.

Tony Beilenson, my former congressional colleague and friend, for giving me the inspiration to do a memoir of my youth. Tony's two-volume autobiography was most enjoyable and filled with interesting and lovely stories of his life.

Mike Smith, the former director of the Walter Reuther Archives and Library at Wayne State University, who was helpful in reading the manuscript and moving the book forward. Mike and I were officemates when we taught at WSU, and I am proud to say we became good friends. Mike introduced me to Charles Hyde and Kathy Wildfong, both of the WSU Press, who read the manuscript and provided valuable suggestions.

Kathy Gille and Ed Bruley, who were vital congressional and political collaborators with me for over forty years. I am grateful to them for participating in the book through their interviews and the book's foreword.

Christine Koch, who, as so often has been the case in the past, was there to offer ideas, suggestions, and memories. From our first days together with Locofoco back in 1972, she has been indispensable.

Martha and Art Mulkoff and Helen Livingston, contemporaries of my parents. Martha, Helen, and Art shared wonderful memories and insights with me. Both Helen and Martha rocked me as an infant and watched me grow into manhood. What a wonderful feeling to have traveled my life with these kind and nurturing friends. They each had rewarding careers and raised amazing families.

Sybil Vera, who was kind enough to read chapters of the manuscript and who also recalled important stories of our family. Her participation was particularly important.

Chris Davis, who worked on my congressional staff in Washington and now works for the Congressional Research Service at the Library of Congress. Chris provided me with valuable records that were helpful in the writing of this book and will aid in the writing of the forthcoming book on my congressional career.

Greg Kowalski, whose several excellent books on Hamtramck bring me joy and fond memories. I relied especially heavily on his book *Hamtramck: The Driven City*.

Christian Korab, who was gracious and helpful in providing guidance on his father's magnificent jacket photo of St. Florian Church and surrounding houses in Hamtramck.

Shawn Pitton, from the University of Iowa, who provided pictures of that campus.

All those who kindly provided hours of helpful, informative interviews. In addition to people mentioned above, Steve Champlin, Cassandra Ulbrich, Tom King, Fred Miller, and Judy Bonior sat for important conversations.

Charlyn Davidson, for the childhood photographs of me that her mother, Joanna, put together. Joanna, Helen Kitzens, and Marge Pilarski were close high school friends of my mother. After Joanna died, her high school friends Helen and Marge were kind enough to pass Joanna's photos to me. I am indebted to Charlyn for her kindness in initiating the process of getting the photos sent my way. Of course, I am also indebted to her late mother for creating a photo album of me and my family and preserving it over so many years.

Jerry Hartz, who worked for me for many years, and Drew Hammil; both now work in the office of House Majority Leader Nancy Pelosi.

Michael Collins, in the office of Congressman John Lewis

Jim Vollman, who provided early stories and information about the apartheid resolution that hangs in Nelson Mandela's home in Soweto.

My daughter, Julie Sutherland, for her picture archive and childhood memories.

My son, Andrew Bonior, for recalling stories and early memories in his life.

Caitlin Conner, for taking pictures in Michigan on the spur of the moment.

Louis Vera, for his photograph of Andy and Vance Bonior.

My publisher, David Wilk, for his patience, creativity, and good advice.

My fact checkers, Kening Zhu and Carolyn Wiener.

My copy editor, Judy Gelman Myers.

My transcriber, Eugene Corey, whose company is Brave New Words.

And finally, and most importantly, my wife, Judy, whose editing skills, proofreading, picture taking, and overall patience, love, and support enabled me to pursue this project. As with Michael Takiff, without her there would be no book.